Williston Wilker

On the Increase of Royal Power in France under Philip Augustus,

1179-1223

Williston Wilker

On the Increase of Royal Power in France under Philip Augustus, 1179-1223

ISBN/EAN: 9783337032340

Printed in Europe, USA, Canada, Australia, Japan

Cover: Foto ©ninafisch / pixelio.de

More available books at **www.hansebooks.com**

ON THE INCREASE

OF

ROYAL POWER IN FRANCE

UNDER

PHILIP AUGUSTUS.

1179—1223.

—

DISSERTATION PRESENTED TO THE PHILOSOPHICAL FACULTY
OF THE UNIVERSITY OF LEIPZIG,

FOR THE DEGREE OF DOCTOR,

BY

WILLISTON WALKER

OF PORTLAND, ME. U. S. A.

LEIPZIG, 1888.

Contents.

	page
Bibliographical Notes	V
Introductory remarks.	

I. Theory of the royal power and position of the royal family.

The monarchy — hereditary or elective?	3
Philip's theory of the royal power	8
Coronation	9
Marriage and coronation of Philip's queens	11
Position of the queen	14
Position of the crown prince	18
Philip's policy regarding his younger children	26

II. The Central Administration.

Philip's majority; when attained. Was he under guardianship? . . .	32
The royal advisers.	
The Seneschal. Philip's policy regarding the post	38
The Chancellor. „ „ „ „ „	42
The Butler. „ „ „ „ „	45
The Chamberlain. „ „ „ „ „	46
Importance of the Sub-Chamberlains	48
The Constable	50
The Marshals	51
Increasing influence of counselors whose relation to the king were personal rather than official	55
The chief counselors	57
Consultation of the council	60
The Assemblies.	
a. Deliberative assemblies.	
Convocation	61
Topics discussed	65
Nature of the assemblies' decisions	66
Value and necessity of the assemblies	68
b. Judicial assemblies.	
Character of the curia regis	70
Procedure	72
Factors in the growing importance of the curia regis . . .	75
1. Progress in the development of a body of judges	76
2. The peers — development of a distinction in the membership of the judicial assembly	77

IV

	page
Attitude of the monarchy toward the peerage	86
Advantages derived from the peerage	88
Policy of the crown regarding the trial of high nobles not peers	88
3. The system of inquests	91
The regency and government during Philip's absence on the crusade of 1190—91	95

III. The Local Administration and the relation of the king to the feudal and corporate elements of the kingdom.

Extent of territory covered by the actual local administration	97
The royal authority and the church	98
The royal authority and the non-noble class; the communes and privileged cities	103
The royal authority and the nobles	106
The extent of Philip's power over the internal affairs of a great fief illustrated by Champagne	108
The policy of the monarchy necessarily one of annexation to the crown domain	110
Methods of annexation illustrated by Normandy	112
Similarity of methods elsewhere	114
Effect of the system of mutual pledges in compelling the vassalage to respect the royal authority	115
Increase in the royal domain effected by Philip	117
by conquest and hereditary succession	118
by exchange and purchase	119
through changes in the succession to fiefs	121
through sharings	122
Extension of the royal authority through protections	123
The local administrative officers.	
Provosts and sub-officers	126
Institution of Bailiffs	129
Their functions	131
Local Seneschals	137
Increase in the revenue through annexation and improved administration	140
Military strength consequent upon improved revenues and administration — paid troops	140
Conclusion	144

Bibliographical Notes.

The writer does not claim to give an exhaustive bibliography, but would indicate the following works as having been used in the preparation of this essay.

I. Historical Sources.

The greater part of the chronicles employed by the writer may be found in the XVII, XVIII and XIX volumes of the "Scriptores Rerum Francicarum" or "Recueil des Historiens de Gaule et de la France", Bouquet, Brial, Delisle and others, 23 vols, Paris 1738—1876. Many have, however, been published separately, with a more accurate text.

Among these chronicles special use has been made of the following:

Rigord, "De gestis Philippi Augusti, Francorum regis," Scriptores, XVII: 3—62. More critically, Fr. Delaborde, "Oeuvres de Rigord et de Guillaume le Breton, Historiens de Philippe-Auguste, publiées pour la Société de l'Histoire de France". Paris 1882, I: 1—167. Such portions of the text as more immediately concern German affairs are edited by A. Molinier, "Monumenta Germaniae Historica," XXVI: 288—294. The author appears to have been born between 1145 and 1150. He pursued the study of medicine and, later, entered the monastary of St. Denis, where his history was doubtless written. The work consists of two parts, of which the first appears to have been composed between 1187 and 1196, and the second added before 1207, at which date the chronicle ends. The narrative is generally accurate, though the first part, especially, is strongly laudatory of the French monarch. The position of the writer was not one of intimate relation to the king, but the central situation of the monastary of which he was an inmate makes his information extensive; and his work is to be ranked among the best of the sources for Philip's early years.

VI

William the Breton. Born about 1165, studied at Mantes and Paris, became royal chaplain and confidential agent of Philip, whom he accompanied on many of his campaigns. He was tutor to Philip's illegitimate son, Carlotus. His intimate acquaintance with affairs at court make his works of prime value, in spite of his evident partiality toward the king and his strong national feeling. He survived Philip. His two works are:

A. "De gestis Philippi Augusti," in prose, "Scriptores," XVII: 62. Later edition, Fr. Delaborde, "Oeuvres de Rigord et de Guillaume le Breton etc." Paris, 1882. I: 168—333. In part in Mon. Ger. Hist. XXVI: 295. This is a continuation of Rigord's work. Three parts are to be distinguished, a, an abridgement of Rigord; b, the body of the work, written, probably, soon after the battle of Bouvines, and covering the period from 1209 to 1215; c, a brief continuation, 1215—1220, to which are added a few notes bringing the story down to the death of Philip. This work has been made a subject of critical study by Fr. Delaborde.

B. The "Philippidos Libri XII," a poem in twelve books of hexameter verse. "Scriptores" XVII: 118—287. Later edition, Fr. Delaborde, "Oeuvres de Rigord et de Guillaume le Breton etc" II, Paris 1885. In part in Mon. Ger. Hist. XXVI: 319—389. The period at which its writing was begun has been variously placed. Brial favors 1215 to 1220 as the era of its composition; Pannenborg, 1220—1225; Delaborde places its beginning in 1218 or 1219 and would attribute some portions to an even earlier period. Its account of Philip's actions is full till 1215. The material employed is substantially that used in the prose work; but the numerous allusions to military and legal customs, the descriptions of places, etc. make it a source of no mean value. It has been critically examined by A. Pannenborg, "Zur Kritik der Philipis", Aurich, 1880.

Further removed from the center of French administration, but more nearly contemporaneous in composition with the early part of Philip's reign, are the following works, printed in the "Scriptores," but published in the better editions here indicated.

"Gesta Regis Henrici Secundi, Benedicti Abbatis," ed. W. Stubbs, 2 vol. London 1867, (Master of Rolls series). This anonymous history, usually known as that of Benedict of Peterborough, is evidently the work of one intimate with the prominent men at the court of Henry II. of England. The close connection of the sovereigns of France and England during this period, the extent and accuracy of the information possessed by the author, make the "Gesta" a source of prime importance. It extends from Christmas, 1169, to the spring of 1192. Four portions may be distinguished, a, 1169—1177, a contemporary composition; b, 1177—1180, probably contemporary; c, 1180—1188, probably compiled from contemporary notes, but containing anticipatory episodes; d, 1188—1192, contemporary.

Roger de Hoveden, "Chronica magistri Rogeri de Houedene," ed. W. Stubbs, 4 vols. London, 1868, (Master of Rolls series). The work of this writer practically continues the "Gesta" from 1192 to 1201. As one of the clerks of Henry II., and a royal agent, a forest justice etc. his acquaintance with the affairs of the day was large. His work from 1170 to 1192 is a rewritten copy of the "Gesta"; from 1192 to 1201 it is original.

Ralph de Diceto, "Ymagines Historiarum", ed. "Radulphi de Diceto, decani Londonensis, Opera Historica," W. Stubbs, 2 vols. London, 1876 (Master of Rolls series). The author became archdeacon of Middlesex in 1152, studied at Paris about 1160 and was made dean of St. Paul's, London, in 1180. He died, probably, in 1202. His work was written between 1188 and 1190; but appears to be based on contemporaneous notes from about 1180 or 1181. It is continued till 1202. In the main well informed, but gossipy and chronologically inexact, its value is less than either of the English sources just enumerated.

Gislebert, "Chronicon Hanoniense". ed. W. Arndt, "Monumenta Germaniae Historica", XXI: 481—601; small reprint, "in usum scholarum", Hanover 1869. A source of prime value. The writer was always a man of affairs at the court of Baldwin V. and Philip of Hainault. Here he occupied the posts of chaplain and of chancellor. He was provost of St. Germain at Mons and St. Albans at Namur. His skill saved Flanders for Baldwin after the death of Philip of Alsace in 1191. A warm admirer of his count, the extent and accuracy of his information and his fairness of mind make his chronicle a most important source for the history of France during the later years of the XII. Century. He died between 1223 and 1225. His chronicle was written shortly after 1200 and covers the period from the latter half of the XI. Century to 1195.

Among sources of less importance the following deserve special notice:

Robert of Auxerre. Chronicle. ed. Scp. XVIII: 247—209; in large part also in ed. Holder-Egger, "Mon. Ger. Hist." XXVI: 219—276. The writer was born in 1156, entered the monastary of St. Marianus at Auxerre in 1172, died in 1212. His chronicle, extending from the beginning of the world to 1211, is one of the best of the mediaeval compilations. As an independent writer he is of less ability. His original work embraces the period from about 1180 to 1211. The composition of the chronicle was begun about 1203; but the record for the last few years of the XII. Cent. is probably based on contemporary notes.

Ralph of Coggeshall, "Chronicon Anglicanum;" ed. J. Stevenson, London 1875, (Master of Rolls series). This chronicle comes from the Cistercian monastary of Coggeshall, and is of limited value. It is at its best in the opening years of the XIII Century.

William of Newbury, "Historia Anglicana"; ed. "Scriptores" XVIII: 1—58. The writer was born in 1136, and became a canon at Newbury. The history was written in his old age and embraces the years from the Conquest of England to about 1197. He is a writer of fair judgment, but inclined to attribute motives to the persons of whom he treats, not always with accuracy. His value as a source of French history is limited.

Roger of Wendover and Matthew Paris. "Matthaei Parisiensis, monachi Sancti Albani, Chronica Majora". ed. H. R. Luard. 7 vols. London, 1872—1883, (Master of Rolls series). This is one of the most valuable compilations among the English chronicles. It is important especially for the later years of Philip. The portion embracing his reign till 1188 is anonymous. From 1188 to 1235 Roger of Wendover is the compiler. He began his work about 1219. Matthew Paris, who became monk at St. Albans in 1217, died in 1259, inserted some additional matter in the work of Wendover, and continued it till near his death.

The "Historia Anglorum" or "Historia Minor" of Matthew Paris, ed. F. Madden, 3 vols. London 1866—69, (Master of Rolls series), is a kind of epitome of the "Chronica Majora", with some additional matter. It was written between 1250 and 1253.

A number of smaller works, contained in the XVII, XVIII and XIX volumes of the "Scriptores", have been cited also in the annotations to this essay. With these may be classed the "Itinerarium Perigrinorum et gesta regis Ricardi," ed. Stubbs, London 1864; an important source for events in Syria during the crusade of 1190—91.

II. Documentary Sources.

L. Delisle, "Catalogue des Actes de Philippe-Auguste." Paris 1856. This remarkable work is an invaluable guide to the charters and letters-patent of Philip. In it a description is given of the extant

IX

manuscript registers of Philip's acts, and the contents of about 2260 documents are summarized. The appendix contains the text of a considerable number of charters.

D'Arbois de Jubainville, "Histoire des ducs et des comtes de Champagne", 7 vols. Paris 1859—69. The author does a work for the documents relating to Champagne similar to that of M. Delisle for the charters of Philip. His "Catalogue" is contained in the III, V and VI volumes of his "Histoire".

The following collections of documentary texts have been used:

Baluze, "Miscellaneorum . . . . . hoc est collectio veterum monumentorum etc." VII; Paris 1715.

Beugnot, "Les Olim," I; preface and notes. Paris 1839.

"Bibliotheque de l'École des Chartes," XXXVII: 381.

Boutaric, "Actes du Parlement de Paris," I, Paris, 1863.

Brussel, "Nouvel examen de l'Usage général des fiefs en France". 2 vols. Paris, 1727. Contains a very large number of charters in the text, the annotations and the proofs. Vol. II contains a complete copy of the treasury account for 1202—1203.

Chantereau-Lefebvre, "Traité des Fiefs", proofs. Paris, 1662.

Felibien, "Histoire de la ville de Paris", proofs. 5 vols. Paris 1725.

"Gallia Christiana, in provincias ecclesiasticas distributa", instruments. 2nd ed. 16 vols. Paris 1715—1865.

Mabillon, "De Re Diplomatica", 3rd ed. Naples, 1789.

Martène, "Veterum scriptorum et monumentorum . . . . Amplissima Collectio". I, Paris, 1704.

Martène. "Thesaurus Anecdotorum" I: Paris, 1717.

"Ordonnances des rois de France de la troisième race". 22 vols. Paris 1723—1847, Chiefly vols. I and XI.

Rymer, "Foedera". 2nd ed. I, London, 1816.

"Scripta de feodis ad regem spectantibus" — collected from the six registers of Philip's record office. "Scriptores," XXIII: 605.

Tardif, "Monuments Historiques," Paris, 1866; especially for the reigns immediately previous to that of Philip.

Teulet, A. "Layettes du Trésor des Chartes" I: Paris, 1863.

Thiery, A. "Recueil des monuments inédits de l'histoire du Tiers État", 3 vols. Paris 1850 etc.

Warnkönig. "Histoire de la Flandre", proofs. ed. A. E. Gheldolf. Brussels, 1835.

Letters. — Between Philip, his ministers, prominent clergy and the popes Lucius III., Urban III., Gregory VIII., Clement III., Celestine III., Innocent III., Honorius III. "Scriptores" XIX: 326—735.

Correspondence with Innocent III, Migne "Patrologia Latina" CCXIV—CCXVI, Innocenti III. Regestorum etc."

Letters of Stephen, bishop of Tournai. The writer was born in 1128, studied law at Bologna, became a member of the monastary of St. Euverte at Orléans in 1155, abbot in 1167; was made abbot of Ste. Geneviève at Paris in 1176 and consecrated bishop of Tournai in 1192. He died Sept. 1203. He was greatly trusted by the king, and his letters throw considerable light on Philip's early years. A selection is given in the "Scriptores" XIX: 282—306.

III. General Historical Works on Philip's reign.

Capefigue, "Histoire de Philippe-Auguste". 5 vols. Brussels, 1830, a work of little critical value.

Dareste, M. C. "Histoire de France", II. Paris, 1884.

Freeman, E. A. "The history of the Norman Conquest of England, its causes and results", V. Oxford, 1876.

Guizot, "Histoire de la civilisation en France", 3rd ed. 4 vols. 1840.

Martin, H. "Histoire de France", IV. Paris, 1839.

Sismondi, "Histoire des Français". Paris, 1823.

Stubbs, W. "Constitutional History of England." I, II. Oxford, 1883.

Todière. "Philippe-Auguste." 4th ed. Tours 1874. Pleasantly written, but wholly uncritical.

Warnkönig, "Histoire de la Flandre" ed. Gheldolf, Brussels 1835.

Zeller and Luchaire, "Philippe-Auguste et Louis VIII." Paris 1884. A collection, in French translation, of extracts from the more important chronicles and poems of Philip's reign, with a few charters and letters.

IV. Special Treatises.

Luchaire, A. "Histoire des Institutions Monarchiques de la France sous les premiers Capetiens, 987—1180". 2 vols. Paris, 1883. A most valuable work, giving the development of monarchical institutions, till the accession of Philip Augustus.

Flach, J. "Les origines de l'ancienne France", I. Paris, 1886.

Bémont, C. "La condamnation de Jean Sans-terre," Revue Historique XXXII. Paris, Sept.-Dec. 1886.

Bernardi, "Mémoire sur l'origine de la pairie en France et en Angleterre", Mémoires de l'Academie des Inscriptions et Belles-Lettres. X: 579. Paris, 1833.

Brial, "Recherches sur l'origine de la pairie en France," "Scriptores" XVII: xiv.

Pardessus, "De la juridiction exercée par la cour féodale du roi sur les grands vassaux de la couronne pendant les XIe, XIIe et XIIIe siècles." Bibliotheque de l'École des Chartes. 2 Series, IV: 281 (1847—48).

Boutaric. "Institutions Militaires de la France". Paris 1863.

Géraud, H. "Les routiers au douzième siècle" and "Mercadier". Bibliotheque de l'École des Chartes, III, pp. 123, 417. (1841—42).

Scheffer-Boichorst, P. "Deutschland und Philipp August von Frankreich in den Jahren 1180 bis 1214". Forschungen zur deutschen Geschichte, VIII, 465. Göttingen, 1868.

Winkelmann, E. "Philipp von Schwaben und Otto IV. von Braunschweig". Jahrbücher der deutschen Geschichte. Leipzig, 1873.

Bréquigny, "Recherches sur les communes", "Ordonnances des rois de France de la troisième race", XI, preface.

Brial, "Scriptores" XIV, preface.

Lefébvre. Les baillis de la Brie au XIII siècle, Bibliotheque de l'École des Chartes". 5 Series I: 179 (1860).

Delisle, L. "Mémoire sur les recueils de judgments rendus par l'éxchiquier de Normandie sous les règnes de Philippe-Auguste, Louis VIII. et Saint-Louis," "Mémoires de l'Academie des Inscriptions et Belles-Lettres", XXIV: pt. 2.

Vuitry. "Etudes sur le régime financier de la France avant la Revolution de 1789". Paris 1878.

The reign of Philip Augustus is a period of great significance in the development of the French monarchy. Whether viewed as an era of large territorial extension, or as an epoch in the consolidation of the royal power, it demands close attention. Its beginning found the authority and dominions of the king of France overshadowed by the possessions and strength of some of his vassals; its end saw the royal domain more than doubled in extent, and the occupant of the throne the most powerful ruler on the soil of modern France.

This increase in the material possessions and in the prestige of the French monarchy was not the result of a radical change in its character. It was a development, due, in large measure, to tendencies which had been less plainly manifested under the earlier sovereigns of the Capetian house, owing to adverse circumstances in their situation; but which were none the less really operative prior to the accession of Philip. The monarchy had, from the time of Hugh Capet onward, a double character. It was predominantly feudal in its relations to its dependents; but its theories, and its practice, were always, to a considerable degree, royal.[1] It was something more than the "great fief", which Mézeray has styled it,[2] even when the power of the monarchs of the third race was most limited. But it was not till the reign of Philip Augustus, that the coincidence of the rule of an able and far-seeing sovereign and a period of unusual weakness in the position of the great vassals and of the neighbouring rulers, gave favorable opportunity for the rapid development of the more distinctively royal attributes of the monarchy.

The increase in royal power a development.

---

[1] Compare Luchaire, „Histoire des Institutions Monarchiques de la France". Paris 1883. I: 51, II: 1 etc.

[2] Quoted by Brussel, „Nouvel Examen de l'Usage général des Fiefs". Paris 1727. I: 147.

Length of Philip's reign. A most obvious advantage enjoyed by Philip is the length of his reign. Born August 21, 1165,[1] he was crowned at All Saints, 1179, and though Louis VII lingered a few months longer, a paralytic invalid[2], from that time onward till his death, July 14, 1223,[3] Philip was king of France. A reign of nearly forty-four years is, in itself, a great opportunity for the development and maturity of a fixed policy. Such a period of rule outlasts the activity of most of its early contemporaries; it affords time to reap the fruits of changes in opinion, as well as to take advantage of the accidents attending the passage of power from hand to hand. So was it in the reign of Philip Augustus. In the course of that long period, the ruler of every great fief of the crown of France was changed at least once of many, several times; and all such transfers naturally afforded scope for the operation of a patient policy of aggression, such as the situation of the French monarchy then required.

More than length of reign essential. But length of reign is not an advantage peculiar to Philip. His father, Louis VII, had been sole occupant of the throne for forty-two years; and though the royal prerogatives had been preserved, and in some respects enlarged, by the wise policy of Suger and other of his counselors, yet the impress left by Louis VII, personally, on the constitutional development of France, was very slight.[4] He lacked the vigor to take advantage of such opportunities as were placed within his reach by his marriage with Eleanor of Aquitaine; or the skill to prevent the growth of a great continental dominion under Henry II of Anjou and of England. Something more than length of reign was needful for increase in the royal power, when menaced by turbulent and energetic vassals. Happily for the future of the French monarchy, those qualities of character which the father lacked

---

[1] Mense augusto, XI kalendas septembris, in festo Timothei et Simphoriani; i. e. Aug. 22, Rigord, ed. Delaborde, "Oeuvres de Rigord et de Guillaume le Breton", Paris 1882, 1: 7, "Scriptores Rerum Francicarum" or "Recueil des Historiens des Gaules et de la France, Bouquet, Brial, Delisle and others, new edition Paris 1878, XVII: 4. Strictly speaking Philip was born on the evening of the 21 st. probably at Gonesse, Delaborde id, note. Delisle "Bibliothèque de l'École des Chartes" 1859, p. 149, 150.

[2] Louis died in 1180: "XIIII kalendas octobris, feria quinta," Rigord, Delaborde I: 22. "Scriptores", XVII: 7.

[3] Delaborde id: 1: 323, "Scriptores", id. 115.

[4] "Vir satis sensatus, pius tamen et mollis, unde Ludovicus Juvenis et Pius nominatus est." John of Ypres, in "Monumenta Germaniae Historica". Pertz and others, Hannover 1826–1888. XXV: 800. Compare Luchaire, "Instit. Monarchiques", II: 262.

were present in the son. Well shaped and merry-faced,[1] quick tem- *Philip's*
pered, a lover of the table and of luxurious habits, Philip was never- *character.*
theless far-seeing in his plans, patient to await their accomplishment,
and forceful and energetic when the moment for action had come.
He was little in sympathy with the religious movements of the time;
but he made the church his assistant in the development of his
policy, and profited immensely from the crusading spirit which it in-
fused into his vassals. His military successes were brilliant; but
they were the fruit of the combinations of a statesman rather than
the genius of a commander, and the victories achieved under him, he
valued more for the aid they gave in the accomplishment of his designs for increasing the extent of the domain and strengthening the
kingly prerogatives, than from any love of war. He used force, where
force seemed necessary; but he was as ready to obtain his end by
bribery or favor. Yet in his policy he had the same aim always in
view; to crush the might of the vassals and exalt the authority of
the crown, was the underlying purpose in all his acts. He attained
so great a measure of success in this work because his patience, skill
and foresight surpassed that of any of the rivals of his later years;
and also because internal quarrels rendered the situation of his opponents, whether in Normandy, Flanders, England, Germany, or southern
France, peculiarly open to the attacks of an aggressive policy.

An inquiry into the state of the French constitution under Philip *Plan of*
Augustus, naturally falls into three main divisions: the theory of *this essay.*
royal power and the position of the royal family itself; the organs
of the central administration; and the relation of the king to the
local government, and to the feudal and corporate estates of the
kingdom.

I. The power of the king under Philip, as under his predeces- *Basis of*
sors, is uniformly recognized, in the charters and on the great seal,[2] *kingly*
as dependent upon God. Philippus Dei gratia Francorum rex,[3] *authority.*

---

[1] "Erat enim forma venustus, corpore decens, facie laetus, capite calvus, colore rubens, potui ciboque deditus, luxuriae pronus, amicis largus, inimicis avarus, in machinis peritissimus, fide catholicus, consilio providus, dicti tenax, judex velox et rectissimus, in victoriis fortunatissimus, vitae timidus, de facili motus, de facili mitigatus, malignos regni primates opprimens eorumque dis-ordias volens, nullum in carcere occidens, minorum consilio utens, nullum nisi parumperde facile odiens." Chron. Turon. "Scriptores," XVIII: 304.

[2] Delisle, "Catalogue des Actes de Philippe-Auguste" Paris, 1856, LXXXIX. Mabillon, "De Re Diplomatica," II: 16: X.

[3] Mabillon, id, II: 3: XXVI, held that Philip introduced the form rex Franciae. Delisle, (Cat. LXIV) denies this, and asserts that Francorum is

is the phrase in which the royal title and the source of the royal authority are set forth.¹ The coronation was preeminently a consecration to a divinely appointed office. The anointing with the God-given chrism was the act in the ceremony which set apart the king as a sacred person; a representative, in some sense, of divine authority.² But the history of the third race, up to the time of Philip Augustus, had exemplified the same struggles between the hereditary and the elective theories of the monarchy which mark the progress of the empire in Germany during the same period. Fortunately a direct heir had never failed in the royal house; but so little settled was the principle of hereditary succession, that none of the Capetian kings had omitted to secure the recognition of his successor during his lifetime.³ This recognition was either a formal designation as

The principles of heredity and election.

---

the only form whose use, as a title, can be proved from the charters. The contraction Franc. is in frequent use, however, and reges Franciae occurs once in the body of one of Philip's charters; while the seal of Louis VIII, as prince, has the inscription Filius regis Franciae, Franciae was certainly in popular use. Compare however the charters printed in Teulet Layettes I: 331, 360 etc. when it would appear that "Francie" is employed in the title.

¹ In letters, Philip expressed first his name and title, then that of the person addressed, save in addressing the pope, when the name of the latter takes precedence in honor. Delisle, Cat. LXV. The king himself added no title to his name save: Dei gratia Francorum rex. In letters addressed to him he is styled usually, when any epithet is given, illustris, as his predecessors of the three races had been. More rarely he is called serenissimus, as in a treaty with Hervey of Nevers. Martène, "Amplissima Collectio" Paris, 1704. I: 1121: serenitas vestra, id. 1114, 1115; serenitas tua, in papal letters, "Scriptores," XIX: 366, 367, 374, 538; serenitas regia, id, 414, 629; celsitudo, id. 366, 403, 646, 667; excellentia, id. 408, 680; excellentissimus, Martène, "Amp. Coll." I: 1145; prudentia, Sep. XIX: 542; sublimitas, id. 538. venerabilis "Gallia Christiana", XIV: 87.

Philip was called: a Deo datus, on account of his birth, as was supposed, in answer to the prayers of his father. "Scriptores", XVII: 4. He gains the title Augustus, by which he is usually known, from Rigord: "Sed forte miramini quod in prima fronte hujus operis voco regem Augustum. Augustos enim vocare consueverunt scriptores, caesares qui rempublicam augmentabant, ab augeo, auges, dictos; unde iste merito dictus est Augustus, ab aucta republica." Prologue to the "De Gestis Philippi". Sep. XVII: 3. Delaborde, "Oeuvres de Rigord etc." I: 6.

² William the Breton, "Philippide", I: 336—360, Sep. XVII: 125. Delaborde id. II: 20, 21.

³ Luchaire, "Instit. Monarchiques", I: 59, points out that association in the crown was practiced also by the later Carolingians, at least by Lothaire in 979.

heir to the throne;[1] or, more usually, an association as king, accomplished by coronation, while the father still lived. In either case the result was the same, — the nobles were obliged to do homage and swear fidelity to the heir.[2]

Something of the old feeling that the succession was a matter of election seems to have remained in the time of Louis VII, notwithstanding the progress of the principle of heredity. But, in spite of the urgency of pope Alexander III that Philip should be associated with Louis on the throne[3], it was not till the latter felt the touch of sickness, that he decided to act. His growing infirmity made him feel, at last, the desirability of laying aside part of the burden of the crown; and he wished to secure the succession of his son according to the precedent of his ancestors.[4] The ready acceptance of his proposition by the assembly before whom he laid it, as well as his delay in following the advice of the pope,[5] shows the strength of the principle of heredity; but the elective idea still existed.

<small>Decadence of the latter.</small>

The election of a new monarch was effected, in the case of Philip Augustus, by an assembly composed of the chief personages of the realm, lay and ecclesiastical, met at the summons of the king, Louis VII. The assembly having come together in the episcopal palace at Paris, the king retired alone to the chapel for a few moments of private prayer. He then addressed the prelates and lay nobles, one by one (a statement that would indicate that the assembly was not numerous, in spite of the imposing title which Rigord bestows upon it),[6] and laid his design before them, asking their consent. The royal proposition was at once approved by the entire assembly, and the council dissolved.[7] Here then was an elec-

<small>Philip's election formal.</small>

---

[1] In the cases of Louis VI and his son Philip. Luchaire, id. 63.

[2] id.

[3] Letter of Alexander III to Henry, archbishop of Reims, "Scriptores" XV: 925. It was written in 1171 or 1172.

[4] "Sentiensque se adversa valetudine paralysi aliquantulum praegravari, convocavit Parisius generale concilium", Rigord, Sep. XVII: 4. Delaborde I: 10.

[5] The youth of Philip would not have prevented an earlier association, had Louis desired it. Robert crowned his eldest son, Hugh, at ten years of age; Henry had Philip I crowned at seven; Louis VII himself received the crown at eleven. Luchaire, "Instit. Monarchiques", I: 60, 61.

[6] "Ludovicus . . . . . convocavit Parisius generale concilium omnium archiepiscoporum, episcoporum, abbatum, necnon et baronum totius regni Francorum, in palatium venerabilis patris nostri Mauricii Parisiensis episcopi." Rigord. Sep. XVII: 4. Delaborde, I. 10.

[7] "Ubi residentibus omnibus, solus Ludovicus capellam ingressus primo, ut in omnibus operibus suis facere consueverat, oratione fusa ad Dominum

tion, as far as form could indicate it; but in reality it was little more than a form. There was no other son of the royal line, as at some previous periods, whose candidacy might form the rallying-point of a faction,[1] nor had opposition ever succeeded in defeating the regular succession of the first-born, in the Capetian house.[2] In the case of Philip, there is no evidence of opposition, or even of discussion, in the elective assembly. The action of that body was formal: its summons was the recognition of an idea that was passing away; its real work was to register the royal will.

<small>No effort to secure the election of Louis (VIII).</small> But, by the end of the reign of Philip Augustus, the principle of election had so far become obsolete that, although he was long an invalid, and, on that account, made his testament some months before his death,[3] he did not attempt to secure the association of his son, Louis (VIII), in the crown, or even to obtain his designation as the future monarch. Several reasons may be given for this course. Louis VIII was believed to be, by right of his mother, a true representative of the Carolingian line,[4] as well as heir of the Capetian race through his father. In him the second and third races were united.[5] But this descent, though possibly appealing to the sentiment of a few, could really have done nothing to make the claims of Louis more plausible to the baronage. No party was interested in a Carolingian restoration. The student monk might delight to

<small>deinde vocatis singulatim archiepiscopis, episcopis et omnibus regni principibus, communicavit eis consilium quod . . . . . filium suum . . . . . cum consilio eorum et voluntate, in regem Francorum sublevare volebat. Audientes autem prelati et principes voluntatem regis, omnes unaminiter clamaverunt, dicentes: Fiat, fiat. Et sic solutum est concilium. id. id.

[1] E. g. under Robert, after the death of his eldest son, Hugh, in 1025; when factions supported the two younger sons, Henry and Robert. Scp. X: 39, Luchaire, "Instit. Mon." I: 64.

[2] From the reign of Hugh Capet to the period now under consideration, the eldest living son had never failed to secure the designation or coronation.

[3] His will was made in Sept. 1222. In it he gives as a reason, "si aliquid humanus nobis contigerit in hac presenti egritudine." He died July 14. 1223. Scp. XVII: 114, 115. Will, Teulet, "Layettes du Trésor des Chartes" I: 540.

"Mox testamento finali, quicquid habebat
Mobilis ipse rei, proprio determinat ore
. . . .
Inde fere totum vexatus febre per annum."
Philippide, Bk. XII: 524—529.

[4] Compare "Scriptores," XIII: 585.

[5] "Rediit regnum ad stirpem Caroli Magni imperatoris, de qua originem ex parte matris dignoscitur contraxisse." Scp. XVII: 302.</small>

point out the relationship of his new sovereign to the hero of the romance of the time, the emperor Charlemagne; but no fear of a rising in favor of the remote descendants of that ruler could have given a serious thought to any Capetian monarch of the twelth century. With far greater probability could it be affirmed that the age of Louis,[1] at the time of his father's fatal illness, rendered an association in the crown at once less desirable, from the independent role that he would have been tempted to play in the government, and less necessary as a means to secure favor to his succession, since his soldierly qualities and his administrative activity had long made him prominent in the eyes of the nobles. The probability of attempted revolt against an heir to the throne who was already thirty-five, was evidently much less than against a boy of fourteen, the age of Philip at his coronation. Some support is given to this view by the conduct of Louis VIII himself on his death bed. The suddenness of his last illness precluded the possibility of summoning an assembly which might designate or elect his twelve year old son, the later Saint Louis, to the throne he was about to vacate. The dying king, however, requested the twelve nobles, that were at his bed-side, to swear to recognize the young prince as sovereign. This they did, assigning a day for his coronation and summoning the nobles of the realm to be present.[2] The intention of Louis VIII was certainly to secure the advantages of a formal designation to his minor son. But at the death of Philip, in 1223, no prospect of contest disturbed the succession. His own victories and firm administration had raised the power of the monarchy beyond that of any of his predecessors of the third race; his son was in the prime of manhood. It is not surprising that under such circumstances of favor the principle of heredity so excluded that of election that even the form of a designation seemed no longer worth preserving.[3]

But if the principle of heredity in the direct line of the royal succession was generally accepted, at the time of Philip's death, the right of election was still admitted, at least tacitly, in case of a failure of immediate heirs to the throne. The testament of Philip *Tacit admission of election in case of failure of the direct line.*

---

[1] Louis VIII was born in 1187, probably Sept. 5. He was therefore nearly 36 at the time of his father's death.

[2] Compare the two charters. Brussel, "Nouvel Examen de l'Usage général des Fiefs" Paris 1727, I: 68.

[3] The length of time which elapsed between the death of Philip and the coronation of his son, July 14 to August 6, shows the entire absence of fear of opposition to Louis' accession.

Augustus, prepared, in 1190,[1] to provide for the administration of goverment during his absence on the crusade, and the course to be followed should he fail to return, makes ample provision for the succession of Louis, then not quite three years old, in the event of Philip's death. It even prescribes the disposition of the royal treasure in case of the demise of both father and son. But it is silent as to the succession, should Philip and Louis both die. It may properly be inferred that the choice of a sovereign would have returned to the hands of the nobles. The principle of heredity, recognized in practice as the rule in the direct line, was not yet sufficiently established to allow the king to make provision for the unelected succession of a representative of a younger branch of the royal house.[2] Philip Augustus himself recognized this dependence of the crown, in the last instance, on the vassals. Wendover reports that in discussion with the papal legate, Walo, in April 1216,[3] regarding the proposed invasion of England by prince Louis, Philip answered to the legate's assertion that the kingdom of England belonged, by gift of John, to the pope: "No king or prince can give his kingdom without the assent of his barons, who are bound to defend that kingdom."[4] And the nobles who heard this reply of their sovereign, gave it their hearty appoval.[5] On the same principle, the converse of this proposition must have been true, at least in theory, — that the barons were bound to defend no prince or king, to whose reception of the kingdom they had not given assent.

Philip's criticism of John.

---

[1] "Scriptores", XVII: 30. Delaborde, "Oeuvres de Rigord etc." I: 100—105.

[2] Had the direct line failed at this time, the succession would not have been an easy question. Louis VII had no other son, and had female succession been excluded, as after the death of Charles IV in 1328, the inheritance would have fallen to the descendants of the sons of Louis VI, the counts of Dreux and Courtenai, none of whom were nobles of the first rank.

[3] At Meulun, (compare as to locality, Bémont, "La Condemnation de Jean-Sansterre" Revue Historique XXXII: 49. Wendover's text has, wrongly, Lugdunum, Lyon, for which Brial suggested Laon), the fifteenth day after Easter, i. e. April 25, 1216. Matthew Paris. edition of Luard, Master of Rolls Series, II: 651.

[4] "Nullus rex vel princeps potest dare regnum suum sine assensu baronum suorum qui regnum illud tenentur defendere". Matthew Paris, "Chronica Majora" id.

[5] "Tunc quoque magnates omnes uno ore clamare coeperunt quod pro isto articulo starent usque ad mortem; ne videlicet rex vel princeps per solam voluntatem suam posset regnum dare vel tributarium facere, unde nobiles regni efficerentur servi." id.

Though it might suit the royal purpose, in a contest with the authority of the pope, to proclaim the ultimate dependence of the crown on the vassals, Philip was no less careful to declare, on other occasions, the superiority of the king in secular matters to any suzerain on the soil of France, whether lay or ecclesiastical. The territories ruled over by the great vassals of the crown were usually aggregations of estates owing homage to many different lords. Thus, for example, the count of Champagne, at the close of the twelfth century, owed fealty for the fiefs composing his domain to more than half a score of over-lords, including, in addition to the king, the archbishops of Reims and Sens, the bishops of Langres and Auxerre, and the duke of Burgundy.[1] The acquisition of new estates by the crown gave rise naturally to many questions as to the homage due for these additions to the domain, particularly in cases where this homage had been paid by the former possessor to an ecclesiastical authority whose right to receive such fealty was not extinguished by the transfer of the actual tenancy of the fief. In all these cases Philip acted on the principle, which he expressly proclaimed in a charter making compensation to the church of Amiens for the homage due for the county of the same name, that the king ought not and could not do homage to any.[2] That this exemption from fealty was not purchased without substantial concessions and the sacrifice of considerable revenue on the part of the king to obtain his purpose, is proof of the importance attached by Philip to this assertion of the supremacy of the crown.[3] *The king can do homage to none*

The formal election of Philip Augustus as associate king having taken place, as has been seen, Louis VII proceeded at once to sum- *Philip's coronation*

[1] D' Arbois de Jubainville, "Histoire des comtes et des ducs de Champagne" Paris, 1859—1869. VII: 57—62.

[2] "Voluit haec ecclesia et benigne concessit, ut feodum suum absque faciendo teneremus, cum utique nemini facere debebamus hominium, vel possimus." Martène, "Amplissima Collectio" I: 965.

[3] At Amiens Philip surrendered the right of entertainment enjoyed by the king and his servants. id. 965, For the homage due for Hesdin Philip relinquished the entertainment due from the bishop of Térouanne id. 1001; that of Gien by a like surrender at Auxerre and Varzi, to the bishop of Auxerre, Sep. XVIII: 726; Various homages due by the nobles of Vermandois to the bishop of Noyon were redeemed, when Philip came into possession of the fief, by the gift, to the bishop, of the royal holdings at Lassigni and Cui, Martène, Amp. Coll. I: 1112. A similar gift of the royal rights over the church of St. Thomas at Crespy, with 60 arpents of land, to the bishop of Senlis redeemed the homage due for the recently acquired fiefs of Crespy, "Gallia Christiana" X: 1409.

mon the nobles of the realm to be present at the crowning.¹ As the illness of the young prince prevented the occurence of the ceremony at the time at first appointed,² Louis, by the advice of his counselors,³ issued a new edict designating All Saints, November 1, 1179, as the day. The place of coronation was, according to custom, at Reims,¹ the seat of the primate of France; and the general usage of the Capetian house was followed, in that the crowning was at the hands of the primate himself.⁵ The ceremony of coronation was performed in the usual fashion, by anointment with the sacred oil,⁶ and the imposition of the crown;⁷ while all the assembly, barons, clergy and people, shouted: "Long live the king".⁸ The event was marked by the absence of Louis VII, too feeble to be moved from Paris;⁹ but the assembly was a brilliant representation of the nobles, nevertheless. Chief in its ranks, and preeminent in the honorary services they rendered, were Henry, son of Henry II of England, and already associated with his father on the throne; and Philip, count

¹ "Ludovicus . . . . publico edicto citari fecit omnes archiepiscopos et episcopos et comites et barones regni Francorum" "Gesta Henrici Secundi", generally styled Benedict of Peterborough, Stubbs Edition, I: 240. The genuineness of the ordinance, attributed to Louis VII, regulating the coronation ceremonies on this occasion, is now generally denied.

² The Assumption of the Virgin, August 15. Sep. XVII: 4. Benedict Petrob. I: 240.

³ "Convocatis consiliariis suis, publico praecipit edicto". Benedict Petrob. I: 242.

⁴ Save in the case of Robert, Hugh his son, and Louis VI, all the Capetian kings were crowned at Reims. Luchaire, "Instit. Monarchiques", I: 66.

⁵ Before Hugh Capet, the dukes of his line had been crowned by the archbishop of Sens, since the archbishop of Reims was a partisan of the Carolingians. Hugh and his successors were mostly crowned by the latter prelate, the only exceptions, after Robert's son Hugh, being Louis VII, whom political exigencies constrained to be crowned at Orleans, by Ivo of Chartres; and Louis VII, who was consecrated by pope Innocent II himself, then at a council at Reims. Luchaire, "Instit.", I: 66, 67.

Philip was crowned by William of Champagne, cardinal, archbishop of Reims, his uncle on his mother's side. The primate was assisted by the archbishops of Tours, Sens and Bourges, and by most of the bishops of the kingdom. Benedict Petrob. 1: 242.

⁶ Philippide, I: 340, Sep. XVII: 125. Delaborde, II: 20, 21. We have, unfortunately, no such detailed account of the coronation of Philip Augustus as we possess regarding that of Philip I. Sep. XI: 32, 33.

⁷ Philippide I: 358.

⁸ "Vivat rex". Sep. XVII: 5. Delaborde I: 13.

⁹ A second stroke of paralysis had deprived Louis VII of the use of the right side of his body. Benedict, Petrob. I: 243.

of Flanders. The former preceeded the youthful Philip Augustus in the procession from the palace to the church, bearing in his hands the crown to be placed on the young king's brow;[1] a service which he rendered by reason of the fief of Normandy.[2] But the count of Flanders was probably the most conspicuous figure among the laymen present at the coronation ceremony. Anxious to perpetuate the influence which he had already acquired at court under Louis VII[3] and to maintain his position as adviser to the young king in the face of the party of the queen-mother, he had come to Reims with a strong armed force prepared to assert his right to carry the sword of state before the youthful monarch in the coronation pageant.[4] He maintained this claim, and obtained even more of a share in the honors of the hour, if we may credit the somewhat doubtful assertion of Ralph de Diceto, that he fulfilled the office of seneschal at the banquet also.[5] Other nobles, whose names have not been recorded, did the lesser services of the festal day.[6]

The influence of Philip of Flanders over the young king soon bore its fruit in the marriage of Philip Augustus, at Bapaumes,

Marriage and second coronation.

---

[1] Benedict Petrob. I: 242.

[2] Ralph de Diceto would have us believe that Henry performed this act simply from a kindly wish that the weight of the crown should not prove burdensome to the young king. Stubbs edition, I: 439. Hoveden gives the far more probable explanation that the service was "de jure ducatus Normanniae" Stubbs edition, II: 194.

[3] Philip had accompanied Louis VII on his pilgrimage to Canterbury to pray for the recovery of Philip Augustus, in August 1179. Benedict I: 241. It had been through Flemish assistance that Louis VII had maintained himself against Henry II. Luchaire "Instit." II: 45.

[4] Philippus .... qui in gestamine gladii regalis jus reclamabat, cum armis et militibus multis venit. Gislebert, edition of Prof. Arndt. "Monumenta Germaniae". XXI: 481—601. Separate edition, Hanover 1869, p. 117, 118; compare Benedict Petrob. I; 242.

[5] "Philippus itaque rex Francorum, tam in gladio perferendo, quam in dapibus apponendis, Philippum Flandriae comitem privilegiatum habuit ministerialem, utentem duplici jure, paterno scilicet et uxorio," Ralph de Diceto, Stubbs edition, I: 438. Philip of Flanders was the husband of Elizabeth of Vermandois, whose father, Rudolph I, had been seneschal under Louis VI and VII, till his death in 1152. But he had bequeathed no hereditary right to the office. If the count of Flanders acted as seneschal, it could have been only for the festivities of the coronation; the real seneschal of France, at this time, was Theobald, count of Blois, uncle of Philip Augustus on his mother's side.

[6] "Multi ducis et comites et barones praeibent et sequebantur illum, diversi diversis deputati obsequiis", Benedict, Petrob. I: 242, 243.

April 28, 1180,[1] to Elizabeth, daughter of the count of Hainault and niece of the count of Flanders. Nothing unusual seems to have marked the ceremony, which was performed by the bishop of Senlis;[2] but the marriage gave occasion for a second coronation, that of the young queen.[3] Though the nobles and clergy of France were summoned to be present, as before, the place for the ceremony fixed at Sens and Pentecost, 1180, as the day;[4] the outward aspect of the whole event was changed by the hostility of the Champagne party, which numbered among its adherents the queen-mother, the archbishop of Reims and the count of Blois, uncles of the young king, and many, who had stood high in the counsels of Louis VII.[5] Their enmity led to an entire change of programme. It would appear that a consulation between the archbishop of Reims and Philip of Flanders was planned, and may possibly have taken place;[6] but the growing opposition of the French nobles to the Flemish influence made a reconciliation difficult, even if it were desired. So threatening was the prospect, that the young king, at the advice of Philip of Flanders anticipated the date set for the coronation of the queen, and instead of allowing the ceremony to take place at Sens, had it hastily performed at St. Denis, early in the morning of Ascension day, at the hands of the archbishop of Sens, assisted by the bishops of Paris and Orleans.[7] By general usage, though the custom was not so definitely fixed as in the case of the king, the archbishop of Reims should have crowned the queen; and William of Champagne was not slow in sending complaints to pope Alexander III, respecting what he deemed the usurpation of his brother of Sens.[8]

[1] Gislebert, small edition, 121.
[2] Sep. XVII: 617.
[3] Elizabeth, daughter of Baldwin V of Hainault and Margaret, sister of Philip of Flanders, was born at Lille in April 1170. She was therefore ten years old at her marriage. Gislebert, 95.
[4] Benedict Petrob. I: 245.
[5] Beside their natural disinclination to see power pass into the hands of the count of Flanders, and their own exclusion from influence at the court of the new king, the Champagne party had a special grievance regarding Elizabeth of Hainault who had been promised in marriage to Henry, son of Henry, count of Champagne. Gislebert, 117, 120.
[6] Compare a letter of Stephen of Tournai, Sep. XIX: 283.
[7] May 29, 1180. "Valde mane, orto jam sole", Benedict Petrob. 1: 246. His assistants are mentioned by Ralph de Diceto, Stubbs edition, II: 5.
[8] Benedict Petrob. 1: 246. While the sole right of queenly coronation was claimed by the archbishop of Reims; even under Louis VII, two queens, Eleanor of Aquitaine and Constance of Castile, had been crowned elsewhere

But what is most noteworthy, even in this hasty coronation, is that it was a true counterpart of the coronation of the king. The queen was set apart for her office, not only by the solemn imposition of the crown, but by anointing as well.[1] At the coronation of his queen, the young king was himself a second time crowned.[2] But it would not appear that Philip was anointed at this time; or that the coronation implied any want of validity in the previous ceremony at Reims. Rather was it in accordance with the custom which led the monarchs to be crowned at solemn assemblies,[3] partly as a recognition of the dignity of the occasion,[4] and partly as an assertion of the divinely appointed character of the kingly office. At this crowning, as at Reims, Philip of Flanders bore the royal sword in the festal procession;[5] but the majority of the nobles, who had graced the previous pageant, were absent.

{Coronation of Philip's queens.}

Fewer details have been preserved concerning the ceremonies attendant on the coronation of Philip's second queen, Ingeburgis of Denmark; but enough is related to show that, in general features, it was similar to the coronation of Elizabeth. The settled state of the kingdom allowed the ceremony to be conducted in a less hurried manner, and by the customary ecclesiastical ministrant; but otherwise it was essentially the same. Philip journeyed to Amiens, and there awaited his bride.[6] On the day of her arrival the marriage took place,[7] and the unction and coronation followed on the subsequent day, the assumption of the Virgin, 1193,[8] at the hands of the arch-

than at Reims, and the latter at the hands of the archbishop of Sens. Luchaire points out that in this case also the archbishop of Reims complained. "Institutions", I: 142. 143. Compare the "Monumenta Germaniae", XXVI: 237.

[1] "Unctio et coronatio", Benedict. Petrob. I: 245. "Inungi et regia corona insignari . . . . fecit". Gislebert. 121.

[2] "Rex Philippus secundo imposuit sibi diadema". Rigord, Scp. XVII: 7. Delaborde, I: 21.

[3] Compare Luchaire "Iustit. Monarchiques", I: 69, 70.

[4] "Ubi ipse ad sue nupte noveque regine honorem, regalem cum ea gestavit coronam". Gislebert, 121.

[5] Gislebert, id. Rigord, Scp. XVII: 7. Delaborde, I: 21.

[6] Scp. XIX: 343.

[7] "Duxit uxorem . . . . in vigilia Assumptionis Sanctae Mariae". Scp. XVIII: 546. "Quae (Ingeburgis) . . . pervenisset Ambianis, ubi rex ipso die desponsavit eamdem". Scp. XIX: 343. August 14.

[8] "In crastino fecit eam coronari et consecrari in reginam". Hoveden III: 324. "In reginam inungi fecit", Scp. XVIII: 701. "Die dominica" id. 546.

bishop of Reims,[1] assisted by many bishops of his province, and in the presence of a large assembly of nobles.[2] Here again, as at the crowning of Elizabeth in 1180, Philip was crowned also.[3]

Sentence of divorce on account of pretended affinity having been passed against Ingeburgis[4], Philip married Maria,[5] daughter of the duke of Meran,[6] apparently at Compiègne, in June 1196.[7] The presence of the archbishop of Reims and some of his suffragans at Compiègne about this time[8] would make it probable that the ceremony was countenanced by the attendance of the primate of France; but it could hardly have been performed by him.[9] The chroniclers of the period, doubtless moved by the opposition of the Roman see, which soon declared the previous divorce and consequently this marriage invalid, have as far as possible avoided giving details of the event.

Significance of the ceremony. We notice in the two royal marriages, regarding which we possess sufficient particulars to warrant a conclusion, three essential factors, corresponding to the three moments in the creation of a

[1] Scp. XVIII: 260, XIX: 343. William of Champagne, archbishop of Reims, cardinal priest titular of St. Sabina and papal legate. He was assisted by the bishops of Arras, Cambrai, Amiens, Térouanne, Tournai, and other suffragans, Scp. XVIII: 546.

[2] "multis Franciae principibus astantibus". id. XVIII: 546.

[3] "fecit eam secum solemniter coronari". Scp. XIX: 343.

[4] By the archbishop of Reims and other bishops assembled in the presence of the king and barons, at Compiègne, 82 days after the marriage — i. e. Nov. 4 or 5, reckoning either from the actual marriage or the coronation ceremony. Hoveden, Stubbs, III: 224, Scp. XVIII: 546. XIX: 343.

[5] Or Agnes.

[6] Bertold IV.

[7] "Mense junio, Baldoinus comes Flandrie fecit hominium regi Philippo apud Compennium, adstantibus Guillelmo Remensi archiepiscopo . . . . . . eodem mense Philippus rex duxit uxorem nomine Mariam filiam ducis Meranie". Rigord, Delaborde, I: 135. Scp. XVII: 46. see also XVIII: 759.

[8] id. see also Delisle, Cat. 498, 500.

[9] In March 1195 Celestine III had ordered William to oppose any second marriage while Ingeburgis lived. "Fraternitati vestrae per apostolica scripta mandamus atque praecipimus quatinus, si forte praefatus rex, conditionis oblitus, ea vivente, aliam superducere voluit, vos, auctoritate freti apostolica, id eidem inhibere firmiter procuretis". Scp. XIX: 340. However inclined to favor Philip William may have been, he would hardly have dared to perform a marriage ceremony in the face of such an inhibition. Moreover when Innocent III recounted the clemency of the Roman see to William, in spite of his offences in the matter of the divorce, he makes no mention of the marriage of Maria to Philip, which would hardly have been omitted had the ceremony been performed by the primate. Scp. XIX: 415, 512.

king.¹ These are the marriage, the unction, and the imposition of the crown. By the first the royal choice was manifested; as the choice of the nobility was, in form at least, expressed in the election of a king. The other moments are alike in the creation of a king or a queen. A royal marriage was therefore to a certain exent a partnership in the royal dignity. The youth and early death of Elizabeth of Hainault,² and the inexplicable antipathy which Philip felt for his Danish wife, Ingeburgis, made the influence of the queen on the course of affairs much less than under some previous Capetian sovereigns. The coronation at marriage, nevertheless, lent something of the royal dignity to the queen, it gave her a position not wholly dependent on the will of the king, but which belonged permanently to one who had been a royal consort. It finds its natural and fitting expression in the position occupied by the queen mother, the widow of Louis VII.

During the ascendency of Philip of Flanders, queen Adela was a prominent object of attack.³ Her estates were siezed and she fled from the kingdom. But the queen mother, supported by her relatives of the Champagne faction, was far too important a personage to be lightly put aside. The interview of Henry II and Philip Augustus, between Gisors and Trie,⁴ by effecting the fall of Philip of Flanders, opened the way for the restoration of her rights. Philip Augustus agreed to provide for his mother a separate and honorable maintenance, as long as Louis VII should live, and at his death the use of her dowry should at once be restored to the queen.⁵ The agreement was carried out.⁶ So far all was a mere act of justice.

Influential position of the queen-mother.

¹ Luchaire Instit. I: 69, points out that the three moments in the elevation of a king were election, unction, coronation.

² She died March 15. 1190. Rigord, Delaborde, 97. She was therefore not quite 20 at her death.

³ "Reginae Alae matri suae dotalitium suum totum at propter nuptias donationem ... auferendo" Scp. XVIII: 141. "Matri suae annuere noluerit ut in sua dispositione habent castella vel villas suae dotae. XVII: 661.

⁴ June 28. 1180.. Treaty, Rymer, Foedera I: 1: 36.

⁵ "Quod praedictae reginae Franciae, matri suae, singulis diebus, quamdiu Lodowicus rex pater suus viveret, septem libras parisinorum ad quotidianum victum solveret; et, post decessum patris sui totam dotam suam, qua rex Francorum Lodowicus eam die desponsationis suae dotavit, in integrum redderet, retentis tantum modo sibi castellis et munitionibus ejusdem dotae". Benedict Petrob. I: 246. In 1217 the allowance for queen Ingeburgis was only 3½ l daily. Brussel I: 552.

⁶ In 1184, 1197, 1206—1219 Philip Augustus confirmed gifts made by queen Adela. — Delisle Cat. 103, 111, 515, 976, 979, 1921.

But the absence of Philip Augustus from France during the crusade of 1190—91 necessitated the appointment of regents for the kingdom, and guardians for his heir,[1] then not three years old. First of the two regents, in the position in which her name is placed in the act regulating the administration of the realm, is the queen mother, Adela.[2] In conjunction with her brother, the archbishop of Reims, she was to have the oversight of the government during the absence of the king. Doubtless had Philip's own wife, Elizabeth, been living, she would have occupied the post of regent, instead of the queen mother. But the position of one who had once been a queen was of such permanent dignity that her appointment as regent was considered fitting and natural.[3] With the return of Philip from the crusade the queen mother relinquished her direct share in the government. She appears to have lived henceforth, till her death, in the quiet enjoyment of her dowry.[4]

Position of Elizabeth and Ingeburgis. Though Philip's first queen, Elizabeth, took no active part in the administration, yet her position was one of such moment in the kingdom, that the heads of the Champagne faction took active measures,[5] in 1184, to procure a divorce on account of the hostility then existing between[6] the queen's father and uncle, Baldwin of Hainault and Philip of Flanders, and Philip Augustus. Happily, cooler counsels

---

[1] "Adele carissime matri sue et Guillelmo Remensi archiepiscopo, avunculo suo, pro tutela et custodia totum regnum Francorum cum filio suo dilectissimo Ludovico commendavit". Rigord, Delaborde, I: 99. Sep. XVII: 29.

[2] "Regina et archiepiscopus" is the order in the will of Philip Augustus, id, Delaborde 100—105, Sep. XVII: 30, 31.

[3] We cannot consider the part played by the barons at Vézelai in the choice of the regents as anything more than a formal assent — "accepta licentia ab omnibus baronibus suis" id. Delaborde, 97, Sep. XVII: 29. — for the will which prescribes the functions of these regents had been decided on by the king, with the advice of his counselors at Paris, previously — "Parisius convocatis amicis et familaribus testamentum condidit, et regni totius ordinationem fecit". id. Delaborde 100, Sep. XVII: 30. But we can at least consider the words of Rigord as indicating that there was no decided opposition to the queen's appointment.

[4] There is no mention of allowance for her expenses in the account for 1202 Brussel II: CXXXIX etc. Philip confirmed gifts and exchanges made by her 1197—8 and 1206. Delisle Cat. 515, 976, 979.

[5] Wm. of Reims, Theobald of Blois, Stephen of Sancerre (the king's maternal uncles), the duke of Burgundy (Hugo), Ralph of Clermont. etc. Gislebert, 139.

[6] Gislebert, id.

prevailed,[1] and the divorce was not consummated; but the attempt shows the importance attaching to the position of queen, and the value set by the faction then dominant in France upon an office so powerful as a means of influence.

The dislike of Philip for his second queen, Ingeburgis, prevented anything like cordial relations between them. Nor was it likely that one who for nineteen years was practically a prisoner,[2] and was even at times in want of the necessaries of life,[3] would have had much personal influence on the course of political affairs. After being received again into favor, in 1213, she had, however, her private establishment, though on a moderate scale,[4] and her own servants.[5] The rather scanty liberality of her husband bequeathed to her 10,000 livres and allowed her some revenues to be expended for religious ends.[6] Her dowry was considerable,[7] and must have yielded her a handsome support. Her charters she was able to confirm with her own private seal.[8] Her title was the same as that

---

[1] Robert, count of Braine, and Robert, count of Dreux, his son, cousins of Philip Augustus, opposed the divorce; together with Philip, bishop of Beauvais, and Henry, bishop of Orleans. id. 140.

[2] In 1213, "Rex... recepit in gratiam et in conjugales affectus legitimam suam Isemburgem reginam, quae per annos XIX repulsa, multo tempore apud Stampas in tenui victu et arcta custodia transegerat dies suos". Scp. XVIII: 281.

[3] Compare a letter of Innocent III. to Philip, April 2, 1207. Scp. XIX: 486.

[4] Brussel, "Usage," I: 552, quotes from the treasury account of 1217, "Pro expensa regina de VII^{xx} diebus, tres minus, usque ad octab. Omnium Sanctorum, IIII^c IIII^{xx} libras, x sol. minus." i. e. 479 l. 10 s. for 137 days, or 3$^1/_2$ livres a day. The queen mother, Adela, had received 7 l. a day, by the agreement made between Gisors and Trie, in 1180.

[5] "Mille autem libras volumus familie nostre distribui.... secundum servitium quod ipse persone nobis fecerunt". Will of Ingeburgis, Sept. 1218. Delisle, Cat. appendix p. 520. She did not die at this time.

[6] He left her 10,000 l. by his will of 1222, Scp. XVII: 114; Teulet, Layettes, I: 549; but he apparently had put a similar sum at her disposal, in case of her death. The will of Ingeburgis, of 1218, provides"; de decem milibus libris quas karissimus maritus et dominus noster Philippus .... nobis dedit pro salute anime nostre distribuendas, et de centum libratis reddituum quas ipse similiter nobis dedit etc". Delisle p. 520.

[7] Charter of dowry given at Amiens, 1193: "Philippus etc..... donamus in dotalitium quicquid pertinet ad praeposituram Aurelianensem et Checiacum, et Castrum-novum et Novillam". i. e. Orleans, Chéci, Château neuf and Neuville; Baluze, "Miscellaneorum" Paris 1715, VII: 245. These provisions are repeated in an agreement between Ingeburgis and Louis VIII at the accession of the latter in 1223. id. 243.

[8] Charter of Ingebergis, 1223: "sigilli nostri auctoritate," Baluze id. 248.

of the king, "Dei gratia Francorum regina";[1] like him she phrased her charters in the first person plural,[2] and she was addressed with similar epithets of honor.[3]

The crown-prince, Louis.

The position of the crown prince, under Philip Augustus, was less important governmentally, than it had been under Philip I, when the greater share of the active administration fell into the hands of Louis VI.; it was not so significant as that of Philip Augustus himself had been during the closing years of the life of Louis VII. The activity of Philip Augustus throughout most of his reign was such that he felt little need of assistance in the control of the administration; and he was doubtless a sufficient judge of men to recognize the want of political skill which characterized Louis (VIII). Even had Philip been more inclined to depend on others than he naturally was, the failure of Louis' attempt to win the English throne would have demonstrated the inability of the prince to carry out enterprises demanding patience and judgment such as most of the efforts of his father had required, and would have prevented any great degree of reliance on him during Philip's later years.[4]

Necessarily an important political factor, but Philip delays bringing him into prominence.

Nevertheless, the role played by the heir apparent could but be a conspicuous one. Heir by right of his mother to one of the richest and most coveted of the lands of northern France[5] and having

[1] Baluze id. Delisle, Cat. appendix p. 520. Letters, Sep. XIX: 322, 323 etc.
[2] Baluze id. Delisle id.
[3] She is addressed, or referred to, as "illustris," Baluze, id VII: 248, Sep. XIX: 323, 406 etc.; "Excellentissima," Sep. XIX: 323; "Excellentia vestra" id. 315, 323; "Gloriosa" id: 315; "Nobilissima," Baluze, id. VII: 245.
[4] It may properly be doubted whether the Capetian dynasty could have been permanently established on the English throne; but the immediate failure of the attempt was due almost as much to a conspicuous absence of those conciliatory qualities, whose presence in his father made the conquest of Normandy possible, as to the death of his chief opponent, John. This folly is especially shown in his alienation of his friends among the English nobility by gifts of castles etc. to French favorites. Matthew Paris, II; 666, 667. The author just quoted was conscious of the great difference between Philip and Louis; he records, in his chronicle of 1223: "Cui successit Ludovicus filius ejus, sed multum dissimiles hic vir et ille."
[5] Arras, St. Omer, Aire, Hesdin — the later Artois — this was the dowry of Elizabeth of Hainault, Louis', mother, and "compositum fuit equidem quod si filia comitis Hanoniensis .... absque proprii corpore herede decederat, predicte possessiones ad comitem Hanoniensem et ejus heredes redirent". Gislebert. 120. 121.

„De justo dotalicio suo tunc domino regi reliquit Sanctum Audomarum et Ariam, que post ipsius Mathildis decessum ad domini regis Francorum filium

a plausible claim to the throne of England through his wife,[1] Louis was certainly one of the political factors of the time with whom it was necessary to reckon. But though this importance of the son was largely the result of the political skill of Philip Augustus, the latter was in no haste to bring him personally into the political arena. Louis was born in the first week of September, 1187 — probably on the fifth day of the month.[2] He was married, May 22 or 23, 1200,[3] to Blanche of Castile, niece of John of England, at Portmort in Normandy, whither the French court was obliged to go for the ceremony, as the interdict laid on France by Innocent III, on account of Philip's refusal to dismiss Maria of Meran, prevented its celebration on French soil,[4] At his marriage Issondun, Graçai, and the fiefs of Berri which were held by André of Chauvigni, had been assigned by John as the dowry of the bride with the promise of large additions should John die without heirs.[5] The young couple had enjoyed a separate

---

parvulum Ludovicum jure hereditario devenire debebant" id 233, 234 anno 1191. St. Omer and Aire had to be given up by Philip to Baldwin of Flanders by the treaty of Jan. 1200 — Martène "Amp. Col." I: 1021; but were relinquished to Louis by a charter of Ferrandus and his wife Joanna of Flanders Febr. 1212. Warnkönig' Hist. de la Fl. I: 346.

[1] Blanche was daughter of Alphonso VIII. of Castile and Eleanor, daughter of Henry II. of England.

[2] There is a curious confusion in the records of the birth of Louis. Gisbert 178 says: "mense Augusto." The "Genealogia Com. Flandriae", Sep. XVIII: 561. "pridie kal. Sept. i. e. Aug. 31. Benedict. Petrob. Stubbs II: 9, says "III nonas sept, die Jovis" i. e. Sept. 3. Rigord, Delaborde I: 81, MCLXXXVII, quarta die Septembris hora tertia fuit eclipsis solis particularis in XVIII gradu Virginis . . . sequente die, videlicet quinta die Septembris, natus fuit Ludovicus . . . . feria secunda, hora XI diei usualis". But the 5 Sept, 1187, was Saturday, not Monday. But this eclipse — reported also as occuring "pridie nonas Septembris, feria sexta, et hora sexta" in England, by Gervais of Canterbury, Sep. XVII: 670 — is so striking a circumstance that Rigord could hardly have failed to note correctly whether the birth occured before or after it — Sept. 5 would therefore seem the correct date.

[3] Rigord, "Delaborde I: 148, says:" MCC, mense Maio, in Ascensione Domini, pax reformata est . . . . Porro sequenti feria secunda, Ludovicus . . . . duxit uxorem." i. e. Mon. May 22. Hoveden, IV: 115, says: "et in crastino, scilicet X kal. junii, feria tertia," i. s. Tues. May 23.

[4] Hoveden IV: 115 — The marriage was by Elias, archbishop of Bordeaux id.

[5] Notwithstanding Hoveden, IV: 107—115, and Rigord, Delaborde I: 148 declare that John gave Evreux and all Philip's Norman conquests, as held at the death of Richard, in dowry to Louis; the treaty of peace of Le Goulet gives the dowry as stated above and makes the transfer of Evreux unconditionally to Philips himself. Rymer. Feodora I: 1: 79. — See also John's charter to Philip

<small>Majority and knighting of Louis.</small> allowance from the royal treasury.¹ But it was not till Pentecost 1209, when he was nearing his twenty-second birthday, that Louis was knighted by his father in the assembly at Compiègne.² This knighting was accompanied by the gift of certain revenues to the young prince, which Philip with his usual care lest power should be concentrated in the hands of a subject, even if that subject were a son, assigned to him, for the most part, in the southern portion of the royal domain and far away from his inheritance in Artois.³ The occasion was one of great festivity, though the details of the ceremony have not been minutely recorded. We know, however, that it was graced by the presence of a large proportion of the nobility of the kingdom, representative of all ranks; and that Philip honored the knighting of his son by conferring the same dignity on a hundred young nobles with him.⁴

The attainment of his majority by the prince is manifested speedily in the charters. The conventions agreed to in July, 1209, between

---

Sep. XVII: 52. John provides that in case of his death without an heir he will increase this dowry by the fief of Gournai, that of the count of Aumale and that of the count of Perche. But all this territory was speedily to be in Philip's hands by actual conquest.

[1] According to the Account for 1202, the provostry of Paris paid Louis and his wife 1800 l., during the year — Brussel "Usage." II: CXLVI, CLXXIV, CLXXXIX. John de Bedford accounted also for an expense of 184 l. 9 s ... for clothing for the young couple during the same period, id. CLVII, CLXXXIII, CCI.

[2] Sep. XVII: 82 — May 17. Arthur of Brittany was knighted by Philip at 16 — id. XVIII: 95. But in his case political considerations hastened the event. Probably Philip intended to put no power into his son's hands till he reached 21, which was the usual period of majority for nobles. — The treaty of peace between Baldwin of Flanders and Philip in Jan. 1200 provides: "Rex faciet dominum Ludovicum filium suum hanc pacem concedere; et ′si forte hoc nollet facere quando habebit aetatem dominus rex neque de terra illa neque de alia partem faceret ei donec id concessisset" Martène, "Amp. Coll," I: 1621—2. Theobald of Champagne and Philip, son of Philip Augustus by Maria of Meran, were both knighted by the father of the latter at 21. Sep. XVIII: 792.

[3] At Lorris, Château-Loudon, Fai, Vitri-aux-Loges, Boiscommun — as well as at Poissi. Philip reserved to himself the right to recall these gifts at anytime. He kept the homage of the territories also. Martène Coll. I: 1090.

[4] Induit Ludovicus ...... cingulum milite de manu patris sui, cum tanta solemnitate et conventu magnatum regni et hominum multitudine et largiflua victualium et donorum abundantia, quanta ante diem illum non legitur visa fuisse. "Guil. Amor. Delaborde I: 226. Ludovicus ..... a patre cingulo militari donatus est, et centum alii nobiles cum eo". Matt. Paris II: 524. If we may trust John of Ypres, writing in the latter half of the XIV century, Louis immediately after his knighting, conferred the same dignity on Robert and Peter, sons of Robert count of Dreux. Sep. XVIII: 603.

Philip and Blanche of Champagne respecting the wardship of the youthful heir of Champagne, Theobald, were repeated and affirmed by Louis in August of the same year;[1] an action which, though done at the order of his father Philip,[2] shows that he was reckoned as of full age and capable of an independent opinion in regard to the point at issue. The care taken to obtain the consent of Louis shows his importance in popular estimation as crown prince; for it is doubtless in view of his possible succession to the throne before the expiration of the time contemplated by the convention that his consent was thought desirable.

A little more than three years after this event, the heir apparent was sent by his father to represent the French monarchy in an interview with Frederick II. then about to mount the throne of the Holy-Roman Empire. At this meeting at Vaucouleurs,[3] Louis negociated a treaty of alliance with Frederick,[4] doubtless by the advice of the prominent nobles who accompanied him, but with full authority as representative.[5]

In the negociations of 1212 with Ferrandus and Joanna of Flanders, Louis treated as one baron with another and not as representative of the monarchy.[6] The question in itself did not involve the rights of the crown. Louis simply attempted to enforce what he deemed to be his inherited right. But the prince of France and the ruler of Artois were not to be separated in the eyes of the men of Flanders, and the consequences of the quarrel between Ferrandus and Louis were of speedy importance to the whole of France. So was it also when Louis took the cross for the Albigensian crusade,

[1] Charter in Martène, Thesaurus Anec. 1: 816, 817.
[2] "Nos autem de mandato domini et genitoris nostri easdem conventiones assecuramus et juravimus praedictae comitissae et Th. ejus filio bona fide tenendas" id. 817.
[3] "Vallem-Coloris, quod est castrum Lotharingiae super fluvium Mosam situm". Sep. XVIII: 281.
[4] The charter of Frederick is dated at Toul, Nov. 19. 1212. "Tullum ... XIII kal. Dec". Martène, Amp. Coll. I: 1111. Toul and Vaucouleurs are near together.
[5] "Non interfuit ipse rex sed Ludovicus .... cum magnatibus regni". Guil. Amor. Delaborde 1: 240. "Philippus misit illuc cum multis regni sui haeredum et filium Ludovicum, ut mutuam hinc inde confoederationem inirent in depressionem Ottonis" id. XVIII: 281.
[6] Louis siezed Aire and St. Omer in Jan. 1212. Sep. XVIII: 563, 564, 574. Ferrandus and Joanna ceeded them to him on his abandonment of his claims to the rest of Flanders on Feb. 25 of that year. Charter, Warnkönig" Histoire de la Flandre" I: 346.

in Feb. 1213. The act in itself was an independent one on his part. It was at his own motion. His father was little pleased with it. But in the political situation of the time the consequences of the act could not fail to affect the whole kingdom. Philip called a council at Paris to discuss the situation and to ascertain who planned to take part in the crusade.[1] For Philip had greater designs regarding Louis than the latter dreamed of, when he plunged hotheaded into the project of an armed pilgrimage against the heretics of southern France. The tyranny of John was driving the baronage of England rapidly toward rebellion, and Philip saw his way cleared, by the pope's sentence of deposition against the English monarch, to crown his victories over John and frustrate the plans of Otho IV. and Reginald of Boulogne, by an invasion and conquest of England in the name of his son.[2] The claims of Louis to the English throne thus made him a factor in the national policy of Philip. The inception of the project came from the latter. It was no independent action on the part of the prince that caused the summoning of the assembly at Soissons in 1213.[3] His plan for the crusade melted away in his excitement at the prospect his father held out to him. His position changes from that of an ordinary baron to that of a prince bearing a part in a far-reaching policy. But the change was no work of his; he was but a puppet in the hands of the master of the game.

Double position of Louis. Louis was in a double position. Of age and a knight, he was in many respects an independent baron in his own domain. As heir apparent, his actions were often important in their consequences to the whole kingdom — as in the quarrel with Ferrandus. Being closely related to the French monarch, he was more under the latter's control than an ordinary baron possessing the same tenures would have been. Even his independence in his own domain was not so great as to exclude the authority of his father in local matters. Philip promised that the serfs of the bishop of Nevers should not be retained either on his own lands or on those of Louis; and he pledged

[1] Rex vero Franciae, audiens quod filius suus cruce signatus esset, multum doluit .... Prima vero Dominica Quadragesimae (Mch. 3.) celebravit rex generale colloquium baronum in civitate Parisiensi, ut ordinaret de motione filii sui et sciret quod et quanti et quales irent cum eo". Petri Hist. Albigensium. Sep. XIX: 78.
[2] Matt. Paris II: 536—7.
[3] April 8. "Crastino Dominice Palmarum", Guil. Amor. Delaborde I: 245. Philip had long desired this opportunity to invade England. He proposed to lead the expedition himself, and he issued an especially imperative summons for army service on this errand. id. Matt Par. II: 537—9.

himself to seize and return such fugitives, by legal process, in both territories.¹ The personal liberty of Louis was limited by a condition attached to his enjoyment of the lands whose revenue Philip had assigned him at his knighting, — that he should not engage in any tournament, except as a spectator.² This twofold position of Louis gives a twofold character to his acts. As royal representative he led the army which opposed John successfully on the Loire just before his father's victory at Bouvines.³ As a noble with other nobles he engaged in the Albigensian crusade of 1215, prominent, indeed, among the pilgrims by his social rank, but no more directly representative of Philip than any other French baron that had taken the crusader's vow.⁴ Being successor to the throne, the alliances of his children were matters of importance sufficient to demand the intervention of Philip Augustus. The treaty which pledged the betrothal of the daughter of Hervey of Nevers to Philip, eldest son of Louis,⁵ was made not only with Louis himself, but with his father; and its fulfillment was guaranteed by the countess of Champagne at

---

¹ Charter June, 1212. "Philippus etc. . . . . . nostro W. Nivernensi episcopo concessimus quod si aliquis hominum suorum de corpore, quem ipse modo tenet ab ipso recederet, et in dominium nostrum sive carissimi filii nostri Ludovici veniret, nos eum caperemus et per legitimam inquisitionem, cui fides de jure debeat adhiberi, Nivernensi episcopo redderemus". Martène "Amp. Coll." I: 1109.

² The Lateran council of 1179 had forbidden tournaments — Benedict. Petrob. I: 226. Whether it was repect for this churchly ordinance or a feeling of the importance of the lives of his sons that impelled Philip, he made abstinence from tournaments a condition of their tenure of estates under him. The promise of Louis is as follows: "Juravimus autem quod non ibimus ad torneamenta; ita quod ea quaeramus, nisi forte aliquod fuerit prope nos, ad quod poterimus ad videndum; neque feremus ibidem arma sicut miles, sed induti haubergeolo et capello ferreo poterimus illa videre. Martène id. 1090. Philip Hurepel made a similar promise at his knighting. id. 1125.

³ "cum militibus a patri suo in partes illas missus" Guil. Amor. Delaborde, I: 255.

⁴ Louis went on the expedition as a pilgrim and returned home promptly at the end of the forty days required by his vow. While on the campaign he put himself under the orders of the papal legate, cardinal Peter of Benevento. "Ludovicus . . . . respondit legato quod ad voluntatem ipsius et consilium se haberet". Petri Hist. Albigensium Sep. XIX: 102. "Ludovicus de voluntate et auctoritate legati faceret dirui muros Narbonae" id. 103. Ludovicus et peregrini, peracto peregrinationis suae termino, videlicet XL dierum ad partes Franciae redierunt". id 104.

⁵ Treaty made in July, 1215. Text Martène, I: 1121 or Sep. XVIII: 783—785. Agnes only daughter of Hervey, count of Nevers, was to be given into the

the command of the father as well as of the son.¹ In the invasion of England, actually accomplished by Louis in 1216 and 1217, the French prince appears also in this double role. His invitation from the English barons was certainly based as much on the belief that his relationship to Philip would render John's French mercenaries practically useless to the latter, as on a recognition of his claims through Blanche of Castile.² Yet those claims of Louis as the husband of Blanche gave the legal justification to the attempt to win the English crown. There is no doubt that Philip countenanced his attempt and wished him success in it. But Philip was far too cool a politician not to see that the victory of Bouvines had removed the dangers which he desired to avert by his proposed invasion of England in 1213, and that the time was ripe for the consolidation of the monarchical power at home rather than for farther conquest, however gratifying to his desire for vengeance on John such conquest might be. The opposition of the church and the dubious prospects of lasting success made Philip the more ready that Louis should appear as if enforcing his own private claims to the English throne rather than as a representative of the French monarch.³ But

charge of Philip Augustus and to be betrothed in Sept. 1217 to Philip, son of Louis. Philip was born in 1206. He died in 1218. The treaty provided that in case Philip should die Louis (IX) should marry Agnes. As a matter of fact, the plan failed of accomplishment, and in May, 1221, Agnes married Guy of St. Paul. Delisle, Cat. 2061—2; see also Brussel I: 162.

¹ "Ego Blancha . . . . de mandato carissimi domini mei illustris Philippi regis Francorum, et domini Ludovici filii ejus, juravi etc." Brussel id.

² "Cumque aliquandiu quem eligerint haesitassent, demum in hoc pariter consenserunt ut Ludovicum filium Philippi regis Francorum sibi praeficerent, et ipsum in regem Angliae sublimarent. Ratio autem eorum erat, quod, si transmarina multitudine, quibus rex Anglorum vallatus incessit, per Ludovicum et patrum suum, de quorum potestate maxima pars eorum fuit, privatus esset, dum a cismarino dictus rex privaretur et destitueretur subsidio, ipse quasi solus remaneret imbellis, et faciens de necessitate virtutem, salubrioribus obtemperaret consiliis". Matt. Paris, II: 647.

³ In the discussion between Philip, Louis and the papal legate Walo at Meulun Apl. 25. 1216, Louis asserted his independence of his father in regard to the English throne: "Domine, etsi ego homo vester ligius sum de feodo quod mihi dedistis in partibus cismarinis, de regno Angliae ad vos non pertinet statuere quicquam" Matt. Paris II: 652, 3. The next day Louis sought his father privately and expressed his determination to invade England. "Videns autem rex constantiam filii sui et animi angustiam, mente voluntate et adjuctorio consensit: sed, praevidens futurorum eventuum pericula, palam assensum non adhibuit, et sic non quasi volendo et persuadendo, sed quasi permittendo, licentiam concessit et cum benedictione dimisit" id. 653.

while Philip might desire that the reponsibility of the undertaking should rest on the shoulders of his son, and prefer that the invasion of England should seem as little the direct work of the French monarchy as the capture of Constantinople by Baldwin of Flanders and other French vassals had been, neither Innocent III. nor the English barons could disassociate the claimant to the English throne from the heir and confidant of Philip of France.[1]

The crown prince, after coming of age, appears, therefore, as a noble and as a prince also. Sometimes the one attribute predominates in his actions, as when he attacks Ferrandus of Flanders, or forms a member of a court to consider the quarrel between the king and the bishop of Paris,[2] or the succession to the county of Beaumont.[3] Sometimes the other characteristic of his station is the more obvious, as when he represents the king in an interview with Frederick II., or commands the royal army on the Loire. His titles and his charters emphasize his relationship to the king of France and, consequently, his princely character.[4] But throughout the reign of Philip Augustus, the heir to the throne occupies a strictly subordinate position in all that appertains to the royal administration. He has not the authority of a "rex designatus", such as Louis VI. had possessed. If he represents the monarch at all, it is only for definite purposes and in a very limited sphere.

[1] Even if we question the accuracy of the picturesque account of the seizure of Innocent III. with fatal illness just after dictating to his secretaries the infliction of church censures on Philip himself. (Guil. Amor. Delaborde I: 308) there can be no doubt that Philip was looked upon by the pope as largely responsible for the expedition, and was put to great trouble to make it appear as if these suspicions were incorrect. "Philippus autem rex . . . . totam terram filii sui et aliorum baronum qui cum eo erant confiscavit, et obtulit se manum contra eos gravare, si ecclesia super his debere amplius facere judicaret. Papa tamen cum nihilominus de favore filii sui suspectum habens etc." id. 307. When Louis visited France in 1217 his father avoided communication with him. id, 312.

[2] Delisle, Cat. 2034. March., 1221.

[3] Martène. "Amp. Coll". I: 1163. April, 1223.

[3] Louis' seal was inscribed; "Filius regis Franciae." Delisle Cat. LXIV. In his address to the abbot and convent of St. Augustin at Canterbury, setting forth his claims to the English throne, he entitles himself: "Ludovicus, domini regis Franciae primogenitus". Rymer, Foedera I: 1. 140. The same title occurs in charters cited in Martène, "Amp. Coll." I: 1090 etc. Many charters made by Louis in Artois close with the formula "astantibus in palatio patris nostri quorum nomina supposita sunt et signa" followed by the names of the five great officers of the crown. Delisle, Cat. LXXX.

|Other children of Philip.| Philip had three children beside Louis; two, a son and a daughter, by Agnes of Meran, who were legitimated by Innocent III. in November, 1201,¹ after the death of their mother.² The third child was an illegitimate son. The legitimation of the children of Agnes was doubtless due to a desire on the part of the pope not to offend Philip too deeply and to smooth over the wounds which the interdict and the enforced dismissal of Agnes had caused the king. It met, nevertheless, with considerable opposition in France.³ But as the bishops of the provinces of Sens and Bourges, and speedily thereafter those of Reims, published sentence of excommunication against all who should oppose the act of the pope,⁴ the validity of the legitimation seems never to have been seriously disputed. During this early period Philip had the children kept at Poissi instead of at Paris.⁵

Philip's policy toward his second son. The younger of the two children of Maria of Meran was a boy born soon after her dismissal in September, 1200, and named after his father, Philip.⁶ His youth and his inferior station as second son made his position inconspicuous compared with that of Louis. Philip Augustus adopted the wise policy of his grandfather, Louis VI. in giving his younger son a place among the nobles of secondary rank, instead of elevating him into a possible rival to the heir apparent by investing him with a duchy like that of Normandy, or a county

---

¹ Letter of Legitimation addressed to the archbishops and bishops of France. Nov. 2. 1201. Sep. XIX: 406.

² "Nuper defuncta" id. "post mortem ipsius Marie" Rigord, Delaborde, I: 151.

³ "quod factum eo tempore pluribus displacuit". Rigord id.

⁴ In Jan. 1202, Peter, archbishop of Sens, Odo, bishop of Paris, Garnier of Troyes, Anseau of Meaux, Gautier of Nevers, Hugh of Orleans, and Hugh of Auxerre, bishops, at Sens; William, archbishop of Bourges and his suffragan, Robert, bishop of Clermont, at Bourges, published their letters. Those of the prelates of the province of Reims were published at Reims Feb. 2, by Reginald, bishop of Laon, Philip of Beauvais, Stephen of Noyon, Lambert of Téronanne and Nivelon of Soissons. Delisle, Cat. 698—711. Teulet. Layettes, I: 231—233.

⁵ The treasury account of John de Bedeford for 1202—3, records the expenditure of 94 l. 13 s. for clothing for the "pueri Pissiaci". In this account the clothing of their attendants and nurses, "camerariae" and „nutrices", is included. Brussel, "Usage", II: clvi, clxxxiii, cci. Among the expenses of the provostry of Poissi for the same period, is: "pro muro gardini faciendo et pro domibus reficiendis, et de pueris regis ducendis apud meduntam (Mante) ix l. xvii s. viii d." id. cxciii.

⁶ Hoveden IV: 138. His nickname was Hurepel, hairy.

like Brittany. Instead of raising Philip Hurepel high enough to be a center about which discontent might rally, he planned to make him an element of strength to the kingdom, by placing in his hands the small but strategically situated, county of Bologne, whose previous possessor, Reginald of Dammartin, was the author of much trouble to the French monarchy. But this, like most of Philip's political achievements, was not accomplished without long preparation. Even before Philip Hurepel had been recognized as legitimate by Innocent III., his father had entered into a treaty with Reginald and Ida of Boulogne, providing that the young prince should be married to their daughter, Matilda, the sole heiress to the county.[1] This treaty of August, 1201,[2] was followed by a second in November, 1209, by which Reginald promised to give certain Norman lands in dowry with his daughter.[3] The marrige probably took place in May of the following year.[4] But the defection of Reginald in 1211, which culminated in his defeat and capture at the battle of Bouvines in 1214, made Philip Augustus anticipate the natural succession of Philip Hurepel to Boulogne. He seized the district in 1211,[5] and henceforward, notwithstanding the death of the countess Ida, in 1216, by whose right her husband, Reginald, had held the territory,[6] it was administered by the heir apparent, Louis, the over-lord of the county.[7] It was

---

[1] The succession to Boulogne fell four consecutive times into the female line in the XII and XIII centuries. Maria, daughter of Stephen, king of England and Matilda, heiress of Boulogne, married Matthew of Alsace, brother of Philip, count of Flanders. They had two daughters, Ida, who married Reginald of Dammartin, in 1191; and Matilda, wife of Henry of Brabant. Reginald and Ida had two daughters, of whom the elder married Philip Hurepel, and their heir in turn was a daughter. Compare Scp. XVIII: 100, Gislebert, 229, etc.

[2] At Compiègne. Delisle, Cat. 674. Text, Teulet, Layettes, I: 226.

[3] Delisle, Cat. 1178. The treaty was somewhat altered in May, 1210, when a charter of Philip Augustus recognized that Reginald had given Philip Hurepel all his possessions in the Norman district of Caux, except Lillebonne and Alizai, a reasonably estimated revenue from which was to be paid by Reginald half yearly. The latter also gave the younger Philip the county of Aumale. Text, Martène, "Amp. Coll." I: 1244. Teulet, Layettes, I: 351.

[4] The charter just quoted would seem to imply that the marriage had taken place. An undated charter of Philip Augustus, recognizing that Philip Hurepel had given his wife Matilda a third of his property in dower, is conectured, by Delisle, to belong to this date. Delisle, Cat. 1219.

[5] Guil. Amor. Delaborde, I: 243.

[6] Scp. XVIII. 557.

[7] Guil. Amor. id. The chronicle of the monastery of Andres records under 1222: "Boloniensis comitatus proprium et principalem comitem non

not till after Philip Hurepel had attained his majority that he became count of Boulogne.

The majority of the second son of Philip Augustus was speedily followed, as that of his elder brother had been, by his knighting at the hands of his father, and apparently in a public and ceremonious fashion, though no details have been preserved. It was, however, at Pentecost, in 1222; and the occasion was employed also for the knighting of Theobald of Champagne,[1] who, though he was almost the same age as Philip Hurepel, had done homage to Philip Augustus for Champagne several years before.[2] The young knight speedily did homage to his father for certain lands and revenues, situated in the bailiwick of Miles de Levis in Normandy;[3] but it would appear that he did not come into full possession of these estates or of the county of Boulogne till his father's death.[4]

Position of second son. The position of Philip Hurepel, under the government of his father, was simply that of a baron of the realm. Philip indeed remembered his relationship to him by the gift of 10,000 livres in his will.[5] He secured him an honorable position among the nobles of

habebat: sed licet Mathildis, haeres ejusdem comitatus .... Philippo regis Francorum filio, nondum militi, desponsaretur, primogenitus tamen regis Francorum dominus Ludovicus curam ejusdem comitatus gerebat. Sep. XVIII: 578.

[1] "Theobaldus comes Campaniensis cingulo militari accingitur in Pentecoste (May 22) cum Philippo regis filio". Sep. XVIII. 792.

[2] Philip Augustus received the homage of Theobald in Aug. 1214, at the request of the mother of the latter, Blanche; but it was with the distinct understanding, recorded in a charter of Nov. of that year, that he should not be free from the guardianship of his mother till his majority. Delisle, Cat. 1504, 1505, 1518. Teulet, Layettes, I: 404, 408.

[3] The charter is undated. Martène, "Amp. Coll." I: 1124, gives it as 1215, but Delisle, Cat. 2158, dates it April, 1222 to July, 1223. The tone of the charter shows that it was made after Philip Hurepel had attained his majority. Miles de Levis was bailiff of Côtentin from 1214 on.

[4] In the charter just noticed Philip Augustus reserves to himself the fortresses of Gavrai and Mortain, and also the right to exchange the lands and revenues concerned for an equivalent. "Dominus autem rex vult quod post ejus decessum, terram praedictam cum proventibus et reditibus ipsius terrae teneam et habeam jure hereditario, cum terra uxoris meae, quae spectat ad eam jure hereditario, si uxor mea vixerit". The Chronicle of the monastery of Andres records under 1223: "Philippus frater Ludovici regis Galliae ab hominibus suis apud Boloniam in primo adventu suo condigne suscipitur". Sep. XVIII: 578. This must have been immediately after his father's death, for in a charter of queen Ingeburgis of August, 1222, the same month in which Louis VIII. was crowned, Philip is recorded as count of Boulogne. Baluze. Misc. VII: 248.

[5] Sep. XVII: 114, 115, Teulet, Layettes, I: 519.

the second rank and placed him where he would be an element of strength to the crown. But he did no more for him then he had done for Reginald of Dammartine or Hervey of Donzai before him. We may imagine that Philip Augustus would have made some use of him representatively, had he attained his majority earlier in the reign, but, whatever may be our conjectures, his station was inferior and insignificant compared with that of the heir apparent.

The other child of Maria of Meran was a daughter, a year or two older than Philip Hurepel,[1] and bearing the same name as her mother.[2] Her chief importance is in the political use which Philip Augustus was able to make of her in various alliances. While still an infant she was betrothed to Arthur of Brittany in 1202,[3] when Philip took the direct homage of Arthur, and prepared to use him against John of England. Arthur's untimely death prevented the marriage; but Philip soon turned his attention in another direction. The conquest of Normandy made Flanders more than ever a quarter from which danger threatened the French crown. This danger had been greatly increased by the union of Flanders and Hainault under the house of Hainault in 1191; and the election of John's nephew, Otto IV., to the German throne in 1198. Philip had long foreseen the peril which threatened him from a union of these two forces, a peril which did not cease till the battle of Bouvines broke the power of the Flemings and the Germans in 1214. Thrust in like a wedge between Flanders and the Empire was the marquisate of Namur, to which Philip, younger son of Baldwin V. of Hainault, had succeeded, on the death of his father in 1195.[4] Though brother-in-law of Philip Augustus through the latter's first queen, Philip of Namur had sided with Richard of England in the contests of 1198—9, and in the latter year had fallen

Political marriages of Philip's daughter.

---

[1] The statement of Hoveden, Stubbs, IV: 185, that Maria was five years old on the day that Philip dismissed her mother: "Genuerat etiam idem rex Franciae de eadem muliere filiam, quae quinquennis erat illa die qua ipse illam dimisit", i. e. Sept 7. 1200, is impossible, for Philip married her mother in Jan. 1196.

[2] Rigord, or a later hand, wrote Johanna, Delaborde 1: 140; but the charters, and other historians, call her Maria.

[3] The treaty of betrothal was made in April, 1202. Delisle, 726. The homage and knighting of Arthur occurred at Gournai in July of the same year. Id. 731.

[4] Namur was held by Philip of his brother Baldwin of Flanders and Hainault (IX. of Flanders and VI. of Hainault), who in turn held it of the Empire. It had been assigned to Philip at the request of his father, Baldwin V. of Hainault, when on his death bed. Gislebert, 273, 274, 292. 293.

into the hands of the French king.¹ The latter, seizing the opportunity to bind his brother-in-law to support the French monarchy, broke off the contract of betrothal existing between Philip of Namur and Matilda, daughter of Peter of Courtnai, then count of Auxerre, but previously of Nevers;² and he apparently imposed other severe conditions before giving the prisoner his freedom.³ Meanwhile the interests of the crown in the contest with John had brought about the engagement between Maria and Arthur of Brittany, which has already been noticed; but the death of the latter ended the project, while new importance attached to Philip of Namur through his guardianship of the two heiresses of Flanders, the daughters of his brother, Baldwin, count of Flanders and emperor of Constantinople.⁴ In August, 1206, Philip Augustus and Philip of Namur entered, therefore, into a formal contract that the latter would marry Maria four years from the ensuing Christmas.⁵ This new relation between the king of France and the marquis of Namur was speedily productive of political advantage to the former. The young heiresses, who, according to the agreement of 1206, were still in the custody of Philip of Namur,⁶ were transferred, in 1208, to the wardship of Philip

---

¹ Philip of Namur was a party to the agreement between Baldwin of Flanders and Richard of England not to make peace separately with Philip Augustus. Rymer, "Foedera", I: 1: 67. He was captured in May 1190. Rigord, Delaborde, I: 145.

² Philip of Namur had entered into treaty of marriage with Mathilda, daughter of Peter, then count of Nevers, in May, 1193. Delisle, Cat. 399. In the contest between Peter of Nevers and Hervey of Donzai, in 1199, Philip Augustus had taken part with the latter, and had compelled Peter to retire to Auxerre, giving up the county of Nevers, with his daughter to Hervey. Sep. XVII: 658, XVIII: 726, Delisle, Cat. 568, 574—577. In Jan., 1200, Philip of Namur formally renounced his treaty of marriage with Mathilda. Delisle, Cat. 591.

³ Philip of Naumur was released from actual imprisonment by the efforts of his sister-in-law, Maria, countess of Flanders. Sep. XVIII: 551. No reliable account has reached us of the exact terms of this release; but we can explain his subsequent compliance with the wishes of Philip Augustus only on the supposition that the conditions were such as to bind him closely.

⁴ Johanna and Margaret. Baldwin and his wife, Maria, both took the cross.

⁵ More exactly within four years after the 20th day subsequent to the next Christmas. Delisle, 1002.

⁶ Delisle, Cat. appendix p. 510. They were not to marry without the consent of Philip Augustus.

Augustus.[1] The marriage probably took place at the time planned.[2] But it was not destined to be of long continuance. The marquis of Namur died in October, 1212.[3] Philip Augustus had, however, further plans in mind; and it was not long before he again sought to make the marriage of his daughter a source of strength to the throne. He had for some years paid a pension to Henry, duke of Brabant, and had planned to use him as a counterweight to Otto IV. in the contest for the German throne. Although the efforts to secure the imperial election for Henry had failed, and Philip had turned his attention to the youthful Frederick II.,[4] yet the position of Brabant and Lorraine and the prominence of their ruler, made him a most valuable ally, were it possible to secure his aid in the approaching struggle with Otto IV. and John. Philip, therefore, entered into negociations with Henry, and at the great assembly at Soissons in April, 1213, the latter agreed to marry Maria, and aid in Philip's proposed invasion of England; while Philip pledged him an income of 1000 livres.[5] Conformably to this convention, the marriage occurred on the 22nd of the same month.[6] The results were not, however, what Philip had hoped. Henry was reconciled to Otto, married his daughter to him,[7] and shared in his defeat at Bouvines.

---

[1] Text of agreement. Id. p. 514. Jacob of Guise, Scp. XVIII: 589, declares that afterwards, at the demand of the Flemings, the girls were sent to Bruges.

[2] Between April, 1210 and April, 1211, Philip of Namur gave a charter assigning a third of his property in dower to his wife Maria, daughter of Philip Augustus. Delisle, Cat. 1206. Teulet, Layettes, I: 361.

[3] Henry, of Brabant and lower Lorraine, did homage to Philip Augustus, in Feb., 1205, and swore fidelity to him against all save Philip of Swabia. Philip Augustus gave him an income of 200 marks silver, payable at Paris. Delisle, Cat. 909. After the murder of Philip of Swabia in 1208, Philip Augustus entered into formal treaty of alliance with Henry, and furnished him money to secure his election as emperor, if possible. Id. 1089, 1090; text, p. 513.

[4] Martène, "Amp. Coll." I: 1111.

[5] April 8. Henry agreed to serve Philip against all, save Frederick II., or, should Frederick die, whoever should be elected „de assensu domini nostri regis Franciae Philippi". He will make no claim on Boulogne, as long as the countess Ida and her daughter live. Philip pledges him 600 livres revenue from Boulogne and 400 from the French treasury. Charters, Scp. XVIII: 687. Henry's first wife, Matilda, and Ida of Boulogne were sisters. Philip thus secured again, as he had done in the treaty of 1208, the undisputed succession of Ida's daughter, Matilda, who had married Philip Hurepel.

[6] Guil. Amor. Delaborde, I: 245. See Scp. XVIII: 657.

[7] She had been betrothed, July 16, 1198, at Aix la Chapelle (Aachen) to Otto. They were married in May, 1214. Scp. XVIII: 615, 630.

In the case of his daughter, as of his younger son, the aim of Philip Augustus was to secure the interests of the throne by the alliances which promised most political advantage. His clear insight into the situation of the time showed him that these interests were to be fostered by the marriage of his daughter with powerful nobles near at hand, rather than with greater rulers at a distance. No touch of sentiment seems ever to have influenced him in giving a husband to his daughter; he valued such alliances solely for their political advantages.

Philip's son Carlotus. The part played by the illegitimate son of Philip Augustus was, as was natural, comparatively unimportant. Peter Carlotus was born, probably, in 1208,[1] and received his early training under the care of William the Breton, who dedicated the Philippide to him, conjointly with the crown prince.[2] He was early designated for the church, and a dispensation from Honorius III. in 1217 removed any bar to ecclesiastical preferment on account of illegitimacy.[3] Soon afterward he was given the treasurership of Saint-Martin of Tours;[4] and, at a very much later period, became bishop of Noyon.[5]

Last acts of Louis VII. II. With the coronation of Philip Augustus, the reign of Louis VII. came practically to a close. One or two acts show that the elder monarch had not abdicated the royal power;[6] but his increasing

---

[1] The address to Carlotus, at the close of the Philippide reads: "Quintus adhuc decimus tibi vix licet annus agatur." Bk. XII: 905. This address was written in the first year of the reign of Louis VIII. (1223—4): "Hic patris fratrisque tui preconia regum excolit .... primo Carmen in octavi Ludovici terminat anno". Id. XII: 912—916. Delaborde, II: 383, 384. Carlotus was therfore born in 1208 or 1209.

[2] "Dogmata quem docui primum puerilia". Id. 902.

[3] April 24. Sep. XIX: 631.

[4] „Carloto thesaurario". Delaborde II. 383. In Jan., 1217, Philip Augustus informed the dean and chapter of St. Martin at Tours that he would recognize Peter as treasurer when they would give him a prebendaryship in their church. Delisle, Cat. 1749.

[5] In 1240.

[6] Gislebert, 118, 119, relates that Roger, bishop of Laon, having been required to purge himself by oath regarding the murder of the men of Laon, and Jan 1, 1180, „infra octavam Natalis Domini," having been fixed as the term of this purgation, and Meaux as the place, Roger asked the intercession of his cousin, count Baldwin of Hainault. "Comes autem cum ipso (Rogero) dominum regem adiit. Quem dominus rex et ejus uxor Adela benigne suscipientes, concesserunt ei ut episcopus Laudunensis constitutam sibi faceret purgationem, quo facto consilium inde bonum et comiti Hanoniensi gratum haberent." This must

feebleness deprived him of any great control of the affairs of state.[1] The young king was easily persuaded to approve the seizure and spoliation of the Jews throughout the royal domain; and, although the act was contrary to the policy of Louis,[2] the latter had become so powerless that the will of his son and his son's advisers was carried out in February, 1180.[3] The growing influence of Philip of Flanders, at this period, as shown in the marriage of Philip Augustus with Elizabeth of Hainault, notwithstanding the opposition of the queen mother and the Champagne party, not only caused the young king to break with his mother and most of his friends in France, but speedily resulted in the removal of the great seal from the custody of Louis VII. himself.[4] Even before his marriage,[5] Philip Augustus accompanied military expeditions to repress the excesses of vassals in Berri, Beaujeu, and Châlons-sur-Saone;[6] and had summoned his army to resist the forces which Henry II. of England was gathering to aid the representatives of the Champagne interest.[7] Evidently Philip, rather than Louis, was the real king of France.

Philip's activity.

But the rule of a boy in his fifteenth year cannot, in the nature of things, be really independent. The youth of Philip was characterized by deference to the will of others, and especially to that of the one who was, for the time being, the object of his admiration. The first few months of his reign show him the tool of the policy

Influence of Henry II. and Philip of Flanders.

have been about Christmas, 1197, for the count spent that day at St. Denis, and then went to Meaux, where the bishop made the required purgation. „Qua peracta purgatione, dominus (Hanouiensis) cum ipso episcopo Parisius rediit, ubi a domino rege impetarunt quod ipsi episcopo bona sua omnia restituit et ei pacem et gratiam suam concessit."

[1] By March, 1180, Louis was bedridden. Ralph de Diceto, II: 4.

[2] Ralph. Id. "Opus quod longo tempore mente clausum gestaverat, sed, pro nimia reverentia quam christianissimo patri sui exhibebat, perficere formidabat. Rigord, Delaborde, I: 14, 15.

[3] There is some confusion in the dates. Rigord and Ralph de Diceto both agree that it was on the Jewish Sabbath. Rigord gives the date as "XVI kal. martii", and Ralph, as "XV kal. februarii". But neither fell on Saturday, in 1180. The date given by Rigord is a Thursday, that of Ralph, Friday. As Rigord was probably an eye-witness, his report as to the month is preferable. Id. 16.

[4] "Ludovicus rex Francorum, quia jus suum et potestatem in Philippum regem transtulerat, ne quid in regno statueret citra filii conscientiam, sigilli sui potestate privatus est". Ralph de Diceto II: 6.

[5] Bapaumes, April 28, 1180.

[6] Rigord, Delaborde I: 16, 17.

[7] Benedict Petrob. I: 245.

of Philip of Flanders;[1] he was no less the follower of Henry II. after his meeting with that astute and persuasive monarch in June, 1180.[2] The mind of the young king had not attained the maturity essential to a self-reliant policy. But if the count of Flanders and the English monarch shaped the main outlines of the policy pursued during the early months of Philip's reign,[3] the actual administration of government was not in their hands. What position, then, did Philip occupy in reference to that administration? The answer to this question involves a reply to the further inquiry; — when did Philip attain his majority? In other words; — were the early years of the young monarch a regency, or was Philip aided by those who were simply his counselors or ministers? The question is not easy to answer. The usually careful chronicler, Robert of Auxerre, expressly declares that Philip was under the guardianship of Robert Clement after the death of Louis VII.[4] Robert Clement survived the old king by a few months only, and was succeeded by his brother, Giles,

Was there a regency?

---

[1] "Interim praefatus Philippus, novus rex Franciae, videns quod pater suus paralytico morbo esset percussus, adhaesit consilio Philippi comitis Flandriae, cujus consilio tyrannidem coepit exercere in populo Gallicano, et omnes quos noverat patri suo fuisse familiares, sprevit et odio habuit". Benedict Petrob. I: 244.

[2] The meeting between Gisors and Trie so completely turned Philip away from the Flanders interest and so closely bound him to Henry II. that, in Dec., 1181, not only Philip of Flanders but the Champagne party were opposing him. The latter party was as little pleased with Philip's liking for Henry as it had been with his inclination toward Philip of Flanders: "Fuit igitur summa et principalis hujus praefatae guerrae causa, quod Philippus rex Franciae, spreto amicorum et avunculorum suorum consilio, adhaesit consilio Henrici regis Angliae ..... Unde factum est quod Willelmus Remensis antistes, et comes Teobaldus, et comes Stephanus, avunculi praedicti regis, dolentes se esse despectos, intebantur in regem nepotem suum insurgere". Id. 284.

[3] M. Dareste, ("Histoire de France", II: 96), is of the opinion that Philip was under the guardianship of Philip of Flanders, and that the government was divided between that count and the queen mother, Adela. Doubtless these two persons were the most influential members of the two rival parties at court during the first few months of Philip's reign, — but M. Dareste certainly goes too far in claiming the division of the government or a guardianship. Louis VII. was still living and had never formally abdicated.

[4] "Hujus autem Egidii frater exstiterat Robertus cognomento Clemens, qui regem a prima etate nutrierat et instruxerat, vir moderatus et prudens regique fidelis et qui regalia industre et strenue administrarat negotia, dum regem post mortem patris habuit in tutela. Huic praedictus Egidius in regni administratione successerat". Mon. Ger. XXVI: 246. This passage was erased by a corrector from the autograph of this chronicle; but the sentence above

in the administration of the kingdom.¹ The chronicler records that the position was soon made vacant again by the removal of Giles from his post.² But in spite of the phrase: "habuit in tutela", which Robert of Auxerre employs to describe the relations between Robert Clement and Philip, it may well be doubted whether Robert was more than the chief of the royal ministers. As a prominent counselor of Louis VII. during the later years of his reign, a man of judgment and integrity, and, above all, as the instructor of the young king in his boyhood, it was natural that he should stand high among the advisers of the young monarch.³ But had Philip Augustus been really under the guardianship of Robert Clement, such a change of policy as was effected by the interview between Henry II. and the young king, near Gisors in June, 1180, would have been impossible. Not only was the reconciliation, there accomplished between Philip Augustus and the queen mother and her friends, opposed by Philip of Flanders, it was directly against the advice of Robert Clement.⁴ The arguments of

Philip his own master

---

quoted was preserved substantially unaltered. Compare Holder-Egger's preface to his edition of Robert of Auxerre, in Mon. Ger. XXVI.

¹ The almost contemporary corrector of the passage just cited writes: "Erat tunc negociorum regis procurator Egidius, vir in rebus seculi sagax". Id. Robert of Auxerre, in the autograph, wrote: "Egidii, tunc a rege pre ceteris in curia sublimati".

² "Garmundus moritur . . . . . Quodque mirandum est; per eosdem dies quibus peste in curia Romana obiit, frater (Egidius) ejus in Francie curia principatum amisit". Id. He probably died at this time, or soon after, (1182).

³ Robert Clement, of Metz-en-Gatinois, was the head of a family long honorably distinguished in the marshalship of France. He appears as one of the judges in the case between the abbey of St. Germain-des-Prés and Barthélemi de Paris in 1178. Luchaire, Instit. I: 312. Tardif, Mon. Hist. 678. His sons, Alberic the Marshal and Henry the Marshal, were early prominent in the counsels of Philip Augustus, (Scp. XVIII: 560), and honorable through their service in arms; the former dying gloriously in the attack on the "Cursed Tower" at Acre, in the crusade of 1191, (Benedict Petrob. II: 173), and the latter, just after the successful repulse of John's army in 1214. (Philippide X: 350, Guil. Amor. Delaborde I: 265). His grandson, John, son of Henry, was given the marshalship, while still under age, in recognition of Henry's services. Guil. Amor. Id. He continued to hold the office under Louis VIII. (Martène "Amp. Col." I: 1175). Robert Clement died in the latter part of 1181 or the early portion of 1182.

Giles was also known as Gilo of Tornella. Scp. XVIII: 783. He served as judge with his brother in 1178. Tardif, Mon. Hist. 678.

⁴ "Rex Angliae senior animum novi regis Franciae nunc blandis nunc asperis adeo emollivit, quod contra consilium comitis Flandriae et Roberti Clement, et multorum aliorum, qui inter ipsum et matrem suam et avunculos

Henry II. were addressed directly to Philip himself and were of a nature fitted to impress a boy.¹ It may be objected that Louis VII. was still living at the time of this interview and that Robert Clement had not, therefore, come into the exercise of the office of guardian. But the whole account of the transaction, as preserved to us by the author of the Gesta Henrici Secundi, an author who was well informed as to the matters he records and who would not, from his nationality, be inclined to flatter the French monarch by representing him more active than he really was, shows that Henry II. dealt with Philip Augustus directly and as fully competent to negociate for himself. If Philip was sufficiently his own master in the summer of 1180 to act contrary to the wishes and interest not only of Robert Clement but of Philip of Flanders as well, then the most powerful counselors in the court of Louis VII. it is not likely that he could have been under guardianship a few months later. Nor have we any evidence of such guardianship, except in the passage quoted from Robert of Auxerre. On the contrary, everything points toward an opposite conclusion. The charters of the early years of Philip Augustus contain no intimation of a regency. Even those which appear to have been issued during the last illness of his father give no hint that they acquire their validity otherwise than by the independent consent of Philip alone.² There is nothing surprising in the fact that Philip Augustus should be considered as of age from the time

after his coronation.

of his coronation. That ceremony did not in itself signify the majority of the one crowned;³ but the young king had already reached the age of fourteen when he was raised to the throne.⁴ The history of the Capetian house before his time had furnished one example of the attainment of his majority by a monarch at fourteen. Philip I. had become free from the guardianship of the count of Flanders in

suos volebant dissidium, omnem malitiam et indignationem quam in animo adversus eos conceperat remisit". Benedict Petrob. II: 246.

¹ Id.

² Delisle, Cat. 1, note, holds that the first few charters on his list were issued before the death of Louis VII. They do not even express the assent of the latter and are worded as on the authority of Philip alone. Great weight cannot, of course, be laid on this representation of the charters; but, if the opinion of M. Delisle is correct, the omission of mention of his father's assent is a fact worthy of notice as showing the independence of Philip Augustus.

³ Philip I. was crowned in 1059, at the age of seven. Louis VII. in 1131, at eleven. The guardianship to which the former was subjected is proof that coronation did not imply majority.

⁴ Philip was fourteen Aug., 22, 1179.

1065.[1] Though the legal majority of nobles in France proper and in Normandy, in the twelfth century, was twenty one,[2] the precedent of the royal house already favored the theory that the king attained his majority with his fifteenth year, — a theory which afterwards became the legal rule of its practice.[3] The exercise of the knightly dignity implied that its possessor had attained his majority;[1] and though the admission of Philip Augustus into the ranks of chivalry has not been recorded, yet William the Breton, in describing the expeditions of the young king against the rebellious nobles of Berri, Beaujeu, and Châlons-sur-Saone, in the opening months of his reign, and while Louis VII. still lived, represents Philip Augustus as a newly created knight.[5] It is therefore safe to affirm that Philip Augustus was his own master

---

[1] Philip I. was the only one of the Capetian monarchs, before Philip Augustus, that came to the throne so young as the latter. On the death of his father, Henry I., in 1060, Baldwin V. of Flanders became the guardian of the young monarch and held this office till 1065, when the latter had barely attained the age of fourteen. Luchaire. "Instit." I: 72—74.

[2] The treaty made between Philip Augustus and Blanche of Champagne, in July or August, 1208, regarding the rights of Theobald, declares: "Et si filiae comitis Henrici, vel aliquis alius, dictum filium meum vel meipsam traherent in causam de comitatu Campaniae, priusquam filius meus viginti et unum annos complesset, filius meus vel ego non teneramur ex inde respondere infra praedictum terminum, quamdiu idem filius viveret, nec dominus rex audiret inde causam: quia usus et consuetudo Franciae talis est, quod nullus ante vigesimum primum annum respondere debet super hereditate, de qua pater ejus tenus esset sine placito cum decederet." Martène, "Amp. Coll." I: 1094. A charter of Henry II. for Normandy, about 1155, says: "Et postquam talis heres fuerit in custodia, cum ad aetatem pervenerit, scilicet XXI annorum, habeat hereditatem suam". Brussel, "Usage," 11. charters, II. The rule was not unbroken, however. Arthur of Brittany was knighted by Philip Augustus and given possession of Poitou and Anjou, as well as Brittany, at 16. Sep. XVII: 54. XVIII: 95. (Really at but little over 15; for he was born March 29, 1187, Benedict Pet. I: 361, and knighted in July, 1202). But we have already noticed that the two sons of Philip Augustus, Louis and Philip Hurepel, and Theobald of Champagne did not come of age till 21.

In Hainault the custom was otherwise. An agreement of July, 1200, between Baldwin of Hainault and Flanders and the barons, declares: "Ad legem aetas hominis est quindecim annorum, feminae vero duodecim". Brussel, "Usage" II: 885.

[3] Philip III. provided, in 1271, that his son should come of age at fourteen. "Ordonnances des Rois de France", XI: 349. Charles V., by an edict of 1374, fixed it permanently at that age. Brussel, "Usage" I: 147, 148.

[4] See Luchaire. "Instit." I: 74, note.

[5] "Sic nova militie gaudens insignia novit Initiare Deo." Philippide I: 472. Delaborde. "Oeuvres de Rigord et de Guillaume le Breton", II: 26.

from the time of his first coronation, and that Robert and Giles Clement were simply the chief among the royal ministers of this early period.

The five great officers of the royal household. At the accession of Philip Augustus the king was still assisted, in the administration, by the five great officers of the royal household, the seneschal, butler, chamberlain, constable, and chancellor.[1] Theoretically they combined the personal service of the king, in the functions which their titles describe, with the administration of the various branches of the government under the royal orders. In general, they had the same functions as the officers of the palace under the Carolingians; yet under the first of the Capetian kings the five great officers just mentioned were so little distinguished from the multitude of palace servants and the nobles occasionally present at the court that, with the exception of the chancellor, they occupy no preeminent station.[2] It was a distinct gain for the monarchy when, by the beginning of the twelfth century, it became able to discharge the routine business of the central administration without the intervention of the promiscuous and indefinite aid of the nobles, chaplains, cooks, marshals, physicians and others, who witness to the charters of the early Capetians.[3] Long before the accession of Philip Augustus, the five great officers had become, in a certain sense, a ministry for the king. Some of their number had commanded the armies,[4] they had administered justice in the king's name, their names were appended as witnesses to every solemn charter and were there recorded with a formula, which, though indicating only that the office was filled by the persons designated, had the appearance of an actual ratification of the royal act.[5] But this theory of admini-

---

[1] This is the order in which their names appear on the charters of Philip Augustus. The chancellor, as the writer of the charter, is always last mentioned; but the order of the others varied greatly at different periods. The order above given became fixed under Louis VII., about 1150. Luchaire, "Instit." I: 164—166.

[2] Compare Id. 159—162. The butler and constable first appear as subscribing charters in 1043, under Henry I. The chamberlain and seneschal appear as subscribers in 1047. In 1048 all except the butler appear on one charter, and first in 1060 all five together. Id. 163.

[3] On the subscriptions of these persons, see id. 160, 161. From the reign of Louis VI., the subscriptions by any, save the five great officers, become increasingly rare.

[4] Not only the seneschal, but also the chamberlain, had had command of the royal armies. Id. 169, 175.

[5] Delisle, Cat. LXXIX—LXXX, proves that the formula: "astantibus in palatio quorum nomina supposita sunt et signa", cannot imply the actual presence in the palace, or even in the country, of the officers whose names

stration with the aid of the five great officers was widely divergent from the actual facts at the beginning of the reign of Philip Augustus; the presentation of these posts to those whose own possessions must have kept them remote from the royal presence a large portion of the year necessarily tended to make these positions more dangerous, on account of the power they gave their holders, if the latter chose to exercise it, than practically useful in the routine of everyday administration. Partly from the awkwardness of the system, but even more by reason of the stormy experiences of Louis VI. and VII. with these turbulent officers,[1] the Capetian monarchs immediately previous to Philip Augustus, had sought to build up an administration conducted by men of lower birth and comparative unimportance,[2] at once more constant in their attendance on the king and more ready to execute his wishes on account of their direct dependence on him for their position. In this effort they had been largely successful. It is only necessary to recall the name of Suger, not to speak of the less known counselors of Louis VII.,[3] to see how completely one of these humbler servants of the king could exercise the authority which might be supposed to belong to the great officers of the palace. But the existence of the great officers was still a standing menace to the royal authority, even when so much of the actual administration was in other hands. The powers inherent in these charges were still vast. They were dangerous to the monarchy just in proportion to the high station and resources of the nobles who held them. There was, indeed, a great difference in the authority attaching to the several offices. The power of the seneschal or the chancellor was far greater, and hence more dangerous to the king, than that of the butler, chamberlain or constable. Hence the policy of Philip Augustus re-

Policy of Philip's predecessors.

appear in the charters of Philip Augustus. Luchaire ("Instit." I: 165 note) is of the opinion that this was also the case under the previous reigns.

[1] For the contest of Louis VI. with the Garlandes, three brothers who had gained the offices of seneschal, chancellor and butler, contemporaneously, see Luchaire. Id. 178, 179. Louis VII. quarreled with his chancellor, Hugh de Champfleuri, in 1172, as he had with Hugh's predecessor, Algrin, in 1140. Id. 188, 189.

[2] Compare Id. 198, 199. Under the earlier Capetians those influential in the ordinary business of the court were mostly nobles; by the reigns of Louis VI. and VII., the counselors had become mostly ecclesiastics of the royal chapel and commoners.

[3] Luchaire, Instit. II: 303—7, gives biographical notes regarding some of the counselors of Louis VII., notably Adam Brûlard, Gilbert la Flèche, Ferri de Paris, Bouchard le Veautre and Thierri Galeran.

garding the several offices was not uniform. He practically suppressed the seneschalship and the chancellorship after the first few years of his reign, while he allowed the three other charges to continue substantially unaltered.

The seneschalship. Character of Theobald of Blois.

At the coronation of Philip Augustus the seneschalship was held by Theobald V., count of Blois, a brother of the queen mother and of the archbishop, William, of Reims. He was already well advanced in years, having been appointed to the office by Louis VII. in 1154,[1] and was a man of high character[2] and wide influence.[3] After his reconciliation with his royal nephew, at the return of the Champagne party to power at court[4], he seems to have been an efficient and valuable, though occasionally self-willed, servant of the crown.[5] Doubtless the qualities which gave worth to the personal character of Theobald were of influence in disposing the king to leave the office of seneschal vacant after his uncle's death; but, as long as the latter lived, the office possessed the ancient prerogatives which made its holder the second personage in the kingdom.[6] Thus in 1180 Theobald exercised judicial functions in the name of the king in the quarrel be-

---

[1] Delisle, Cat. LXXXI. He was appointed by Louis VII. The treatise of Hugh de Cleves, representing the seneschalship as a fief of the house of Anjou, has been shown to be undeserving of confidence. Mabille, "Introd. aux Chron. des contes d'Anjou", XLIX–LII, cited in Luchaire, "Instit." I: 176. The statement of Giraldus Cambrensis, "De instructione Principis", Sep. XVIII: 141, that Philip of Flanders had given the seneschalship, (which he is said to have inherited from Rudolph I, of Vermandois, through his wife, Elizabeth, Rudolph's daughter), in sub-fief to Theobald, is without foundation.

[2] He was known as the "Good". "Thibaldus pius et misericors regis Francorum senescallus". Rigord, Delaborde, 1: 113.

[3] He was made one of the three rulers of the camp of the crusaders before Acre in Nov., 1190. The two others were archbishop Baldwin of Canterbury and Frederick of Swabia. "Itinerarium Regis Ricardi", Stubbs. 116.

[4] His flight into Normandy with the queen mother and appeal to Henry II. for assistance, Benedict. Petrob. I: 245, have already been noticed. He united with the rest of the Champagne party in their opposition to the influence of Henry II. at the French court in 1181. Id. 284. But he conducted the expedition against Philip of Flanders in 1185 conjointly with his brother the archbishop of Reims. Rigord, Delaborde, 1: 42.

[5] He united with Philip of Flanders in compelling Philip Augustus to discuss terms of peace with Henry II. in 1188, refusing to fight till after the crusade. Benedict. Petrob. II: 48, 49.

[6] In his letter to pope Alexander III., denouncing Henry II. for the murder of Becket, 1171, Theobald gives himself the title of "Blesensis comes et regni Francorum procurator". Benedict. Petrob. 1: 15.

tween the clergy of Mâcon and Gerard, count of Vienne.¹ The seneschal shared with the monarch, at Orleans at least, the exclusive power of summoning before the royal court.² He also possessed the right, under Philip Augustus as under his predecessors, to conduct unmolested within the precincts of a commune one who had offended against the communal laws.³ This right was usually enjoyed by the king and seneschal alone.⁴ He had a share in the revenue of some communes conjointly with the king⁵, and an income from certain provostries⁶, as well as a fee for oaths of fidelity sworn to the crown by bishops, abbots, and other prelates.⁷ He commanded the royal army, on at least one important expedition, when the king himself was

Rights of the seneschal

---

¹ "Subjecerat autem utraque pars se nostro arbitrio. Unde comes Th. avunculus noster nostri auctoritate arbitrii de querimoniis clericorum, quod praedictum est, judicavit." Martène, "Amp. Coll." I: 945.

² "Item ut neque prepositus neque aliquis serviens noster aliquem de burgensibus ante presentiam nostram, nisi ex precepto nostro vel dapiferi nostri, submoneat.". Delisle, Cat. appendix p. 498.

³ "Nemo autem praeter nos et dapiferum nostrum, poterit conducere in villam Suessionensem hominem, qui forefactum fecerit homini qui hanc communiam juraverit, nisi forisfactum emendare venerit secundum judicium eorum qui communiam servaverint". Charter of Soissons, confirmed by Philipp Augustus in 1181. Ordonnances XI: 220. The charters of Vailli in 1185 (id. 238), Compiègne in 1186 (id. 242), Sens in 1189 (id. 263), Villeneuve in 1200, (modelled on the charter of Soissons of 1181), id. 279. Crespi en Valois in 1215, (modelled on that of Vailli of 1185), id. 306, have substantially the same clause.

⁴ There were local exceptions; at Vailli the "heirs of Milo" shared the right with the king and seneschal. Id. 238. The charter of Amiens, 1190, provides that the king, seneschal, provost, bishop or mayor might bring anyone, not guilty of certain heinous crimes specified, into the city once a year, although under banishment. Id. 267.

⁵ The charter of Pontoise, 1188, provides: „Ad hoc prefate communie preposituram nostram Pontisare et minagioem concessimus in hunc modum, quod de prepositura nostra, singulis annis reddent nobis quingentas libras, et senescallo nostro triginta libras". Id. 255.

⁶ The accounts for 1202—3 report the sum of 176 l. 17 s. 6d. paid, "de senescalcia", by 18 provostries. These vary from 46:17:6, for Sens, to 1:10 for Boisses. These payments were made at the All Saints term of the accounts. The seneschalship was already vacant, and the revenues due to that office were apparently retained by the king for the benefit of the treasury. See Brussel, I:509. (where he has added the sums wrongly) and the „Account", Id. II.

⁷ In the receipts for the May term of the treasury account in 1203, Guy de Béthisi, bailiff, reported the following items: "Et debet C. l. et c. s. Pro abbate et pro katalaunis, VIxx l. Et pro Renaudo Mapas CL. l. Et pro senescalcia katalaunensi X. l. "Brussel II: CXCVI. Rotro, bishop of Châlons, died in 1202 and was succeeded by Gerard de Douay in 1203. A charter of Philip IV.,

present with it[1]. As commander of those armies he had the right to summon to army service, as well as the monarch. Naturally, however useful a man of such authority might be, when favorably disposed toward the occupant of the throne, his powers trespassed too closely on those of the king himself to make the existence of such an officer desirable under a vigorous monarchy. But Philip could not have dispensed with the seneschalship while Theobald lived. As a brother of the queen mother, the archbishop of Reims, and the count of Sancerre, and brother and uncle of successive counts of Champagne, his connection with that Champagne interest, which formed the main defence of the French throne against attack from Normandy or Flanders, was too intimate to allow Philip to discard him, had he desired to do so. Philip was wise enough to wait till death had removed the vigorous count of Blois, during the siege of Acre in January, 1191.[3] Even then the office was not formally abolished. But Philip left it unfilled: and though his charters, and those of the kings long after him, bore the inscription, Dapifero nullo, and thereby recognized the office as existing potentially, the seneshalship had really ceased to be.[4] Its authority and privileges were partly retained by the king, and partly transferred to the new order of royal ministers, the bailiffs, and to the hitherto comparatively unimportant constable.

Philip practically discontinues the office.

The conduct of Philip Augustus toward the other great post of influence among the five palace officers was similar to his treatment of the seneschalship. The chancellorship, under Louis VI. and VII., was a source of frequent anxiety to the crown and was often in open

Philip leaves the chancellorship vacant and employs members of his council.

of 1309, gives a clue to the meaning of this entry: "Quod in emolumentis, quae ratione juramentorum fidelitatumque ab episcopis, abbatibus, abbatissis et aliis praelatis regni nostri consueverat praestari, certam videlicet decem librarum summam in quodlibet juramento, ratione dapiferatiae vel senescalliae Franciae, quam in manu nostra tenemus etc." Ordon. I:472.

[1] E. g. in the campaign against Philip of Flanders in 1185. „Tunc comes....... principem militie regis Theobaldum comitem Blesensium, Francie senescallum, vocavit." Rigord, Delaborde, I:42.

[2] The privilege of St. Martin of Pontoise, given by Philip provides: „Ita tamen ut quod expeditionis nostras et equitatus nostros in hominibus in praedicta terra morantibus retinemus, qui neque a praeposito, neque ab aliquo ministrorum submoneantur, nisi ex praecepto nostro, vel dapiferi nostri." Ducagne "Glossarium." sub „Senescalcus."

[3] Jan. 20, 1191. Bened. Petrob. Stubbs. II: 148 note.

[4] This indication of the vacancy of the seneschalship continued till the XIV. century. Luchaire "Instit." I:181.

opposition to the king.¹ It was second only to the seneschalship in authority. The office had remained vacant from the dismission of Hugh of Champfleuri, bishop of Soissons, in 1172, till it was again filled by Louis VII. in 1179, some months before the coronation of Philip Augustus.³ The new chancellor, Hugh, son of the celebrated Hugh de Puiset, bishop of Durham,⁴ seems to have held the post but little more than a year.⁵ He was succeeded by a chancellor who also bore the name of Hugh, but who appears, on the evidence of a charter of 1186, to have been connected with Béthisi.⁶ The latter held office till 1185.⁷ From that time till the close of the reign of Philip Augustus the chancellorship remained vacant. Its functions were discharged by various counselors of the royal court. One of these was Walter of Nemours, son of Walter de Capella, both of whom enjoyed the office of sub-chamberlain⁸ under Philip. Walter "the younger",⁹ as he is often called, occupied an influential position as a royal counselor; he was even more prominent as a soldier,¹⁰ and

Walter "the younger".

---

¹ Stephen de Garlande, Algrin d'Étampes, Cadurc, Simon the nephew of Suger, and Hugh de Champfleuri, all incurred the hostility of their king; and several of these chancellors stood in armed opposition to their sovereign. The monarchy seems to have suffered more embarrassment from the chancellors of the XII. century than from the seneschals. See Luchaire, "Instit." 1:188, 189.

² Id. 189. Delisle, Cat. LXXXV.

³ Of the five charters of Louis VII., given in 1179, which are contained in Tardif, Mon. Hist., two (nos. 679, 683) are given "vacante cancellaria." The others (nos. 680, 1, 2) are subscribed "per manum secundi Hugonis cancellarii". As the year was than reckoned from Easter, Hugh must have been appointed after April 1, 1179.

⁴ "Hanc autem cartam receperunt praefati monachi (S. Trinitatis Cantuariae) ex dono Lodowici regis Francorum, per manum Hugonis de Puteaco, cancellarii sui, filii Hugonis Dunelmensis episcopi". Benedict. Petrob. I:241.

⁵ His successor was in office by Nov. 1. 1180. Delisle Cat. LXXXVI.

⁶ Id. The subject is somewhat obscure. A charter of 1186 confirms to the church of St. Adrian at Béthisi certain gifts made for the commemoration of the chancellor, Hugh, buried in that church. A second charter, of the same year, mentions the executors of the will of "Hugh, chancellor of the king." Id. 172 A., 176.

⁷ Delisle, LXXXVI. Between April and October.

⁸ I have ventured so to designate the office. Both bear the title "camerarius" in the charters, e. g. Delisle, page 497, 503, 515; but they never subscribed the royal charters as among the five great officers. Id. LXXXVI. compare. Rigord, Delaborde I:64.

⁹ "Galterus junior." Guil. Amor. Delaborde I:257. 272 etc.

¹⁰ He was one of the body-guard of Philip Augustus at the battle of Bouvines, and distinguished himself in the contest. Guil. Amor. Id. 272, 284.

— 44 —

exercised the marshalship during the minority of John Clement,[1] but his work for the royal archives was of equal value. It was to him that the restoration of the charters and rolls of the kingdom was entrusted after the loss of the French archives at the battle of Fretteval in July, 1194.[2] He was the founder of the Trésor des Chartes, and William the Breton will be readily believed when he calls this a work involving great labor. If Walter of Nemour was actively connected with the preservation of the royal charters, Frater Guarinus, a brother of the order of the Hospital, was principally concerned with their expedition. From Nov. or Dec., 1201, his name frequently appears at their conclusion.[3] Like Walter, he was active in the councils of the king,[4] and he was a soldier of even greater distinction. The ordering of the battle of Bouvines was his work.[5] But neither his military activity nor his election, in 1213[6], to the see of Senlis, interrupted his labor in the expedition of charters. On the accession of Louis VIII., he became chancellor in title;[7] a distinction which he would doubtless have attained long before, had it not been the settled policy of Philip Augustus to keep the office in his own hands. As it was, the chancellorship was inconspicuous under Philip's rule. His wise management of this office, as of the seneschalship, prevented the occurence of quarrels between the king and his officers such as turmoiled the reign of Louis VI. It immeasurably strengthened the monarchy, by placing under the immediate control

Brother Warren.

Effect of this policy.

He was prominent in the crusade of 1218, during which he was captured by the infidels. Sep. XVIII:287.

[1] Guil. Amor. Id. 265.
[2] Philippide IV ; 569. Delaborde II : 120:
"Profuit huic operi Galterus junior: ille
Hoc grave sumpsit onus in se, qui cuncta reduxit
Ingenio naturali sensusque vigore
In solitum rectumque statum."
[3] Delisle, LXXXII. "Per manum fratris Garini" or „Guarani", is the formula.
[4] „Frater Garinus, qui, cum esset frater professus Hospitalis Hierosolymitani, regis Philippi magnanimi specialis consiliarii effectus, in aula regia propter prudentiam et incomparabilem consilii virtutem ..... ita laudabiliter se habebat, quod quasi secundus a rege negotia regni inculpate tractabat." Guil. Amor. Delaborde, 1:256. „regis specialis amicus." Philippide. X : 729.
Nobiles et majores de consilio suo misit, scilicet B. de Roya, fratrem Guarinum familiarem clericum suum, vices cancellarii agentem." Chron. Rotomagensi, Sep. XVIII : 359.
[5] Guil. Amor. Delaborde, I : 275, 276.
[6] Id. 256.
[7] Baluze, Misc. VII: 218. Ordon. XI: 317 etc.

of the king the power which had been exercised by the great officers in semi-independent fashion.

The three remaining great offices, of butler, chamberlain, and constable, were not otherwise treated under Philip Augustus than under his immediate predecessors. They were comparatively uninfluential. Their holders came from the less powerful nobles, for the most part, and there was less ground for royal dislike than in the case of the seneschalship or chancellorship. Philip was not a man to change established order simply for the sake of novelty; and, therefore, though he left the seneschal's post and chancellorship vacant during the greater part of his reign, he continued the three other offices with fresh appointments. *More conservative treatment of the three minor offices.*

The treatment of the butlership is a good example of Philip's conservatism, where the interests of the crown were not imperilled. The family of La Tour, of Senlis, had held the office, with the exception of a brief period during the ascendency of the Garlandes, continuously since the accession of Louis VI.[1] Their faithfulness to the crown, their ability, and the comparatively small possessions of their house, contributed to win the favor of Louis VI. and VII., which made theirs the only instance, in the history of the French monarchy during the twelfth century, of the possession of a high royal office by many successive generations of the same family.[2] The same policy was pursued by Philip Augustus. At his accession he found the office held by Guy III.[3] of Senlis, who had succeeded his father, William le Loup, about 1149.[4] Philip allowed him to continue in undisturbed possession of the butlership till about 1186, when the charge was transferred from the doubtless enfeebled Guy III. to his son, Guy IV.[5] The latter retained the office till his death in 1221.[6] For some reason, Philip Augustus left the butlership vacant after the death of Guy IV., so that it remained without an incumbent till the accession of Louis VIII. The new king at once appointed Robert de Courtenai to the office;[7] and the butlership went from the control *The butlership.*

---

[1] See the notes on the butlers of Senlis, under Louis VI. and VII. Luchaire, Instit. II: 300.

[2] Id. I: 172.

[3] I follow the numbering of Luchaire. Delisle, Cat. LXXXII, numbers him II.

[4] Delisle, Id.

[5] Id. Guy III. died in 1187.

[6] Id. Possibly Oct. 16. He left a son of the same name. Id. 2057.

[7] Baluze, Misc. VII: 248. Martène, "Amp. Coll." I: 1177.

of the family of La Tour. Whatever may have been the reason for this change of policy in the closing months of Philip's reign, he made no departure from the policy of his father and grandfather till over forty years after the death of Louis VII. The infrequency of reference to the butler in the sources of our information concerning the period makes it difficult to affirm, with exactness, in what the privileges of the office consisted.[1] The occupant of the butlership plays no such important part under Philip Augustus as under his father,[2] and, though the name of the butler immediately follows that of the seneschal in subscriptions to the charters, the holders of the office appear to have had less share in the administration under Philip than the chamberlains or constables.

The chamberlain's post becomes largely honorary.

On his accession, Philip found the chamberlain's office in the hands of a certain Reginald, who had held the post since 1175.[3] His subscription appears on but two of the charters issued by the young king: and he cannot have held office later than the summer of 1180.[4] He was succeeded at that time by Matthew III., count of Beaumont-sur-Oise.[5] Two members of the family of Beaumont, Matthew I. and II., had already held the same office under Louis VII., previous to the appointment of Reginald.[6] The chamberlain's post no longer possessed the authority which had attached to it under Henry I. and Philip I., when it had exercised the military functions appropriated later by the seneschalship.[7] We find Matthew III. serving as a judge, with other barons, regarding the claims of the vicedominus of Châlons to the regalia of that see.[8] But, in the main, his position was not one of great administrative importance. Though he signed the royal charters as chamberlain, the office, as held by him, must have been largely honorary. Indeed, so completely was he outshone by the sub-chamberlains, that it seems sometimes to have been forgotten that

Matthew de Beaumont and Bartholomew de Roie.

---

[1] The account of the provost of Paris, for the year 1202—3, show a payment to the butler of 10 livres in each of the three periods into which the financial year was divided. Brussel "Usage". II. cxlvii, clxxiv, clxxxix.

[2] See the remarks on the prominence of Guy III. at the court Louis VII. Luchaire, "Inst." II: 300. 301.

[3] Delisle, Cat. LXXXII.

[4] Id. Nos. 1 and 2 in the catalogue of M. Delisle.

[5] Id.

[6] Luchaire, "Inst." 1: 169.

[7] Under Henry I. the chamberlain was "princeps exercitus Franconum", Id. (from Sep. XI: 207). Under Philip I., the chamberlain, Galeran, was the most influential officer at the royal court. Id.

[8] Text of the judgment, Delisle, Cat. appendix p. 503.

Matthew was chamberlain at all. The title is seldom given to him outside of the formal subscriptions to charters, while the sub-chamberlains, Walter de Capella, and his sons, Ursio and Walter the younger, are recorded constantly as camerarii.¹ Matthew de Beaumont retained the post till 1208.² He was succeeded by Bartholomew de Roie,³ who continued to hold the office under the reign of Louis IX.⁴ The new chamberlain was a man of much more distinction in the royal service than Matthew de Beaumont. But his prominence was acquired before his appointment to the chamberlain's office and seems to have been little increased by the attainment of his new dignity. Philip had long employed him on business of importance. In January, 1194, he had sworn the royal assent, as representative of the French monarch, to the treaty made by the latter with John while Richard of England was still in captivity, and Richard's treacherous brother hoped to prevent his return and secure the favor of Philip, at the sacrifice of a large part of the Continental possessions of the house of Anjou.⁵ He had been one of the sureties of the peace of Goulet, made with John, then become king of England, in 1200,⁶ and of the truce with the citizens of Rouen in 1204.⁷ In the summer of 1206, Philip had sent him to Courtrai to meet Philip of Namur, and to take the oaths of the barons and communes of Flanders and Hainault to support the treaty made between the king and the marquis of Namur, respecting the wardship of the heiresses of Flanders and the marriage of the daughter of

¹ In the document just cited Matthew is styled simply "comes Belli-Montis", while the title of camerarius is given to Walter de Capella. Rigord and William the Breton give Matthew the title of camerarius in their own texts, while Walter de Capella has the title uniformly, and Walter the younger usually, in their writings. But, in spite of this, we cannot give rank among the five great palace officers to any camerarii except Reginald, Matthew de Beaumont and Bartholomew de Roie, for they alone signed the charters in that capacity.

² Probably till Sept., 1208, certainly till May. Delisle, Cat. LXXXIII.

³ In Sept. or Oct., 1208. Id.

⁴ "Videbant enim regni Franciae pervasores per manus mulieris et pueri (Blanche of Castile and Louis IX.), necnon et cujusdam senis, scilicet Bartholomaei de Roya eorumdem consiliarii, regnum Franciae gubernatum." Chron. Turonense. Scp. XVIII. 319.

⁵ "Ego vero (Johannes) in propria persona juravi quod ego praedictas conventiones observabo, et bona fide et sine malo ingenio eas tenebo. Rex autem Franciae Bartholomaeum militem suum fecit jurare quod ipse bona fide et sine malo ingenio omnes praedictas conventiones observabit". Scp. XVII: 40.

⁶ Id. 53.

⁷ Id. 59.

Philip Augustus to Philip of Namur.[1] He, apparently, secured the approbation of his sovereign in the execution of this trust, for he speedily thereafter received the gift of a fief in Normandy from the royal hand.[2] He had served as a judge in the investigation concerning the regalia of Châlons,[3] with Matthew de Beaumont, then still chamberlain; and had been one of the special messengers sent by Philip to induce the chapter of Rouen to relax the interdict imposed on that city in 1207.[4] No wonder the chronicler of Rouen styles him one of the chief of Philip's counselors.[5] His appointment to the post of chamberlain brought no change in his relations to his sovereign. He was one of the judges in the quarrel between Philip and the bishop of Paris in 1221,[6] and in the dispute concerning the succession to the county of Beaumont in 1223.[7] He was soldier enough to be one of Philip's body-guard at Bouvines;[8] and the confidence of the king in his integrity is shown by his appointment as one of the three executors of Philip's will.[9] Yet it may properly be doubted whether his position as chamberlain really signified much more than the possession of an honorary title.

Prominence of the sub-chamberlains, as royal counselors, not due to their office.

Throughout the reign of Philip Augustus, the names most frequently mentioned in connection with this office are those of the sub-chamberlains of the family of Walter de Capella, of Villebéon. Though not of high birth,[10] the founder of the family had long enjoyed the favor of his sovereign and held an influential position at court. He appears as camerarius, in the palace of Louis VII., as

[1] "B. de Roia, salutem. Mandamus vobis quatinus eatis in Flandriam; in octabis Sancti Johannis Baptiste sitis apud Curtraium, sicut ordinatum fuit, in occursum comiti Namurcii, et securitatem recipiatis ab omnibus baronibus Flandrie et communiis et Hanonie et omnibus militibus qui sunt ibi alicujus nominis, sub hac forma. Quod etc." Delisle, Cat. appendix p. 511.

[2] Aquigni, dept. Eure. Charter given between Nov., 1206, and Apl., 1207. Id. no. 1007.

[3] Id. appendix p. 503.

[4] Scp. XVIII: 359.

[5] "Nobiles et majores de consilio suo misit (rex), scilicet B. de Roya, fratrum Guarinum familiorem clericum suum, vices cancelarii agentum, etc." Id.

[6] Delisle, Cat. 2034, Text Teulet, Layettes, I: 514.

[7] Martène, "Amp. Coll". I: 1164.

[8] Guil. Amor. Delaborde I: 272, 284.

[9] "Hujus autem testamenti executores constituimus dilectos et fideles nostros Garinum Sylvanectensem episcopum et Bartolomeum de Roia Francie camerarium, et fratrem Haimardum tessaurium Templi." Teulet, Layettes, 1:549.

[10] "Galterus senior, regis Franciae camararius, qui fuit nobilior gestis quam genere". Scp. XVIII: 769.

early as 1167.¹ The post brought him certain privileges, which show that the office was a fief, having certain rights and properties attached to it and belonging to the office itself;² but our information is too scanty to enable us to ascertain the extent of these tenures. Certainly, however, the chief activity of the sub-chamberlain was connected with the general administration of the kingdom, rather than with duties such as are indicated by the title he bore. Thus, in 1186, Walter became provost of Poissi;³ in 1193, he sought to aid Philip in his attempted divorce from Ingeburgis;⁴ in 1200, the punishment to be imposed on Thomas, provost of Paris, for indignities inflicted on the students of the great University, was left to his discretion.⁵ But the most striking proof of the influence of Walter de Capella is the prominence attained by his sons. Of the seven born to him,⁶ three devoted themselves to the church, and gained eventually the important bishoprics of Noyon, Paris, and Meaux.⁷ Four followed him in the royal service and bore the title of camerarii. Of these sub-chamberlains, one, Walter the younger, has already been noticed in connection with the chancellor's office, to the efficiency of which he so materially contributed by his labors in the restoration of the lost archives. Another, Philip, died comparatively young;⁸ and a third, John, was not specially distinguished.⁹ The remaining one of the four, Ursio,

The family of Walter de Capella.

---

¹ Tardif, "Mon. Hist.", 606.
² Luchaire, "Instit." II: 299, publishes a charter of 1172, by which Walter de Capella remits the taxes due from a certain house at Paris to the chamberlain's office, the house having been given to the poor. A charter of Matthew de Beaumont, of 1155, also given by Luchaire, (id. 301), speaks of property at Pont-aux-Moines near Orléans, claimed "de feudo camere".
³ Rigord, Delaborde, I: 64.
⁴ Hoveden, III: 224.
⁵ Sep. XVII: 606.
⁶ The wife of Walter de Capella was Aveline de Nemours, Sep. XVIII: 769. His brother, Stephen, had attained the archbishopric of Bourges (Tardif. Mon. Hist. 656). His brother-in-law, Theobald the Rich, (Delisle Cat. 570), was a prominent burgher of Paris, and active in the administration during Philip's absence on the crusade of 1190. Walter died in 1204.
⁷ "Et ita fuerunt tres fratres uterini simul episcopi et contemporanei, Stephanus Noviomensis, Petrus Parisiensis et Guillelmus Meldensis; filii Galteri quondam Francie camerarii, fratres Galteri junioris, viri satis virtute laudabiles et in palatio regis praeclari, et in scholis, quantum expediebat, sufficienter exercitati". Guil. Amor. Delaborde I: 257, see also Sep. XVIII: 769. Stephen was bishop of Noyon from 1188 to Sept. 1221; Peter, of Paris, 1208 — Dec. 1219; William, of Meaux, 1214 — Aug. 1221.
⁸ He was dead in Aug. 1191. Delisle, Cat. appendix p. 501.
⁹ He is mentioned in Delisle, Cat. 1662, 1663. see also XVIII: 769.

was as prominent, and almost as many sided, in his service to the king as his brother, Walter the younger. He appears as one of the three royal commissioners who signed the truce of July, 1194, between Philip Augustus and Richard of England.¹ Soon after he was sent on a special mission to the archbishop of Rouen, to assure that prelate of the cordial welcome of the French monarch, if obliged to leave Normandy on account of Richard's seizure of church lands for his fortress of Andeli.² He appears as one of the sureties of the peace of Goulet in 1200;³ and, as one of the representatives of the king, he swore to observe the truce made with John after the battle of Bouvines.⁴ His services as judge were called into requisition in the quarrel with the bishop of Paris,⁵ and the disputed succession to the county of Beaumont,⁶ already noticed. Evidently, Ursio and the family of which he was a member were more than simple sub-chamberlains.⁷ Their prominence was not due to the tenure of an office alone; they were the trusted counselors of the king on matters of general administration, and their employments were as varied as the exigencies of the royal service.

<small>Philip's policy respecting the office of constable.</small> The office of constable was in a transition state under the reign of Philip Augustus. As long as the seneschalship existed, the holder of the latter post exercised a higher authority in the army than the constable. Under Henry I. the chamberlain had been the commander-in-chief.⁸ There is no evidence that the constable pos-

¹ Between Verneuil and Tillières, July 23. 1194. Sep. XVII: 570.
² Id. 652.
³ Id. 53. In 1202—3 Ursio was in military service near Goulet. "Ursio cambellanus, de LXVI. diebus, LXVI. l." Brussel II: clxxxvi.
⁴ Sep. XVII: 104.
⁵ Delisle, Cat. 2034, Teulet, Layettes, I: 514.
⁶ Martène, "Amp. Coll." I: 1164.
⁷ Ursio has usually the title of camerarius. In the text of the truce after the battle of Bouvines, he is designated as cambellanus, (Sep. XVII: 104); and he bears the same title in the text of the decision regarding Beaumont, (Martène, "Amp. Coll." I: 1164). This shows the indefiniteness of the usage. The cambellani, proper, were subordinate officers, having actual charge of the royal apartments. Such were Andrew (Delisle, Cat. appendix p. 501), Brice (Id. Cat. 790), Hugh (Id. 344), Reginald (Id. 224). Yet even these could attain considerable prominence. Andrew was, apparently, one of the council at Paris during Philip's absence on the crusade of 1190—91. Delisle, Cat. LXII. The distinction in title is not fixed. Brice is called camerarius, Sep. XXIII: 612.
⁸ Luchaire, "Instit." I: 169.

sessed any supreme command under Philip Augustus.¹ But the office, in itself, as far as it was active rather than honorary, tended to bring its holder more into military affairs than that of butler or chamberlain, and made it natural that he should succeed to the military powers of the seneschal on the suspension of the charge of the latter functionary. Such an increase in the authority of the constable did not, however, take place during the vigorous reign of Philip Augustus. The latter pursued the same policy toward this office that he employed with reference to the posts of butler and chamberlain. He filled the charge, when it became vacant; but he allowed the real activity to pass, to a great extent, into the hands of ministers of lower rank and greater probable subservience to the royal will.

The constable, at the accession of Philip Augustus, was Ralph, count of Clermont-en-Beauvaisis, who had held the post since 1164.² He was prominent at the court of his sovereign, but apparently more as an adviser than as a military commander.³ In the opening months of the new reign his influence was exerted to bring about the marriage of the young king with Elizabeth of Hainault,⁴ which Philip of Flanders had at heart. But after the break between the latter and his sovereign, Ralph adhered to the party of Philip Augustus, and was consequently attacked by Philip of Flanders.⁵ It was at the advice of Ralph that the French monarch refused to give back the lands of his uncle, the count of Sancerre, who had sided with the count of Flanders in the contests of 1181.⁶ The

Ralph, count of Clermont-en-Beauvaisis.

---

¹ The constable is placed after the marshal, in the charter conceeding the regalia of Mâcon to the bishop of that city and his successors in 1209. "Exercitus etiam in praedictis regalibus non simpliciter, sed tantum hoc modo retinemus; si nos, vel filius noster, vel marescallus, vel senescallus, vel constabularius Franciae, de mandato nostro, versus partes illas duceret dictus Matisconensis episcopus usque Divionem et non ultra, in nostrum exercitum cum armis et militibus venire teneretur." Martène, "Amp. Coll." I. 1087.

² Delisle, Cat. LXXXIV.

³ "Comes Flandrie et Radulphus comes Clarimontis et alii quidam precipue regis Francorum familiares et consiliarii", Gislebert. 120. "Radulphus.... prepotens in consiliis ipsius regis." Id. 125.

⁴ Gislebert, 120.

⁵ Philip of Flanders had demanded of Ralph the castle of Breteuil, which the latter held of him. Gislebert, 125.

⁶ „Comes vero Flandriae petiit sibi et Stephano comiti (of Sancerre) restitutionem fieri, Sed rex, per consilium comitis Claro Monte, eam reddere noluit." Benedict. Petrob. I : 284.

peace of the following spring assured to Ralph the possession of Breteuil, and settled the quarrel between the monarch and his vassal of Flanders, for the time being.[1] The peace, too, brought the Champagne party into greater prominence at court; but Ralph still continued an influential royal adviser. Thus, in 1184, he supported the archbishop of Reims, who had been, since 1182, the king's chief counselor in the almost successful effort to bring about a divorce between Philip Augustus and his queen, Elizabeth.[2] Like many of his friends and opponents, he took the cross in 1188,[3] and died during the siege of Acre,[4] where so many of the nobles of France found their graves.

Drogo de Mello.

Although Drogo de Mello, the next constable, was present at Acre at the time of Ralph's death, and Philip had distinguished him on the crusade by marks of special favor,[5] it was not till July, 1193, that the king appointed him to the post.[6] Certainly, a constable was no pressing necessity for the French military establishment, or an earlier choice would have been made. Drogo de Mello was already distinguished as a soldier. He had acquitted himself brilliantly, although severely wounded, in battle with the forces of Richard, afterward king of England, at Mantes in 1188.[7] But when we consider the office that he held, his warlike exploits after attaining the constable's post were inconsiderable compared with those of William des Barres, or Bartholomew de Roie, or half a score of others. He does not appear as a commander. His name is not mentioned in connection with the battle of Bouvines, where frater Guarinus, the bishop elect of Senlis and Philip's vice-chancellor, was in command. Probably he was infirm through illness or age;[8] but, what-

[1] Benedict. I: 286.
[2] Gislebert, 139.
[3] Rigord, Delaborde, I: 84.
[4] Rigord, Id. 113. A charter of Philip Augustus dated at Acre, July, 1191, and announcing the last wishes of Ralph, makes it certain that he died before Philip's departure for France. Delisle, Cat. 341.
[5] Philip had given him 200 ounces of gold at Messina, on account of losses by shipwreck. Rigord, 107. After the capture of Acre, Philip appointed him commissioner to superintend the division of the prisoners and spoil with Richard of England. Benedict Petrob. II: 179.
[6] Delisle. Cat. LXXXIV.
[7] Philippide, III: 565 et seq.
[8] He had a son of the same name, who was prominent in the fight at Mantes in 1188. (Id.) It was to this son that the charge of the important castles of Loches and Châtillon-sur-Indre was committed by Philip in 1205. Martène, "Amp. Coll" I: 1053.

ever may have been the reason, the constable's office, as held by Drogo, had none of the preeminence in military matters that it enjoyed under later kings. He had prominence enough at court to be one of the three commissioners to make the truce, of July, 1194, with Richard of England,[1] and to procure the gift of the castles of Loches and Châtillon-sur-Indre to his son, Drogo, in 1205. He signed the charters as constable till May, and possibly till July, 1218.[2]

The last constable to hold office under Philip Augustus was Matthew II. de Montmorenci,[3] a soldier of great experience and long prominent in the royal service.[4] The peaceful close of Philip's reign, however, afforded little opportunity for the exercise of the duties later peculiar to the constable, even if they were conferred on him, of which we have no evidence. A single incident shows that his military ability was rather feared than trusted by his sovereign.[5] His chief duties, however, seem to have been to share in the judicial activity of the royal court.[6] He survived Philip and Louis VIII., and continued to hold the office of constable in the opening years of the reign of Louis IX.[7]

Among those connected with the office of chamberlain, the chief activity in the royal service was displayed, as we have seen, by the subofficers rather than by the great officer whose name appears at the close of the royal charters. So it was also with the station of constable. The officers of whom most frequent mention is made in the documents

Matthew de Montmorenci.

---

[1] Scp. XVII : 570.
[2] Delisle, Cat. LXXXIV.
[3] Id.
[4] In 1198 he was unhorsed by Richard of England, personally, at the battle near Gisors. Scp. XVII : 589. He received 300 ounces of gold from Philip at Messina, Rigord, 107. He was in the first line at the battle of Bouvines, Guil. Amor, 276. In 1216 he was employed, with William des Barres, to summon Blanche of Champagne to be present at the trial of her claims to Champagne (Brussel "Usage" I : 651). Previous to the trial, he was royal messenger to receive the assurance of her consent to a truce with her rivals, Érard of Brienne and his wife, Philippa. (Delisle Cat. 1658.)
[5] In Nov., 1219, Philip made him promise not to fortify an island below St. Denis. In May, 1220, Philip, having demolished a fortified house on the island, belonging to one of the sergeants of Matthew de Montmorenci, allowed another of his sergeants to build a house, on condition that it should not be fortified. Delisle, Cat. 1938, 1969.
[6] E. g. in the case of the bishop of Paris (Teulet I : 514), and that of the succession to Beaumont. (Martène, "Amp. Coll." 1 : 1163), which have already been cited as employing other of the court officers.
[7] Charter of Louis IX, April, 1229. Scp. XIX : 223.

of the period, and who seem to have been most actively engaged in the military service of the French monarch, are the marshals, rather than the constables themselves. This office was not new. It had existed, certainly, since 1047;[1] and like the sub-offices of the chamberlain's charge, the marshalship was not confined to a single individual, but was held simultaneously by several persons.[2] Like those offices, too, the marshalship was exercised throughout the reign of Philip Augustus by various members of the same family. The sons of Robert Clement attained as great prominence in the royal service as those of Walter de Capella: and the marshalship continued in the family for three generations under Philip Augustus, though never transmitted by hereditary right.[3] But they had no monopoly of the office; and, though there was always a marshal of the name of Clement during the reign, there were others also.[4] The career of the family of Clement has been noticed already in our consideration of

Prominence of the marshals.

The family of Clement.

[1] Luchaire, "Instit." I: 167 note. Boutaric, ("Institutions Militaires de la France", 271), is in error in representing Philip as the creator of the office.

[2] Under Philip I., in 1068, there were at least three marshals contemporaneously. Id. The existence of several marshals under Louis VII. is proved by a charter of 1166, in favor of the abbey of St. Denis. Id. Tardif, Mon. Hist. 576.

[3] William the Breton, in recording the appointment of John, son of Henry Clement, to the marshalship made vacant by the death of the latter, adds: "Et hoc totum fuit de benignitate regis, quia hereditaria successio in talibus officiis locum non habet." Delaborde I: 265. On the accession of Louis VIII., in 1223, this John gave a charter recognizing the non-hereditary character of his office: "Ego Johannes Marescallus Domini Ludovici regis illustris: notum facio universis praesentes literas inspecturis, me super sacrosancta jurasse ipsi domino regi, quod non retinebo equos nec palefridos nec roncinos redditos ad opus meum, ratione ministerii mei quod habeo de dono ipsius domini regis. Nec ego, nec heredes mei, reclamibimus marescalliam jure hereditario tenendam et habendam. In cujus rei etc. . . . Actum apud Suessionem anno Domini M°CC°XXIII°, mense Augusto." Martène, "Amp. Coll." I: 1175.

[4] Among these were Nivelon of Arras, who was bailiff of that city in 1202, and already held the title of marshal. Brussel II: cliii. In 1217, Philip employed him to receive guarantees of fidelity concerning Alard de Bourghelles and Walter de Vormizeele. Delisle, Cat. 1718, 1725, 1726, 1738. Teulet, Layettes, II: 412, 413.

Peter the Marshal, who had held office under Louis VII., was appointed one of the receivers of the royal revenue during the crusade of 1190. Will of Philip Augustus, Delaborde, I: 103.

Matthew de Bourges was marshal 1185. Delisle, Cat. 121.

John, not John Clement, appears as marshal, in the accounts of 1202—3, in active military service. Brussel II: clxxiii, clxxx: And there is mention of a „Stultus marescallus" in the same record. Id. clxxxix.

Theobald was marshal in 1209. Delisle, Cat. 1145. William de Tournel in 1221, Id. 2034.

the relations of Robert Clement to Philip, during the opening years of the latter's reign. The prominence of Alberic and Henry in the councils of the king,[1] the glorious death of the former at the Cursed Tower of Acre,[2] the military services of the latter in Aquitaine and elsewhere,[3] the general grief at his death in 1214,[4] and the gratitude of Philip for the services of Henry, as shown in the appointment of his minor son, John, to the vacant post,[5] all exhibit the prominence which it was possible for a family of comparatively humble origin to attain in the service of the king. But it was a prominence which was made possible only by the preference of the monarchy to use men of lower rank and to divide authority between several representatives, rather than to leave power in the hands of great nobles or high palace officers whose semi-independence was a constant menace to the king.

The consideration of the great offices of the crown, under Philip Augustus, has shown the completion under him of a process already begun by his grandfather and father. The great court offices, which the limited extent of the royal possessions under the early Capetians, and the intimate association of the nobles of the Ile-de-France with the king in the administration of the government, made useful under Henry I. or Philip I., had proved dangerous to the growing strength of the monarchy and unwieldy in administrative practice. Louis VI. and Louis VII. had tried to limit their power. Philip Augustus practically abolished the two posts of greatest prominence, and, by his employment of men of lower position, made the three remaining offices chiefly honorary. No feature of this policy was original with Philip. It was that of his grandfather and father. But

Philip completes the work of his father and grandfather,—

---

[1] Scp. XVIII: 560.

[2] Benedict Petrob. II: 173. Compare this essay, p. 35, note 3.

[3] In 1208, in conjunction with William des Roches, Henry overran the territories of the viscount of Thouars and Savari of Mauléon, who had been threatening the French possessions in Anjou. Delaborde I: 225. The accounts of revenue for 1202—3 show that Henry was actively engaged in the royal service in Normandy at that time. Brussel II: clxvi, vii & viii. William the Breton declares of him:
"Henricus vero modicus vir corpore, magnus
Viribus, armata nulli virtute secundus,
Cujus erat primum gestare in prelia pilum,
Quippe marescalli claro fulgebat honore." Philippide, VIII: 283.

[4] Guil. Amor, Delaborde I: 265, Philippide, X: 350.

[5] Guil. Amor. Id.

he carried it out with a vigor and thoroughness which they lacked,[1] and the consequence was a very considerable strengthening of the royal authority in the central administration. The position of the royal servants became, by this process, increasingly one of personal relation to a master rather than connection with an office or fief. The central administration was emerging from the feudal stage, where the semi-independent exercise of rights, granted once for all to the tenant, is the characterizing feature, and where the peaceful limitation of those rights by the sovereign, during the life of the possessor, is almost impossible. It had not yet reached the plane of development where the royal servants become exclusively associated with single departments of administration. Thus, on the one hand, it is difficult to discover the performance, by the holders of the three great court offices, which Philip suffered to remain after the suspension of the seneschalship and chancellorship, of any weighty act by reason of their posts of butler, chamberlain or constable; and, on the other, the counselors of the king frequently united the most diverse employments in the same individual, — as when Warren the Hospitaller exercised the functions of a vice-chancellor, a high military commander, a receiving officer of the treasury, and, when occasion demanded, of a judge, while holding an important ecclesiastical preferment.

by giving increasing prominence to men of low rank.

After the suspension of the seneschalship, the most influential of the royal counselors were the tenants of none of the great court offices under Philip Augustus. But Philip had no hesitation in using a man of high position, if he was in accord with the policy of the king, as freely as the servants of his own creation. He placed great dependence on his uncle, the archbishop of Reims, whose position as primate of France gave him an influence second to that of no noble of the realm; and, on the other hand, he bestowed a confidence hardly less great on Bernard of Grammont,[2] or

But he uses men of every station freely.

---

[1] Louis VI. had left the seneschalship vacant for four years, Louis VII. for two, but neither had the strength or the courage to make the vacancy permanent.

[2] Peter Bernard de Coudrai, or de Bré, was originally a knight. He took orders and became fifth prior of Grammont, afterward "corrector" of the "Bonihomines" of the order of Grammont, in the wood of Vincennes. His influence was so great that, in 1168, he was ordered by Alexander III. to admonish Henry II. of England for his treatment of Thomas à Becket. Sep. XII: 441, XVI: 332. It was on his advice, in 1181, that Philip remitted debts due by Christians to Jews, reserving a fifth for the royal treasury. Rigord, 25. Philip had such confidence in him, that, in his direction for the government of the kingdom during the crusade, he ordered: "Si prebenda vel beneficium aliquod

Haimard,[1] the royal treasurer at the Temple. During the absence of Philip on the crusade of 1190, the regency was administered by William of Reims and the queen mother; but the great seal was intrusted to a council composed, in part at least, of Paris burghers,[2] and the oversight of the payments of the revenue into the treasury was their charge.[3]

But though the number of persons, who stood in positions of more or less confidence under the king, is hardly less impressive than the variety of their occupations, there was always one more prominent than all others in the royal councils, one who constited in a certain sense a prime-minister. Naturally, the degree of influence of this chief of the royal advisers was greater during the early years of the reign than after Philip had obtained full powers of manhood. The relation was one designated by no office or title, and depending simply on the preference of the sovereign and the ability of the minister, but the primacy among the royal advisers was none the less real. Several such chief counselors are to be distinguished in the period under consideration; men of very different rank and ability. The coronation of the young king was followed by the preponderence of the influence of Philip of Flanders. It is to that noble, that the mariage with Elizabeth of Hainault, and the exile of the Champagne party, was due. But the meeting between Philip Augustus and Henry of England in June, 1180, put an end to the influence of the count of Flanders. The return of the Champagne party was not, however, followed by their immediate attainment of power at the

The prime minister.

At the opening of the reign.

---

ecclesiasticum vacaverit, quondo regalia in manu nostra venient, secundum quod melius et honestius poterunt regina et archiepiscopus (i. e. the regents) viris honestis et literatis consilio fratris Bernardi conferant." Id. 102, (Ed. Delaborde).

[1] Haymard was a brother of the Templar order. He served as treasurer of the kingdom, and, as such, receipted for most of the payments in the account of 1202—3. Brussel, Usage II. In 1204 he was instrumental in changing the monetary standard of Normandy from that of Angers to that of Tours. Delisle Cat. p. 507 appendix. He is one of the three executors of the will of Philip, Teulet, Layettes, 1: 549.

[2] A charter of Dec., 1190, is witnessed: "In presentia nostrorum burgensium, qui sigillum nostrum custodiunt" Delisle Cat. LXIII. This was the special seal used in France, while the regular chancery followed the monarch on his crusade.

[3] "Precepimus quod omnes reditus nostri et servitia et obventiones afferanter Parisius per tria tempora; primo ad festum Sancti Remigii, secundo ad Purificationem beate Virginis, tertio ad Ascensionen; et tradatur burgensibus nostis predictis, et P. Marscallo". Will of 1190. Rigord, Delaborde, 1: 103.

court of the young monarch.¹ The mind of the boy ruler was filled with admiration for Henry of England and his son, the younger Henry; but, though the advice and aid of [the English rulers was sought by Philip, the everyday routine of the administration could not be in their hands; and in this the young king seems to have depended on the advice of his old instructor, Robert Clement. The position occupied by this counselor has already been somewhat discussed, in considering the period at which Philip attained his majority. It certainly made him the administrator of the ordinary business of the kingdom,² till his death, in the latter part of 1181, or the opening months of 1182, put the routine administration into the hands of his brother Giles.³ But though the latter secured the election of his brother Garmund to the see of Auxerre,⁴ it may be doubted if his influence was greater with the young monarch, during the winter of 1181—2, than that of Ralph of Clermont,⁵ the constable, who directed the military policy of Philip against Philip of Flanders and Stephen of Sancerre, to the annoyance of Henry of England⁶ and the distress

---

[1] „Philippus rex Franciae, spreto amicorum et avunculorum suorum consilio, adhaesit consilio Henrici regis Angliae, filii Matildis imperatricis." Benedict. Petrob. I: 284.

[2] Though, as has already been seen, we cannot admit that Robert exercised a full guardianship over Philip Augustus, we must take the statement of Robert of Auxerre that Robert was: "Vir moderatus et prudens regique fidelis et qui regalia industrie et strenue administravat negotia" (Mon. Ger. XXVI: 246), to mean, at least, that Robert was the chief among the royal ministers. This interpretation is confirmed by a passage in a letter of Stephen, abbot of St. Geneviève at Paris, later bishop of Tournai, written to Raymond, his prior, in the latter part of 1181, or the first month or two of 1182: "Si quid inter vos circa exteriora negotia natum fuerit quaestionis, propositum ad B. olim praepositum referte, cui dominus Robertus ex parte domini regis injunxit ut quidquid in negotiis vestris postulaveritis, ope et opera ejus fiat vobis," (Sep. XIX: 284', where the reference is almost certainly to Robert Clement.

[3] We have here again to depend largely on the testimony of Robert of Auxerre (Mon. Ger. XXVI: 246) when he tells us: "Huic (Roberto) praedictus Egidius in regni administratione successerat."

[4] Robert of Auxerre. Id. "Ipso anno (1182) Antissiodorenses canonici Garmundum quartum abbatem Pontinensem elegerunt in presulem; non tam ipsius merito, quam sollicito studio fratris ejus Egidii, tunc a rege pro ceteris in curia sublimati."

[5] Radulphus comes Clarimontis, prepotens in consiliis ipsius regis." Gislebert, 125. Compare Benedict. Petrob. I: 284.

[6] Henry waited on the English coast from about January 1st to March 4th, 1182, hoping for a fair wind to allow him to reach the continent and bring the war between Philip Augustus and Philip of Flanders to an end. It was

of the Champagne party. The peace effected by the English monarch after Easter, 1182,[1] was followed by a reconciliation between the offended interests; and the administration of the kingdom was thenceforward largely in accordance with the advice of the king's uncle, William, archbishop of Reims. His hand, probably, is to be seen in the severity of the dealings with heretics which characterize Philip's early reign.[2] By the following year, 1183, the influence of the cardinal[3] archbishop had become so great that Philip styles him: "in consiliis nostris oculus vigilans, in negotiis dextra manus,"[4] and the evidence of this preeminent station is seen in his share in the contest with Philip of Flanders in 1185,[5] and, especially, in his appointment as co-regent during the absence of the king on the crusade of 1190—91. But though William of Reims never ceased to be among the most trusted of the royal counselors,[6] the growing manhood of Philip made the king himself more and more the con-

The archbishop of Reims.

---

not till the latter date that he was able to make the voyage. Benedict. Petrob. I: 285.

[1] Id. 385, 286. At Senlis. "post clausum Pascha," Ralph de Diceto II: 10.

[2] In conjunction with Philip of Flanders, William condemned many heretics at Arras, and other places, after Christmas, 1182, Rigord, Delaborde I: 35. Scp. XVIII: 536, 555. The expulsion of the Jews from the kingdom, in the spring and summer of 1182, may be attributed with probability to his influence.

[3] He was made cardinal priest, with the title of St. Sabina, at the Lateran council of 1179. Benedict Petrob. I: 222.

[4] The passage occurs in an undated letter of Stephen, then abbot of St. Geneviève at Paris, to pope Lucius III. Brial assigns the letter to 1183, Delisle prefers to place it at the beginning of 1184. The abbot, writing in the name of Philip, assigns the reasons why William has been retained by the king in spite of the pope's summons to Rome. The king accredits Stephen to the pope:" Impugnant adolescentiam nostram....... Adsistit nobis super omnes amicos et fideles nostros carissimus avunculus noster Willelmus Remensis archiepiscopus, in consiliis nostris oculus vigilans, in negotiis dextra manus, cum vel ad tempus recedere a nobis succedere est hostibus nostri.... In articulo summae necessitatis nostrae, confidentes de praecipua dilectione vestra, retinuimus eum, clavum in oculis hostium nostrorum, et in lateribus eorum lanceam, sine ipso fieri nihil sustimantes, sive de pace, sive de bello, cum hostibus sit agendum." Scp. XIX: 285.

[5] "Comes (Philippus).... principum militiae regis Theobaldum.... Franciae senescallum, vocavit, et G[uillelmum] Remensem archiepiscopum, ipsius regis avunculos, quibus sicut regis fidelibus cura rerum gerendarum eo tempore commissa fuerat." Rigord, Delaborde, I: 42.

[6] His activity in favoring the divorce of Ingeburgis was marked. Hoveden, III: 224. In 1194 he was sent as one of the French commissioners to Vaudreuil to make truce with Richard of England, Id. (569), and he was sent,

Brother Warren. trolling force of the administration, and brought humbler and more dependent servants of the crown into greater prominence. No one, thereafter, exercised the commanding influence on the course of affairs which had been wielded by Philip of Flanders or William of Reims. But of the numerous counselors of the later years of Philip's reign, none was so active or so trusted as brother Warren of the Hospitallers, later bishop of Senlis. Long before the death of his sovereign left him the first named executor of Philip's will,[1] he was chief among the royal advisers.[2] His activity extended to all departments of government, but was especially manifested as vice-chancellor, military commander and judge.[3] He merits well the description given of him by William the Breton: "specialis consiliarius" and "quasi secundus a rege."[4]

Advice of the counselors. While the advice of this body of counselors is not generally recorded, evidence is not lacking that it was frequently taken by Philip, not only during the early years of his reign, but on most important occasions. Such consultation embraced not merely the details of local

with William, archbishop of Ely, the English representative, to the emperor Henry VI. to obtain his assent to the peace there agreed upon.

The Necrology of Chartres notices his death as follows: "VIII idus Septembris, (1202) obiit vir magnificus Willelmus Remensis achiepiscopus.... Hic dum vixit, regis et regni consiliarius, quasi secundus rex habebatur." Sep. XVIII: 766.

[1] Teulet, Layettes, I: 549.

[2] It is impossible to find any sharp line of demarcation between the prime ministry of William of Reims and the ascendency of Warren.

[3] His prominence as vice-chancellor, and his command at Bouvines, have already been noticed. His employment as judge was no less marked. A few instances may be given. In 1214, he was one of three arbitrators between the "vice-dominus" of the Laonnois and the bishop of Laon. Delisle, Cat. 1522. In 1215, between the count of Blois and the chapter of Chartres. Id. 1573. 1216 saw him one of the judges in the great case of the succession to Champagne, Brussel, "Usage," 651. In 1219, he adjudged the contest between the nuns of Fontevraud and the archbishop of Tours. Delisle, Cat. 1928. In 1220, with Robert de Béthisi. he investigated the right of the archbishop of Reims to conduct into Péronne, Id. 1986. The quarrel with the bishop of Paris claimed his attention in 1221, Id. 2034; and the same year he arbitrated between the bishop of Chartres and the mayor of Pont Gonin, and between Matthew de Montmorenci and the monks of St. Denis, Id. 2047, 2090. He was one of the judges of the succession to Beaumont in 1223, Martène, Amp. Coll. I: 1163; and decided between the bishop and chapter of Noyon and the commune of that place. Delisle, 2216.

[4] Delaborde I: 256.

policy, such as the erection of markets at Paris,[1] it extended to the terms of peace with vassals,[2] to reforms in administrative policy, such as were brought about at the appointment of the regency in 1190;[3] and to the summoning of general councils of the magnates of the kingdom to consider important questions of public policy, or to participate in the ceremonies of state.

It is difficult to draw any sharp distinction between the advisory functions of these amici regis,[4] familiares[5] or consiliarii,[6] as the body of counselors we have had under consideration is styled, and those of the assemblies which Philip, like the Capetian monarchs who had preceeded him, called to his aid in the consideration of any unusual phases of administration. The counselors were, most of them at least, continuously in the immediate neighborhood of the king. It was through their aid that the ordinary routine of business was despatched; their advice was taken by the king in the preparation of matters requiring care and deliberation; the special abilities of many of them led to their employment on errands of responsibility, — they were, in short, a standing council for the monarch.

But constant as was the use made by Philip of his counselors, he supplemented their advice, on any occasion of special moment, by the summons of an assembly of the whole or a portion of the nobles of the realm. Such an assembly was usually entitled a curia,[7] a colloquium,[8]

The Assemblies. How convened.

---

[1] Rigord, Delaborde Id. 34.

[2] 1186. Contest with duke of Burgundy: "habito rex cum amicis suis saniori consilio, illa tria castra duci restituit." Rigord, Id. 53.

[3] "Convocatis amicis et familiaribus testamentum condidit et regni totius ordinationem fecit." Rigord, Delaborde I: 100.

[4] Id. 53, 100, XIX: 285, Philippide X: 731 etc.

[5] Rigord, 100, 119, Gislebert 120, etc.

[6] Gislebert 120, 139, Scp. XVIII: 766, Guil. Amor. Delaborde I: 256 etc.

[7] Curia, under Philip Augustus, was chiefly used of the assembly in its judicial capacity. e. g. "Volebat (rex) quoque secularium rerum causas non nisi sua in curia diffiniri." Robert of Auxerre, Scp. XVIII: 248. "Vobiscum in curia domini regis habeo judicare". Gislebert 166. "Super praedictis autem petiit utraque pars sibi judicium in curia domini regis". Charter of decision in care of the succession to Beaumont, Martène "Amp. Coll." I: 1163.

[8] The consultations between the sovereign and other monarchs, to which the nobles were also summoned, were nsully styled colloquia — e. g. with Henry II., Benedict Petrob. I: 217, 272, 276. 312 etc. Rigord, Delaborde, 83; with Richard, Hovedel IV: 3. 80. Scp. XVIII: 50, 57. XIX: 299; with John, Ordon I: 31; with Frederick Barbarossa, Gislebert, 180, Chron. Mosomense, Scp. XVIII: 698. But the same designation was employed regarding councils between the king and his barons. E. g. the divorce of Ingeburgis,

or concilium,[1] often with the added epithet solemne or generale,[2] if the occasion was one of special moment. The summons of the king is usually described by the expression convocavit.[3] This covocation was effected, as under the earlier Capetians, by a personal letter of summons addressed to the more prominent clergy and nobles,[4] if not to all whose presence was desired, and enjoining attendance in terms which did not admit of refusal, save on grounds of absolute inability to comply with the invitation.[5] The summons

---

Sep. XVIII: 546. Various features of the Albigensian crusade. Id XIX: 15, 78; the double marriage between the families of Champagne and Hainault, Gislebert 171; internal affairs, Sep. XVIII: 116, 551.

[1] The assembly to elect Philip as king is styled a "generale concilium", Rigord, 10. So is that which met to consider the question of a crusade, in Jan., 1185, id. 47; and again in March 1188, id. 84. The great meeting in Soissons in 1213, to consider the invasion of England, is described as a "concilium". Guil. Amor, Delaborde, I: 245.

[2] See instances in the previous note. Many might be added. The assembly at Villeneuve, in 1209, which effected the agreement concerning the division of fiefs is styled, by Peter of Vaux-Sarnei, a "solemne colloquium". Sep. XIX: 15. Compare Sep. XVIII: 698, XIX: 78, 299 etc.

[3] Rigord, 41, 43, Guil. Amor. 245. Sep. XVIII: 31 etc. Beside this usage of the historians, we have that of the charters, e. g. "Convocavimus". Delisle, Cat. appendix p. 503. The summons of an accused person before the curia will be considered in treating of the legal administration.

[4] The customs regarding assemblies differ so little, under Philip Augustus, from those described by Luchaire ("Inst." 1: 246—268) as obtaining under the monarchs immediately previous, that most of that author's observations could be transferred to the reign of Philip. The following letter of Stephen, then bishop of Tournai, asking his metropolitan William of Reims to excuse him from attendance on the consecration of the bishop of Châlons, is, however, of interest. The letter lacks a date, but is ascribed by Brial to 1196. "Inter haec timor et tremor venerunt super me, prope jam tremulum senem, in duabus citationibus vestris et tertia tamquam peremptoria a domino rege facta: prima ad jucundum festivumque domini mei et amici carissimi Catalaunensis electi sacrum Remis, dominica qua cantatur Oculi (Mch. 24); secunda ad solemne colloquium domini regis, dominica qua cantatur Laetare (Meh. 31) juxta Vallem-Rodolii; tertia Parisius, dominica qua cantatur Isti sunt dies (Apl. 7), propter causam quae vertitur inter episcopum Parisiensum et ecclesiam de Kalu (Chelles), ad quam dominus rex sub multa attestatione et adjuratione me citavit." Sep. XIX: 299.

[5] The letter just quoted shows that Stephen of Tournai considered the summons of his sovereign more imperative than that of his metropolitan. Yet, though he begged for excuse from the latter, on account of physical inability to perform the journey, he did not dare refuse and, in the end, went to the consecration to which his archbishop summoned him. If the call of his metropolitan had such influence over him, the "peremptoria" citation of his so-

expressed the nature of the business and appointed the time and place of meeting.[1] It would appear that, when addressed to high ecclesiastical dignitaries and nobles of prominence, the latter summoned the attendance, in some instances, of their suffragans or vassals.[2] But the king was free to invite whom he chose. The character and rank of the persons summoned, as well as their number, depended largely on the nature of the business to be discussed. If a matter of peace and war,[3] a marriage alliance with a foreign sovereign,[4] a question of feudal policy, like the regulation of the

Those summoned.

vereign must have had even more. On no other ground than that of the uniformly recognized imperative nature of a summons can we account for the frequent attendance of the high clergy and baronage on these assemblies, attendance involving great labor and expense. How serious a matter this was is shown by the statements of Gislebert regarding the count of Hainault, who was not a vassal of France. He attended Philip's coronation in 1179, at the request of Philip of Flanders: "Ad cujus comitis preces comes Hanoniensis, qui in nullo regi Francorum obligatus erat, quia nec hominio quocumque nec confederatione aliqua vel familiaritate eidem regi tenebatur, cum 80 militibus et armis ad illum coronamentum in propriis expensis venit." Gislebert, 118. He was present at the colloquies with Henry II. in 1180: "Quibus colloquiis .... in magnis et arduis propriis expensis semper intererat." Id. 122.

[1] See letter of Stephen of Tournai, just quoted. In 1184 Baldwin of Hainault wished to enter into alliance with Philip: "Deinde dominus comes Hanoniensis ad dominum regem Francorum Parisius cum paucis venit. Ubi facta cum domino rege contra comitem Flandrie confederatione, quia ipse eciam rex ibi cum paucis erat, dominus rex ei diem constituit Suessionis, ut ibi plures principes et nobiles Francie haberet." Gislebert 151, 152.

[2] From the letter of Stephen of Tournai it apears that his summons to the "solemne colloquium" at Vaudreuil was through the metropolitan, rather than direct from the king. Philip of Flanders attended the coronation assembly of the young monarch "cum armis et militibus multis." Gislebert 118.

[3] E. g. 1182, peace with Philip of Flanders: "cum archiepiscopis, episcopis, abbatibus et Francorum proceribus." Scp. XVIII: 535. For the same object in 1185: "Philippus Augustus apud .... Compennium ... omnes principes terre sue convocavit." Rigord, 41. In 1196 peace was made with Richard: "convocatis ut inque archiepiscopis, episcopis, et baronibus." Id. 133. In 1202 Philip determined to invade Normandy: "habito ..... cum principibus et baronibus suis consilio." Id. 152. The invasion of England was proposed to such an assembly in 1213: "convocavit Philippus rex concilium in civitate Suessionensi .... cui interfuerunt omnes proceres regni ...... Ibidem igitur tractatum fuit de transfretando in Angliam, et placuit sermo iste baronibus universis." Guil. Amor. 245. (ed. Delaborde).

[4] Bela, king of Hungary, sent messengers to Paris in 1186 asking the hand of Philip's sister Margaret: "Quorum petitiones benigne suscipiens, convocavit archiepiscopos, episcopos et principes regni majores, quorum consilio

succession to fiefs,[1] the recognition of a claimant to a great county, when such recognition involved political rather than legal problems;[2] all such questions were discussed with the prelates and nobles, as being those most directly concerned. On the other hand, if the question was one involving intricate legal points, the king frequently summoned to his aid, in addition to a representation of the nobility, a number of men of legal knowledge, taken from any rank, but coming, naturally, largely from the bourgeois class.[3] The latter were, however, summoned simply on account of their experience and ability. They were not, as were the clergy and nobles, representatives of the rank to which they belonged. It was only on occasions affecting the interests of the entire population, like a crusade,[4] or at the great

et sapientia in negotiis suis pertractandis frequentius uti consueverat." Rigord, Delaborde I: 67.

[1] The charter forbidding sub-infeudation, issued at Villeneuve May 1., 1209, declares: "Philippus Dei gratia Francorum rex, O(do) dux Burgundiae, Herveus comes Nivernensis, Renaldus comes Bolonensis, Guillelmus comes Sancti Pauli, G(uido) de Domnapetra, et plures alii magnates de regno Franciae, unanimiter convenerunt et assensu publico firmaverunt, ut a primo die Maii in posterum ita sit de feodalibus tenementis etc." Brussel, Usage. II:874. Text also Teulet, Layettes, I:331.

[2] In March, 1215, Philip announced to Innocent III. that he would not entertain complaints against the title of Theobald to Champagne till the majority of the latter: "Noverit paternitas vestra quod nos cum dilecta et fideli nostra Blancha comitissa Companiae, per consilium baronum nostrorum, et per consuetudinem in regnum Franciae hactenus approbatam, tales conventiones fecimus etc." Sep. XIX:598.

[3] E. g. the question concerning the regalia of Châlons, in 1202. Delisle Cat. appendix p. 503, where those summoned on divided into three classes; "Convocavimus sapientes homines nostros, Belvacensem, Parisiensem, Meldensem episcopos, et alius viros litteratos, Lotharium Cremonensem, Renulfum archidiaconum Bituricensem, magistrum Galfridum de Pissiaco, magistrum Nicholaum de Carnoto. Convocavimus etiam barones nostros comitem Belli Montis, comitem Pontivi etc. The inquiry into the succession to Beaumont, in 1223, may also be cited. Martène, "Amp. Coll" I:1163. This subject will be further considered in treating of the legal administration.

[4] Rigord records: "Anno Domini MCLXXXVIII, mense martio, media Quadragesima, Parisius celebratum est generale concilium a Philippo rege, convocatis omnibus archiepiscopis, episcopis, abbatibus, et totius regni baronibus, in quo innumerabilis militum multitudo seu peditum sacratissima cruce signati sunt; et propter hanc instantem necessitatem (oppido enim iter Hierosolymitanum rex affectabat), cum assensu cleri et populi, quasdam decimas ab omnibus esse accipiendas eo tantum anno decrevit, que dicte sunt decime Salahadini", Delaborde, I: 84, 85. Yet, though the lower classes were present, their part in the decision was very small. Rigord simply indicates some expression of approbation by the whole assembly when he says: "cum assensu cleri et populi"

spectacular events, such as a coronation[1] or a knighting,[2] that the presence of the lower classes, as such, in the assemblies is recorded, and even then their attendance was due to their own impulses of curiosity[3] or their position in the retinue of those of higher rank,[4] rather than to any direct summons from the king.

The range of topics submitted to the consideration of such an assembly embraced nearly all departments of administration. Anything outside the ordinary routine of business which was despatched by the palace counselors, called for the summoning of such a gathering. Not only great problems of public policy, such as war and peace, crusades, alliances, the appointment of regents, or the regulation of fiefs, were laid before the assemblies;[5] such comparatively minor matters as the institution of a body-guard[6], or the settlement of disputes in an order of monks[7], were the occasions of these gatherings also. The great field embraced by the activity of the curia regis called for the frequent convocation of portions of the clergy and baronage, together with those experienced in the law — a form of the

Subjects of consideration.

---

for the notice of the decision of the assembly, which he preserves, declares: "Constitutum est a domino Philippo Francorum rege, consilio archiepiscoporum, episcoporum et baronum terre sue quod etc.", showing that the deliberation was confined the high nobles of the domain. Id. 85.

[1] The same author, in describing Philip's coronation, says: "convocatis archiepiscopis, episcopis, et omnibus terre sue baronibus .... coronatus est .... cum omnibus archiepiscopis, episcopis, ceterisque regni principibus et universo clero et populo clamantibus: "Vivat rex, vivat rex!" Id. 12, 13. Here a certain participation of the lower orders in recorded, but there is no statement implying any special summons to them to be present as a class.

[2] In 1209 Louis, the crown prince, was knighted at Compiègne: "cum tanta solemnitate et conventu magnatum regni et hominum multitudine ... quanta ante diem illum non legitur visa fuisse." Delaborde, "Oeuvres etc." 1: 226.

[3] Beside the instances just cited, showing the reasons for the presence of the lower orders on these occasions, we have an interesting statement of Rigord regarding the second coronation of Philip: "Interea dum multa turba populi de circumpositis civitatibus, suburbiis, vicis et villis, cum magno gaudio ad tantum solemnitatem videndam convenisset, et ut viderent regem et reginam diademate insignitos etc." Rigord, Delaborde, I: 21.

[4] The large retinues brought to these coronations by Philip of Flanders have already been noticed. Gislebert, 118.

[5] Instances have already been given.

[6] William of Newbury, Scp. XVIII: 31.

[7] "Rex Francorum .... convocatis baronibus suis et ecclesiasticis personis prudentibus et religiosis, partes ad concordiam et pacem commovit et commonuit". 1190. Letter of Stephen, later bishop of Tournai, to Celestine III., regarding the quarrels of the order of Grammont." Scp. XIX: 289.

assemblies which we shall further consider in treating of the legal administration under Philip Augustus. Advice was thus sought by the monarch, or at least consent to his acts obtained, regarding most of the problems of government. One class of questions, however, was not ordinarily laid before these councils; a class, too, which occupies perhaps the most prominent place in the discussions of modern assemblies. The usual royal revenues, being considered the private property of the sovereign, were not subject to the advice of the assembly. It was only when an **extraordinary levy** was sought for a purpose aside from the ordinary exigencies of government, as, for instance, the tenths which it was attempted to raise for the crusade in 1188, that general consent was deemed necessary.[1] In regard to the amount or collection of the regular revenue the assembly was not consulted. In cases where a dispute as to the right to receive a particular revenue raised a question of legal title between the king and another suzerain, the judgment of the curia regis was invoked to decide between the claimants.[2]

Nature and authority of the Assemblies.

It would be an error, however, to represent the assembly, under Philip Augustus, as a coördinate branch of the government. It was rather an advisory council, a convenient means of ascertaining the sentiments of the prelates and baronage, of announcing and publishing the royal purposes, and of obtaining the assent of the vassals of the crown to the enterprises which the king had in view. It was not a body representative of a nation. The members came together as individuals, summoned by the king for a special purpose. They had no power to initiate business, though when once assembled, they, in one instance at least, exercised the right of petition;[3] they met at

---

[1] See this essay, p. 64, n. 4.

[2] E. g. The quarrel between the king and the "vice-dominus" of Châlons over the regalia of that see, in 1202, Delisle, Cat. appendix p. 503.

[3] We have an instance of the exercise of petition in the assembly which came together in May, 1200, to ratify the peace then made with John of England. (Date Delisle, Cat. 619, Brial assigns it to 1214). "Philippus ... universis amicis et fidelibus baronibus, et aliis ad quos praesentes literae pervenerint, salutem et dilectionem: Noveritis quod universi cruce-signati et omnis clerus qui ad colloquium convenerant inter nos et dilectum et fidelem nostrum J. regem Angliae, intuitu Dei requisierunt absque violentia et absque districtione aliqua tum summi pontificis, tum cleri, tum alicujus alterius, quod nos ad auxilium Terrae Jerosolymitanae quadragesimam partem reddituum nostrorum unius anni mitteremus. Et nos praedicto modo absque consuetudine et districtione aliqua et absque violentia aliqua in posterum requirendis, intuitu Dei eis hoc concessimus". Ordon. I: 31. But it is to be noticed that this request was by a particular and privileged body of men, the "cruce-signati," and for

no stated times and in no fixed place;[1] they were called together by the king and acted on the propositions presented by him.[2] There is reason to believe that in most instances their action was wholly formal, the real discussion having taken place in the more intimate circle of the palace counselors, and the proposition of the king being

a religious purpose which was universally recognized as having special claims. No inference as to the conduct of assemblies in regard to the ordinary affairs of the kingdom can properly be drawn from it.

[1] It has often been said that the assemblies met chiefly on the great church festivals. However this may have been under the early Capetians, it was by no means the rule under Philip Augustus. Philip was crowned at All Saints. The coronation of his first queen was originally fixed at Pentecost and then changed to Ascension. Prince Louis, Theobald of Champagne, Philip Hurepel and Philip of Namur were knighted at Pentecost; but, with these exceptions, few impotant assemblies for the consideration of other than legal questions were held on these festivals. The councils to consider the crusade in 1185 and 1188, were held, respectively, in Jan. and at Mid-lent. That at Vezelai in 1190, in July. That at Soissons in 1213, to consider the invasion of England, on the Monday after Palm Sunday. The colloquies with foreign sovereigns were seldom held on a great festival. The absence of special reference in the chronicles to the majority of legal trials, and the custom of dating charters simply by the month, make an affirmation concerning them more difficult. In regard to the place of assembly no fixed custom prevailed. Naturally, Paris, as the ordinary residence of the king, was the scene of a large proportion. But the colloquies with the sovereigns of England and Germany were held at, or near, the respective frontiers. Out of 28 assemblies, not of a judicial character, and not exclusively colloquies with other sovereigns, 9 were held at Paris, 4 at Compiègne, 2 each at St. Denis, Senlis, Sens and Soissons, and one each at Amiens, Laon, Poissi, Portmort, Reims, Vezelai and Villeneuve.

[2] A good example is the council called together by Louis VII. to elect Philip. The king presented his proposition and, "audientes autem prelati et principi voluntatem regis, omnes unanimiter clamaverunt dicentes Fiat, fiat." Rigord, Delaborde, I:10. The course of proceeding, as related by William the Breton, in describing the council at Soissons, in 1213, is so similar that we can affirm its essential truth, even if we ascribe the words put into the king's mouth to the fancy of the poet.

"Francigenum ductor prelatos ecclesiarum
Et toto proceres de regno congregat omnes,
Quorum stans medius placide sic incipit ore . . . . .
Dixerat. At proceres, verandaque curia sancti
Concilii, palmas alacras ad sidera tendunt,
Et conclamantes voto communiter uno
Tam sanctam regis, tam commendabile laudant.
Propositum."
Philippide, IX: 162—165, 193—197. Delaborde, II: 254, 256.

simply accepted or ratified by the assembly. But whether this action was occasionally deliberative or not, we have no recorded instance, under Philip Augustus, where the body failed to assent to the proposition submitted by the king. This assent carried little binding force beyond the range of the personal influence of those who gave it.[1] Hence the few laws which were enacted by Philip Augustus and his assemblies are far more of the nature of treaties than of statutes. They are, with one or two exceptions,[3] agreements between the monarch and the individual vassals, and were no further binding than the personal territories of the contracting parties extended.

The Assemblies necessary for the king, —   But it would be an error no less great to suppose that, because the convocation of an assembly was so dependent on the royal will,

---

The assembly having thus expressed its approbation, the members swore individually to accompany the king.

"Seseque in idem discrimen ituros
Una promitunt, promissaque pignore firmant
Juris jurandi. Primus Ludovicus, et Odo
Allobrogus, Comes Herveus, et Bellijocensis
Guiscardus jurant etc" . . . .
Omnis baro, comes, dux, rector, episcopus, abbas,
Cum reliquis membris regni, se federe firmo
Sponte ligant regi, viresque in prelia spondent."
                                        Philippide. IX: 197—201, 227—229.

The assembly which met at Vezelai, on the eve of the crusade in 1190, ratified the choice of regents, and, apparently, the regulations for the government of the kingdom, which had been made by Philip, with the aid of his "amici et familiares", before leaving Paris. Rigord, Delaborde, I: 100.

[1] The agrement between the king and his barons respecting sub-infeudation, made at the assembly at Villeneuve, May 1, 1209, was not shared in by Blanche of Champagne. We have the testimony of Brussel ("Usage" II:874) that division continued in practice in Champagne without regard to this convention of Villeneuve.

The tenths, agreed upon by the assembly of 1188 for the crusade, were to be collected from all not joining in the expedition, "omnes illi crucem non habentes, quicumque sint, decimam ad minus dabunt," except the lepers and three religious orders. Rigord, Id. 88. But, though the assembly which consented to the tax was unusually large, Philip found himself unable to collect it, owing to the opposition of the clergy; and was compelled to abandon the attempt. In a letter to the archbishop of Reims and the clergy and laity of his province, he declares: "Et ne damnatae exactionis occasio sibi, vel contra se, alicui praescriptionem portat, et ne quis ex ea vel augeri vel minui, vel in aliquo se sentiat praegravari, volumus ut omnia in eo sint in quo erant 40 dies quando occurere assumpsimus." Ordon. XI:255—57. This was not the feudal aid, which was not recognized as due for a crusade till the XIII. cent. Compare Luchaire. "Instit." I:120.

[2] The ordinance of 1215, concerning champions, will be considered later.

and its action usually little more than an assent to the royal proposition, that Philip could have dispensed with such assemblies altogether. The same individualism and semi-independence which made it difficult to execute the king's purpose, even where strengthened by the consent of the assembly, would have made it impossible for the king to have succeeded at all, had it not been for the ratification of his plans thus obtained. In the feudal state of the twelfth and thirteenth centuries, the king could pursue a definite course of action only by winning for his support the assent of a sufficient number of his vassals to overawe, and if needful to crush, opposition. To do this without the assemblies would have been impossible. The loosely joined elements of the nobility, jealous of their personal rights and ready for rebellions and conspiracies if they thought them endangered, must be secured for the side of the monarchy at every new phase of the political situation, if the monarchy was to have help to meet the difficulties of the hour.[1] The assembly gave the king an opportunity to publish and explain his projects, and secure the personal

---

[1] A good illustration of Philip's use of the support of his baronage is his action when the pope attempted to check his victorious career in Normandy in 1203. Philip secured letters, authorizing him to resist the papal demands, from Reginald of Boulogne in June; in July he obtained similar guarantees from Odo, duke of Burgundy, and Hervey of Nevers, at Vaudreuil, and in which William of Sancerre a little later joined; while at the assembly which was convened at Mantes, in August, by the papal legates themselves, he secured the same endorsement from Matthew of Beaumont, Eleanor of St. Quentin and Valois, Blanche of Champagne, Catherine of Blois and Clermont, Ralph, count of Soissons, Enguerran de Courci, and Guy de Dampierre. Delisle, Cat. 762, 770—779. The letter of Odo is printed in Sep. XVIII: 77 note. Teulet, Layettes, I: 243. A similar case occured in 1205, when Innocent III. assumed protection over the persons and goods of the crusaders, and freed them from the payment of interest on their debts. These privileges were to be enforced by church censures. Philip, then at Chinon, consulted his baronage, who committed their decision advising resistance to writing, and promised aid to the king. These were Robert of Courtenai; William, count of Sancerre; Peter, count of Auxerre; Hervey, count of Nevers; Enguerran, count of Perche; and Guy of Dampierre. Teulet, Layettes, I: 291, 292. Probably it was soon after this event that Philip consulted Odo of Burgundy, by letter, regarding the policy to be pursued in the matter. Odo replied: "Super his igitur excellencie vestre per litteras nostras patentes et nuncium nostrum notificamus quod non videtur nobis justum vel racionabile nec licitum domino Pape vel alii quod in regno vestro institucionem faciat, nisi de consilio vestro et vestrorum, quare vos vel vestri barones et fideles servicium et justicias hominum suorum debitas perdant. Id. I: 292. Delisle, Cat. p. 510.

consent of those most directly affected by their execution.¹ It enabled him to feel the pulse of the baronage and to ascertain from what quarter opposition threatened.² Its investigation gave an authoritative definition to royal rights, and its action endorsed the limitations which the royal justice sought to put on the claims of the clergy.³

<small>and for the clergy and baronage.</small> Nor was the assembly less valuable for the vassalage. Through it their share in the royal administration was made real. Their presence witnessed the agreements of the vassals with the sovereign, their voice ratified the conditions of peace or the declaration of war; their opinion influenced, if indirectly, the public policy of the king; and the assemblies, even when simply ratifying the royal will, asserted by the act itself their right to participate in the government and their importance in the body politic.

<small>Policy of Philip.</small> Philip continued the policy of his immediate predecessors in regard to the assembly; his stronger hand enabled him to put the routine business of daily administration more completely than they had been able into the care of the counselors of the palace. With those counselors he deliberated in regard to administrative changes and public policy. He doubtless sought, as far as possible, to concentrate the real power in, as well as to confine actual discussion to, the *familiares* of the palace. But he could not dispense with the assemblies. His use of them was constant; and through his consultation of his subjects and his care to secure their support in his acts, the course of development was furthered which was to result, within less than a century after Philip's death, in the regular summons of the États Généraux.

<small>The curia regis.</small> By far the most frequent employment of the assembly was as the royal judicial court, the *curia regis*, as it was customarily called, its title of *parlamentum* not coming into use till the reign of Saint Louis. The same dependence of the king on the good-will of his clergy and baronage, which made the assemblies for consultation a necessity to the monarchy, rendered the participation of his subjects

---

¹ E. g. the council at Soissons in 1213, where the king secured the oaths of the clergy and baronage to accompany him on his projected invasion of England.

² It was the hostility of the count of Flanders, first made evident at the Soissons council, which showed the danger threatening the royal plans. Guil. Amor. Delaborde, I: 245, 246.

³ The articles drawn up in 1205 or 1206, at Paris, contain a statement of the claims of the clergy regarding their rights of jurisdiction, tithes, gifts of land, and excommunication. Each article is followed by a response asserting the rights of the king and barons: "In hoc concordati sunt rex et barones". Text Brussel, II: xxvii. Martène, "Amp. Coll." I: 1083.

and vassals even more essential in the determination of legal cases of moment. The general feudal principle of the assistance of the suzerain by his vassal, which was expressed in his promise of aid, counsel and service, required the fief-holder to further with his advice the administration of justice by his lord, when summoned by the latter for the purpose. The further principle, which antedates feudalism by far, and which feudalism adopted, that the accused should be judged by those of like rank and station, by his equals, made the presence of the vassals in the royal court a necessary element in its constitution, in a kingdom which was still so largely feudal as that of Philip Augustus. But, as we have several times had occasion to notice, the Capetian monarchy was not wholly feudal. If the king could summon his vassals as suzerain, as prince he could equally require the assistance of his subjects, including therefore, in a broad sense, all who had sworn fidelity to him.[1] Hence the appearance in the assemblies, whether judicial or deliberative, of those who held no fief from the crown, of representatives of the non-noble class who were among the counselors of the king. The growing importance of the royal advisers, the greater difficulty and numerousness of the cases consequent upon the extending jurisdiction of the court, the necessity which was increasingly felt for the advice of those more learned in the law and custom than the fighting barons could possibly be, — a necessity which reliance on oral and documentary evidence, rather than the duel, rendered yearly more evident, — made the feudal element in the curia regis of decreasing importance. These tendencies characterized the institution at Philip's accession[2] and their working continued throughout his reign; but though its royal, rather than its feudal, character increasingly asserted itself, both in the prominence of counselors in its decisions and the extent of its jurisdiction, it never ceased to be in a true sense a function of the assembly, while Philip was on the throne.

---

[1] This distinction between the right of justice of the king as prince over those who had sworn fidelity to him, and as suzerain over his vassals, has been pointed out by Flach. In practice, the two classes became confounded and all were called before the curia regis, which was, in principle, royal, rather than feudal; and was composed of all the fideles that the king chose to summon. Flach. "Les origines de l'ancienne France." I: 227—246.

[2] Compare Luchaire. "Instit. Monarchiques" I: 269—325 for the state and tendencies of the curia regis under the predecessors of Philip. Its form of procedure during the same period is treated at length in the passage cited. (314—325).

Procedure. Complaint and summons.

The methods of procedure in the royal court were substantially unaltered under Philip. Its decisions were based on pleas and inquests, more rarely on an appeal to the judgment of God. As under his predecessors, the action began with a complaint adressed personally to the king.[1] If the latter entertained it, he summoned the accused, by word of mouth or by messenger, to appear at a fixed time and place and give answer. Were the suit one which both contestants were ready to submit to the judgment of the king, the summons became, naturally, a simple notification of the trial, given to both parties. In cases of moment, the king then sent calls to be

Place and composition of the court.

present to a greater or less number of his clergy, barons, and advisers;[2] in minor affairs he apparently left the composition of the judicial assembly to selection, at the time of trial, from the attendants on the royal person, whom governmental duties or temporary circumstances were sure to bring together wherever the king

---

[1] The procedure of the royal court, under Philip, is well illustrated by the charter recording the judgment assigning the castle of Vertaizon to the bishop of Clermont, because its holders had received the enemies of the bishop. Jan., 1205. "Notum etc. Quod propter clamorem quem dilectus et fidelis noster Rothom. (Rothbertus), Claramontensis episcopus nobis facit de l'ontis de Captolio et de Jarentona uxore ejus, nos ore proprio summonuimus eos apud Silviniacum, et assignavimus diem ad quem ipse et uxor ejus coram nobis comparerent responsuri sufficienter ad clamorem ipsius episcopi. Ad quem nec venerunt nec pro se miserunt. Secundo autem, dum essemus apud Castrum-Radulfi, fecimus eos summoneri et eos diem assignavimus propter predictum clamorem, ad quam diem predictus Pontius non venit, sed uxor ejus venit, sed non venit sicut debuit. Tercio vero eandem uxorem viva voce summonuimus et Pontium maritum ejus fecimus summoneri per certum nuncium, et certum diem dedimus ad quem ipsi venirent responsuri coram Hugone de Capella, ballivo nostro. Ad quem ipsi nec venerunt nec miserunt, sed nobis per litteras mandaverunt quod coram rege Arragonum responderent super clamore isto. Episcopus autem ad singulos ante nominatos comparuit in propria persona, paratus probare quod ipsi scilicet P[ontius] homo ligius episcopi et Ja[rantona] uxor in castro Vetaisonis quod ab eo tenebant et eo juraverunt in proditione et dolo capitales inimcos episcopi nocte receperunt ad capiendum ipsum et suos perdendos. Unde propter hoc, communicato cum baronibus nostris consilio, ipsum castrum et pertinencia adjudicavimus episcopo et ecclesie Claromontensibus, ut a nobis et heredibus nostris ea perpetuo jure teneant, sicut alia regalia nostra, dominium sicut dominium, feodum sicut feodum. Tam de castro quam de pertinenciis ipsum episcopum publice saisivimus de dominio sicut de dominio, de feodo sicut de feodo. Actum Parisius, anno Domini M°CC° quarto (old style), mense januario." Boutaric, "Actes du Parlement de Paris" I: ccxcix. Martène, "Amp. Coll." I: 1044.

[2] Regalia of Châlons, 1202. Delisle Cat. p. 503: "diem eidem assignavimus Parisius, super audiendo judicis ... et ad diem illum convocavimus sapientes homines nostros ... convocavimus etiam barones etc."

might be. The court had no fixed seat, though the preference of the king for Paris as a place of residence made that city the more usual scene of its sessions, as of the meeting of the assemblies to discuss political problems. The presence of the king, or of his representive, was still the factor determinative of its place; and its constitution at any particular session depended on the royal summons, — a summons directed, however, with some degree of reference to the rank of the persons to be brought before its bar. On the day appointed the plaintiff presented himself. If the defendant did not appear, the king renewed the summons and designated the time and place of trial afresh. This process was repeated, if necessary, two or three times. Should the accused then fail to make answer, in person or by representative, judgment was given against him in default.[1] In the ordinary course of events, however, both parties presented themselves before the court.

The trial opened with the statement of the complaint by the plaintiff and its answer by the defendant, each giving his arguments and adducing such testimony and documentary evidence as he was able.[2] These proofs were thereupon considered by the judges in the light of customary usage, or the principles of the Roman law, then beginning to assert its sway in the western world.[3] The deliberation

Trial and decision.

---

[1] "Radulfus de Roia, mi'es, homo ligius regis, occidit quendam militem in castillania Roie; frater militis interfecti conquestus est domino regi quod ipse Radulfus occiderat maliciose fratrem suum; rex assignavit diem Radulfo, et ipse deficit de die; et propter hoc, pro defectu, rex fecit dirui domos suas de Garmeni et cepit catella ejus". Inquest concerning the right of justice at Roie. Beugnot, "Les Olim" I: 963. The condemnation of John in 1202 is the most conspicuous case.

[2] An illustration may be found in the arguments presented at the trial regarding the succession to Beaumont in 1223. Text, Boutaric, "Actes du Parlement de Paris." I: ccci. Martène, "Amp. Coll." I: 1163.

[3] "Qui (sapientes homines, viri litterati et barones) facta diligenti inquisitione, librato diu consilio, judicaverunt vicedominum Cathalaunensem nichil habere juris in regalibus nostris, hiis quatuor rationibus que secuntur; Quia jus commune (custom law), quod in aliis regalibus per alias regni nostri ecclesias habemus, quibus nullus aliquid juris habet nisi nos, manifeste contra ipsum faciebat. Privilegium patris nostri bone memorie regis quondam Ludovici, quod super regalibus illis factum fuerat, similiter contra ipsum manifeste faciebat. Jus etiam scriptum (the Roman law), in quo dicitur quod fiscalia non prescributur tempore, similiter contra ipsum faciebat. Tandem testimonia illorum quos pro se induxerat nichil pro eo probabant. Alia multa testimonia manifeste pro nobis et contra ipsum manifeste faciebant." Trial regarding the regalia of Châlons, about 1202. Delisle, Cat. appendix pp. 503, 504.

took place in the presence, and often with the participation, of the king, who approved the finding and pronounced judgment.¹ This decision was speedily thereafter embodied in a charter, stating the time and place of the court, the allegations of the parties in contest, and the ground and nature of the sentence.² The names of at least a portion of the judges were also given, in cases of importance, and so dependent was the monarchy still on the good-will of its great vassals that, in weighty trials, charters similar to that of the king were issued by the more prominent members of the judicial assembly.³ In ordinary controversies the certification of the king was sufficient to attest the judgment.

If the trial was a civil contest, a compromise was, if possible, effected before the parties left the court, or the consent of the defeated suitor to the decision was sought.⁴ In the event of a criminal condemnation it had been a maxim of legal procedure, previous to Philip's reign, that no arrest should take place in the court itself, but that the convicted person should have freedom to retire.⁵ The principle finds expression in one of Philip's earlier charters;⁶ but by the time

---

¹ "Judicatus est ibidem a paribus regni nostri etc. . . . nobis audientibus et judicium approbantibus, quod etc." Succession to Champagne trial. 1216. Chantereau-Lefebvre, "Traité des Fiefs," proofs 68, 69. Brussel, "Usage" I : 651, 653.

Judicatumque fuit in curia domini regis apud Vernonem ab ipso domino rege et ab archiepiscopo Turonense, episcopo Andegavensi . . . . . et pluribus aliis. Judicatumque fuit concorditer ab hiis omnibus, quod etc." Beaumont trial, 1223.

² Compare the three charters just quoted, etc.

³ The controversy respecting the succession to Champagne resulted in at least two such instances. Philip ordered those acting as judges in the trial at Melun to prepare letters-patent recording the judgment and conformed to his own: "Dilecte mandamus et requirimus vos, quatenus juxta tenorem litterarum nostrarum patentes litteras vestras faciatis, de judicio et orramentis habetis et apud Meledunum recitatis." Chantereau-Lefebvre, "Traité des Fiefs," proofs 69. The same collection contains letters from sixteen of the judges, prepared in conformity with this order. Another instance is to be found in D'Arbois de Jubainville, "Histoire des ducs et des comtes de Champagne." V. p. 111.

⁴ Compare Delisle, Cat. 1337. "Hoc autem judicium praedictum concesserunt praedicti Erardus et Philip[pa] et ea die qua istud judicium factum fuit, nichil amplius quaesierunt a praedicta comitissa Campaniae et ejus filio." Succession controversy, trial of 1216.

⁵ Luchaire. "Instit. Monarchiques" I : 322.

⁶ Charter for Orleans, about 1187: "Quisquis autem burgensis per submonitionem nostram ad curiam nostram venerit, sive pro forifacto, sive pro quacunque causa cum submonuerimus, si placitum nostrum noluerit vel non po-

of the controversy with John the strength of the monarchy had become sufficient to enable the king to enforce his judgments without delay, if he so chose. According to the account of Matthew Paris, the only hope of avoiding personal seizure, in the absence of a royal safe-conduct, lay in refusal to obey the summons;[1] an act which involved condemnation in default. A decision of the question in dispute by recourse to the duel was infrequent in the proceedings of the curia regis, though still common in the local courts of the royal agents.[2]

Increasing authority of the Curia regis under Philip

But if the judicial administration of the royal court shows little change in the form of procedure during Philip's reign, the competence of the tribunal was enlarged and its authority over the king's subjects enforced as never before; — in such manner as to make it a mighty agency in increasing the political power of the monarchy. It is this enlarged practical authority, rather than any radical change in the methods of adjudicature, which marks the progress of the curia regis under Philip. The local courts, rather than the central tribunal, are the scenes of his chief administrative reforms. But it was, nevertheless, the development of three factors, in addition to the energetic will and the political sagacity of the sovereign, which made this growth in the actual power of the curia possible. Two of these factors were due to causes already operative in the composition of the royal court; namely the formation of the lawyer class, and the development of a distinction in the membership of the court itself, the peers. The one is the natural consequence of the right of the king to summon to the legal assembly such of his subjects as he chose, the other a corollary from the principle of trial by equals. The third factor was the system of inquests into the civil rights of the king

---

tuerit, nos eum non retinebimus, nisi in presenti forifacto fuerit interceptus; sed habeat licentiam redeundi et per diem suum in domo sua morandi. Deinceps autem tam ipse quam omnes ejus res in nostra voluntate erunt." Delisle, Cat. appendix. pp. 496, 499.

[1] Matthew Paris II: 658. "Et Episcopus: Domine, et redeat?" Et rex: "Ita sit, si parium suorum judicium hoc permittat."

[2] Philip discouraged the use of the duel. In 1200 he provided that any person maltreating the students of Paris should be brought before the king's court and could not free themselves by the duel or ordeal. Ordon. I: 23. In 1204 he declared than any questions arising as to the condition of serfs freed by the chapter of Orleans should be decided by testimony and not by the duel. Delisle Cat. 861. For the employment of the duel and ordeal see Delisle Cat. appendix 522. Beugnot "Les Olim" I: 963, 969.

and his subjects, and into grave criminal offenses, conducted by commissioners appointed by the monarch.

Growth of a corps of judges. The growth of a corps of judges in the curia regis is contemporary with the prominence of the simple counselors in the business of the palace. As has already been seen in considering the royal advisers, influence in the deliberations of the king was wielded by many of high rank, — the preeminence of the cardinal archbishop of Reims among the royal servants is a conspicuous example. So was it also with the legal advisers. They were by no means exclusively from the ranks of the lower nobility or the burgher class. But the important fact to notice is that, whether noble or non-noble, they were summoned for their legal knowledge. In their selection the royal right to command the services of the subject, rather than the claim of the suzerain to the advice of his vassals, is manifested. To the trial of the pretention of the vicedominus of Châlons to a share in the regalia of that bishopric, Philip summoned three bishops, the fame of one, at least, of whom, as a lawyer, was sung by a contemporary poet;[1] he convoked also four men of much inferior station, one of whom was apparently of foreign origin,[2] and whose sole influence in the counsels of the king must have been due to their familiarity with the written law, the study of which was beginning to be pursued with zeal at Paris.[3] The tendency here shown is one which shifted the decisive weight in the legal assembly from the baronage to the immediate servants and dependents of the king. This prominence of the royal advisers in judicial questions had begun to be marked in the later years of Louis VII.[4] Under Philip Augustus not only the regular counselors take part in a majority of the trials, but many members of the lower orders of the clergy,

---

[1] The bishops were those of Beauvais, Paris, and Meaux. Giles of Paris, in his Carolinus thus sings of the latter:
"Cum superexcellens legum jurisque peritus,
Ille inter patres, intraque palatia, magni
Nominis Ansellus, quem cum majoribus orbis
Meldis episcopio promovit gratia sensus,
Hic tulerit curas."
Aegidii Parisiensis Carolinus. Sep. XVII: 298.

[2] Lothaire of Cremona; Ranulf, archdeacon of Bourges; Geoffrey of Poissi, and Nicholas of Chartres. The two latter are distinguished by the title of Magister.

[3] "Cum itaque in eadem nobilissima civitate (Paris) non modo de trivio et quadrivio, verum et de quaestionibus juris canonici et civilis . . . . plena et perfecta inveniretur doctrina." Guil. Amor. Delaborde I: 230.

[4] Luchaire, "Instit. Monarchiques," 1: 312.

clerci, and other non-nobles, who appear to have been employed in the royal service in no other than a judicial capacity, are reckoned among the judges in cases of moment.[1] The skill of these servants of the crown in legal studies is attested by pope Innocent III.[2] There is no reason to suppose that their participation in the court was simply as advisers,[3] or that they were not true judges. On the contrary, as those acquainted with law and custom, as able to read and to weigh the value of documentary evidence, their voice must have had great weight in any decision in which they took part; and the share of the barons in the judicial assembly must have been more and more a mere acceptance or rejection of the conclusions reached by their more learned associates. And in so far as this result was accomplished, the judicial assembly became a royal tribunal rather than a feudal court.

The second factor in the development of the power of the curia regis, is the complement of the tendency already noticed. Few problems have been more contested than that of the origin of the peers. No solution as yet proposed is wholly satisfactory. But, fortunately for our present purpose, the question of their origin is less important than the fact of the recognition of such a distinction in the membership of the royal court during the reign of Philip Augustus. The falsity of the document purporting to describe the duties of the peers at Philip's coronation has frequently been pointed out.[4] Our first distinct notice of their action is in connection with the trial of John; though a single instance of the use of the title is to be met with earlier.[5]

The Peers. Obscurity of their origin.

---

[1] Beside those already noticed as present at the trial regarding the regalia of Châlons, the adjudication of the succession to Beaumont, 1223, may be cited: "judicatumque fuit in curia domini regis apud Vernonem ab ipso domino rege et . . . . . . Henrico thesaurario Bellovacensi, Roberto Balbo, Jacobo de Dinant, Milone de Crociaco, clericis, etc." Boutaric, "Actes du Parlement de Paris" I: ccci. Martène, "Amp. Coll." I; 1163.

[2] Letter of Innocent III., July, 1202: "Qui consiliarii ejus (Philippi) et familiares existunt, et in utroque sunt jure periti." Scp. XIX: 414.

[3] This is the opinion of Beugnot, "Les Olim" I: lxix, lxv. The charters already cited show them in no different light, as regards full judicial competency, than the members of the same assemblies who were drawn from the baronage.

[4] Brial, "Histoire littéraire de la France" XIV: 22; Bernardi: "Memoires de l'Académie des Inscriptions." X: 612—617; Luchaire "Instit. Monarchiques" II: 294, 295.

[5] The earliest employment of the designation peer, as a title, is to be found in a letter of Bernard, prior of Grammont to Henry II. of England, in

<small>Was John twice condemned?</small>

The majority of writers have accepted two trials for John, both resulting in condemnation in default, one in 1202, on the complaint of the barons of Poitou, and the other in 1203, for the murder of Arthur of Brittany. Our information as to his alleged condemnation for the latter crime is by no means satisfactory, however. The story rests on Wendover's account of the interview of the ambassadors of prince Louis with the pope in 1216;[1] and on a letter of the same prince to the monks of St. Augustine at Canterbury, written, apparently, just after his landing in England, in May of the same year. The latter is explicit in its statement of the ground and nature of the condemnation.[2] But, as a recent writer has pointed out, there is grave reason to doubt the fact of the trial of John for the murder of Arthur at all.[3] None of the contemporary historians of France record it, though abundant in their denunciations of Johns misdeeds. On the other hand there is considerable evidence of his condemnation, in default, on the complaint of his Pontivine vassals in 1202,[4] a con-

---

1171, in which he speaks of the archbishop of Reims (Henry, brother of Louis VII.) as: "dominus princeps Henricus de Francia, par Franciae, dux et archipraesul Remensis." Sep. XVI : 473. The instance is, however, wholly isolated and exceptional, being the only reference to the peerage before the reign of Philip.

[1] Matthew Paris. Chron. Major. II : 657. In the account of the discussions with the papal legate at Melun in 1216, regarding Louis' expedition to England, Wendover makes Philip say: "Item si aliquando verus rex (John) postea regnum forisfecit per mortem Arthuri, de quo facto damnatus fuit in curia nostra." Id. 651.

[2] "Praeterea satis notum est, quomodo de murdro Arturi nepotis sui in curia karissimi domini regis Franciae, cujus ambo erant homines ligii, per pares suos citatus et per eosdem pares tandem fuit legitime condempnatus; quod quidem murdrum ejusdem temporis pluribus in Anglia et pluries praedictus Johannes est confessus, per quem condempnationem bona sua ubicumque essent aut undecumque ea haberet, per usitatas consuetudines forisfecit, et tunc iterato nobis tanquam vero haeredi cessit jus regni Angliae, maxime cum adhuc de carne sua haeredem non haberet." Rymer, Foedera I : 1 : 140.

[3] Bémont, "La condemnation de Jean Sans-terre", "Revue Historique" vol. XXXII (Sept. Nov., 1886), two articles.

[4] Probably on April 28 of that year. Bémont, Id. p. 307, 308. Both Rigord and William the Breton record the summons addressed to John to appear before the king and his court and make answer to the charges laid against him. William the Breton further narrates that, after much negociation, John pledged two castles, Botavant and Tillières, as guarantee of his appearance before the court. Both writers agree that he failed to appear in person or by representative. While neither expressly declares that sentence in default was passed on John, both accounts seem to imply it. Rigord says: "Sed quoniam rex Angliae ad diem prefixum nec in propria persona venit nec responsalem suffi-

demnation which immediately preceeded the invasion of John's territories by Philip, and was its legal justification. The text of the decision rendered at this trial has not come down to us, if it was ever put in writing; but the English writer, Ralph Coggishall, records that John was summoned thither to respond to his peers.[1] This declaration is supported by a statement of Hoveden, regarding the answer given by the barons of Poitou to John's demand that they should appear for trial before him.[2] This concurrent testimony makes it extremely probable that the judgment of the English monarch by his peers, cited by Louis in his proclamation addressed to the people of England through the monks of Canterbury, and urged upon the pope thirteen years after the alleged event, was really that pronounced in 1202, on complaint of the vassals of Poitou. The lapse of a few years would leave the generally accredited murder of Arthur and the forfeiture of John's lands (a forfeiture which would naturally

cientem mittere voluit, habito rex Francorum cum principibus et baronibus suis consilio, collecto exercitu Normanniam ingressus, munitunculam quamdam quam Botavant vocabant, funditus evertit etc." Delaborde I: 151, 152. This was the first move in the war which cost John his territories.

A contemporary English writer is much more explicit, while his statements, as for as comparison is possible, are in substantial agreement with those of the French historians. Ralph Coggeshall relates: "Rex Johannes coepit acriter expugnare comitem de Marchis, scilicet Hugonem cognomento Brun, et fratrem ejus comitem de Eu, quia rebellaverant contra eum pro filia comitis Engolismensis, quam Hugo praedictus prius affidaverat. Sed cum regis infestationem comites illi ferre diutius non possent, conquesti sunt regi Philippo, quasi capitali domino, de nimia infestatione regis Angliae domini sui. At rex Philippus multoties mandavit regi Angliae quatinus ab eorum expugnatione quiesceret, et cum hominibus suis aliquam pacis concordiam componeret. Sed cum rex Angliae nullatenus mandatis aut precibus regis Franciae adquiescere voluisset, summonitus est per proceres regni Francorum, quasi comes Aquitaniae et Andegaviae, quatinus ad curiam domini sui regis Franciae Parisius veniret, et judicium curiae suae subiret, domino suo de illatis injuriis responsurus, et juri quod pares sui decernebant pariturus.... Tandem vero curia regis Franciae adunata adjudicavit regem Angliae tota terra privandum, quam hactenus de regibus Franciae ipse et progenitores sui tenuerant, eo quod fere omnia servitia eisdem terris debita per longum jam tempus facere contempserant, nec domino suo fere in aliquibus obtemporare volebant. Hoc igitur curiae suae judicium rex Philippus gratanter acceptans et approbans, coadunato exercitu, confestim invasit castellum Butavant etc.". Chron. Anglicanum, ed. Stevenson, 135, 136.

[1] See previous note.

[2] "Eodem anno (1201) Johannes rex Angliae, volens appellare barones Pictaviae, de sua et fratris sui proditione, multos conduxit et secum duxit viros, arte bellandi in duello doctos, et de terris suis cismarinis et transmarinis electos. Sed barones Pictaviae inde praemuniti ad curiam illius venire noluerunt, dicentes quod nemini responderent nisi pari suo." Hoveden IV: 176.

appear coextensive with Philip's conquests) the two most striking memories of the contest; and a connection between the events in men's minds would be the easier because Philip had entered into possession of most of the territories claimed by the murdered Arthur. It is not likely that Louis would have scrupled, in his proclamation claiming the English throne, or in his representations to the pope, to attribute the sentence of forfeiture, which really was passed in 1202, to the generally accepted murder of Arthur in 1203, — a prince wh was looked upon by many in England as the rightful heir to the Plantagenet throne. Such a condemnation would have justified itself to the sympathies of the English baronage much more than a sentence based on the grievances of a few of John's vassals in Poitou. Belief in the unscrupulousness of Louis, statement is confirmed by the affirmation, which he couples with the declaration of the condemnation passed on John, that the sentence involved the forfeiture of the criminal's goods, wherever situated, and the loss of the English throne;[1] though he was doubtless well aware that a condemnation in the court of the French monarch could deprive John only of the fiefs held from the French crown, of which the realm of England was not a part.

Some condemnation by John's "peers".

But, though we may question the accuracy of the representations of prince Louis as to the ground of John's sentence, his statements and the record of the historians leave us no room to doubt that there was some action, in the curia regis, condemnatory of John, by a rank of vassals denoted as the peers, pares, of the English sovereign in his dependence on the French crown as duke of Aquitaine or of Normandy. That action has been shown to have taken place, almost unquestionably, in 1202. We must therefore conclude that the designation "peer" was in recognized use at that time. No document, however, gives any certain information as to the identity of those thus distinguished at this trial.

Who were peers? Contested succession to Champagne.

The first definite statement as to the persons constituting the rank of peers is given in the letters-patent recording the judgment rendered by the judicial assembly at Melun, in July, 1216, refusing the demand of Érard de Brienne, that the king should receive his homage for the county of Champagne, which he claimed as the right of his wife Philippa, the alleged heiress of the late count Henry, to the exclusion of Theobald IV. and the latter's mother, Blanche, then in actual possession of the fief. In this charter we are told

---

[2] See this essay p. 78, note 2.

that the decision was by the peers of the realm, namely, the archbishop of Reims, the bishops of Langres, Châlons, Beauvais, and Noyon, and the duke of Burgundy, and also by many other bishops and barons, whose names are likewise given.¹ But, as Bernardi has long since pointed out,² the sole distinction accorded to the peers is that of enumeration at the head of the list of adjudicators. As judges their rights at the trial were no other than those of the ecclesiastics and nobles whose names follow in the record. Philip Augustus himself, in a letter to pope Honorius, speaks of it simply as a judgment of the barons of France.³ But in enumerating the judges he mentions by name only the peers; and he expressly declares that the amend made by the bishop of Orléans for having spoken against this decision was made to, and in the presence of, the king and the peers, whose names he has just reported to the pope.⁴ The letters-patent of the judges at the trial at Melun all attest the distinction in title attaching to the peers.⁵ A similar instance occurs in regard to a trial, in March of the next year, 1217, involving the same parties. Here, as before, the decision is recorded as given by the barons, i. e. by the entire assembly. But the letters patent which attest it are those of the six peers who are prominent in 1216.⁶

Superiority in titular rank could not long be openly acknowl-

¹ "Judicatum est ibidem a paribus regni nostri, videlicet A[nselmo], Remensi archiepiscopo; Willelmo, Lingonensi; Willel[mo], Cathalaunensi; Ph[ilippo], Belvacensi,; Stephano, Noviomensi, episcopis; et O[done], duce Burgundiae; et a multis aliis episcopis et baronibus nostris, videlicet Altissiodorensi; R[eginaldo], Carnotensi; et Silvanensi; et J[ordano], Lexoviensi, episcopis; et Guillelmo, comite Pontini; R[oberto], comite Drocarum; B. [Petro], comite Britanniae; G[alchero], comite sancti Pauli; Willelm[o], de Rupibus, senescallo Andegavensi; Willem[o], comite Juvigniaci; J[ohanne], comite Belli-Montis; et R[oberto], comite de Alençon, nobis audientibus et judicium approbantibus, quod etc." Chantereau-Lefebvre, "Traité des Fiefs" 68, 69. Brussel, "Usage", I: 651, 652, Teulet, Layettes. I: 431, 432 etc.

² "Mémoires de l'Académie des Inscriptions", X: 644. (1833).

³ "Judicium baronum Franciae", Chantereau-Lefebvre, "Traité des Fiefs" proofs, 62. The letter was written in April, 1217, (new style) to inform the pope that the bishop of Orléans had made amends for his misconduct.

⁴ Id. "Super qua temeritate in praesentia nostra et parium praedictorum, per recordationem eorundem publice comitis idipsum, nobis et paribus emendavit."

⁵ They were all formed on the model of that of the king. Sixteen may be found in Chantereau-Lefebvre, 70—86.

⁶ D'Arbois de Jubainville, "Histoire des ducs et des comtes de Champagne", IV: I: 139, V: 111, 112.

edged without some effort on the part of its possessors to make their position a distinction of practical importance. Such an attempt occurred speedily after the death of Philip, and is of interest for the light it reflects on the composition of the curia regis, and on the non-independent position of the peers during the reign of the monarch that had just closed. In 1224 John de Nesle entered complaint against Johanna, countess of Flanders, one of the peers of France, on account of her refusal to do him justice.[1] Louis VIII., then king, summoned her to appear and make answer before the royal court, sending two knights as messengers. The countess claimed that she could be cited only by a peer. The question, being submitted to the judgment of the court, was decided against her, and the competence of the summons sustained. The countess then affirmed her readiness to do justice to her vassal. The court decided that the case, having been brought to its cognizance, could not be dismissed. The peers present in the judicial assembly thereupon urged that the ministers of the royal household, the chancellor, butler, chamberlain, and constable, should not sit with them in judgment on a peer. The servants of the crown, whose rights were thus called in question, answered, however, that they were entitled to their place by the established usage of the curia regis in cases involving members of the peerage; and the court sustained them in this claim.[2] The point is of interest, for none of these officers took part in their ministerial capacity in the trial involving the succession to Champagne, in 1216.[3] Possibly we have here a hint as to the composition of the royal court at the condemnation of John, in 1202. It is evident that, whatever dignity attached to the peers under

Side-note: No exclusive jurisdiction over their own order.

---

[1] Text, Boutaric, "Actes du Parlament de Paris," I: cccii. Martène, "Amp. Coll." I: 1193. The process has been criticised by Pardessus, "Bibliothèque de l'École des Chartes," IV: 296, 297, (1847—48).

[2] "Preterea cum parcs Francie dicerent quod cancellarius, buticularius, camerarius, constabularius Francie, ministeriales hospitii domini regis, non debebant cum eis interesse ad faciendum judicia super pares Francie; et dicti ministeriales hospitii domini regis e contrario dicerent se debere ad usus et consuetudines Francie observatas interesse cum paribus Francie ad judicandum pares. Judicatum fuit in curia domini regis, quod ministeriales predicti de hospitio domini regis debent interesse cum paribus Francie ad judicandum pares, et tunc judicaverunt comitissam Flandrie ministeriales predicti cum paribus Francie, apud Parisius anno Domini M. CC. XXIV." Id.

[3] The office of chancellor was held, in 1224, by Warren, bishop of Senlis, who was one of the judges in 1216 in his capacity as bishop. He did not receive the chancellor's title till accession of Louis VIII.

Philip, they had no exclusive jurisdiction over the membership of their own order.

The traditional number of the peers is twelve; and of those assigned by Matthew Paris to this rank,[1] we find ten actually indicated, between 1202 and 1224, as members of the curia regis or as summoned before its bar. The decision of 1216 was rendered by five of the ecclesiastical peers, the archbishop of Reims, the bishops of Langres, Châlons, Beauvais, and Noyon. The same letters-patent show the duke of Burgundy to be one of the lay peers; and the proceedings on that occasion, at the trial of John in 1202, and of Johanna of Flanders in 1224, make evident the peerage of the possessors of the counties of Champagne and Flanders, and of the duchies of Aquitaine and Normandy. Only two of the twelve are thus unevidenced, the bishop of Laon and the count of Toulouse. The absence of the latter from the record is easily explicable, as the count of Toulouse was a declared heretic, for whose forfeited lands Simon de Montfort had just done homage to Philip.[2] The new possessor had returned to Languedoc just after this act of fealty to his sovereign.[3] The recently elected bishop of Laon had, probably, not yet been consecrated.[4] There being thus evidence of the recognition, under Philip, of ten of the twelve peerages of later fame, and no mention of any outside that circle as holding the title under his reign, the probabilities become overwhelming that the peerage was already in the early years of the thirteenth century considered an attribute of the twelve great posts, six ecclesiastical and six lay, to which tradition attaches the title.

Number of peers.

The question of the origin of this peerage is involved in much difficulty. While the lay peers are obviously the heads of the great semi-independent fiefs of France, the ground of the distinction in the case of their six spiritual companions is much less evident. There is no reason to suppose that the peerage of the clergy was of later recognition than that of the lay nobles.[5] As a matter of fact, it is to an ecclesiastic, the archbishop of Reims, that the title of peer is

Origin of the peerage.

---

[1] Matthew Paris, "Chronica Majora", Luard, V: 606, 607. The list is inserted in an account of the events of 1257.

[2] Charter of homage, Sep. XIX: 646. April, 1216.

[3] Sep. XVIII: 284.

[4] Robert, brother of the count of St. Paul, was elected bishop of Laon in 1209, and died in 1215. He was succeeded by Anselm de Mauny. Compare Delisle, Cat. 1630.

[5] Compare Bernardi, "Mémoires de l'Académie des Inscriptions". X: 629.

first ascribed.[1] The spiritual peers are the chief representatives of the dignity in every trial under Philip Augustus. But why the peerage should belong to such prelates as the bishops of Langres and Noyon, and not to ecclesiastics like the archbishops of Sens, Bourges, or Tours, or the bishops of Paris and Orléans, is not easy to explain. The theory of Bernardi, though imperfect, is probably the best as yet propounded, — that these prelates possessed the dignity because, in addition to their ecclesiastical station, they held fiefs as dukes or counts, an authority in secular matters not appertaining to the other archbishops and bishops, who have been cited.[2] But this explanation must be taken with much allowance. It is no more true to affirm, with Bernardi, that the ecclesiastical peers were the only prelates who held suzerainties directly from the crown, than to declare that their lay associates were the sole barons exercising complete local sovereignty and owning immediate allegiance to the king, as monarch, rather than as duke or count. The bishop of Auxerre, for example, was a territorial suzerain important enough to number the counts of Champagne[3] and of Nevers[4] among his vassals, and Philip himself was glad to purchase from him the homage of a fief.[5] Even the archbishop of Sens, though a much less extensive territorial lord than his suffragan of Auxerre, was the feudal suzerain of the count of Champagne, for a few fiefs.[6] But, in principle, the theory we have just noticed is correct. It was as territorial rulers, not as ecclesiastical dignitaries, that the clerical peers had their importance; and, as secular suzerains, the prelates designated as peers were more prominent than any other of the bishops of France. It was the extent of his possessions, rather than any difference in his relations to the crown, which made the duke of Burgundy, for example, a greater personage among the royal vassals than the seignior of Bourbon.[7] And so was it with the ecclesiastical peers. Their superior dignity was

---

[1] See this essay, p. 77, note 5.

[2] Bernardi, Id. 627, The archbishop of Reims, the bishops of Laon and Langres ranked as dukes; the bishops of Beauvais, Châlons and Noyon as counts. Beugnot, "Les Olim" I: 1.

[3] D'Arbois de Jubainville, "Histoire des ducs et des comtes de Champagne", IV: 888, VII: 61.

[4] Delisle, Cat. 1586.

[5] Gien, 1204, Sep. XVIII: 726.

[6] D'Arbois de Jubainville, Id. IV: 887, VII: 60.

[7] Compare on the direct relations between the crown and the counts or seigniors of Auxerre, Bourbon, Couci, Foraz, Nevers etc., Luchaire, "Inst. Monarchiques" II: 31.

based on superior power and independence as territorial suzerains; but this superiority to their fellow bishops was originally one of degree rather than kind.

Many writers have held that the peers were instituted by the monarchy,[1] but no satisfactory evidence of such designation or appointment has ever been advanced. These dignitaries, both lay and ecclesiastical, were rather those whose importance as feudal proprietors was such as to secure the recognition of a certain degree of superiority to their fellow-vassals, independent of any royal designation. The representatives of most of these peerages were frequent in their attendance on the royal person, and participant in the administration of justice and in the political assemblies. Most of them were thus often brought into comparison with the other vassals of the crown. And whatever dignity attached to these could hardly be denied to those of the twelve who were seldom, or never, at the royal court, — the duke of Normandy and Aquitaine, by far the mightiest vassal of the crown, and the count of Toulouse, whose fief Philip himself pronounced one of the chief tenures of the kingdom[2]. This view of the peerage, as originating simply in prominence among the vassals, is confirmed by a declaration of Philip regarding certain of the nobles of Vermandois. In the charter confirming the commune of St. Quentin, 1195, the king says: "When first the commune was obtained, all the peers of Vermandois, who at that time were considered the greatest [of the nobles] .... swore to maintain etc."[3]

Not of royal appointment.

A considerable number of the prelates and barons, probably twelve, being thus regarded as, in some sense, more important than their fellows, it was entirely consonant with the principle of trial by equals, which underlies all the jurisprudence of the feudal period, that those thus held in honor should deem any judicial assembly met to judge one of their number incomplete, which did not contain some representative of their rank. As the curia regis came more and more under the control of the royal counselors, men taken, for the most part, from the lower nobility and the non-noble class, the

Distinction between the peers and other members of the judicial assemblies.

---

[1] This is the view of Bernardi, of Beugnot ("Les Olim" I: preface), of Brial, (Sep. XVII: preface), etc.

[2] Delisle, Cat. Appendix p. 513.

[3] "Cum primum communia acquisita fuit, omnes Viromandiae pares, qui tunc temporis majores habebantur, et omnes clerici, salvo ordine suo, omnesque milites, salva fidelitatis comitis, firmiter tenerandam juraverunt." Ordon. XI: 270.

distinction in rank between the more influential portion of the court and the high vassal before it would necessarily become more sharply defined, and the desire for trial before those of like station would be emphasized. Such, in reality, was the course of events. The period of the recognition of the distinction in dignity between the peers and the other members of the judicial assemblies is that of the marked increase of the influence of the royal counselors in the general administration of justice. Thus, in the record of the trial of the duke of Burgundy, on complaints made by the bishop of Langres, in 1153,[1] no mention appears of any inequality in judicial rank between the contesting parties and the members of the court, though the latter included at least one non-noble counselor of the king.[2] The judicial assembly was composed as usual, and no doubts as to its competency were raised by the duke of Burgundy. Our information as to the constituency of the tribunal, which passed sentence on John in 1202, is meager; but the emphasis laid on the presence of his peers shows that all members of the assembly were no longer looked upon as the full judicial equals of the high vassals of the crown. By 1216 the distinction attaching to the high vassals was so marked that the court, before which the claims of Erard de Brienne and Philippa to Champagne were discussed, contained none who were not of noble rank, and the peers are clearly distinguished. In 1224 the claims of the peerage had risen to the point of an attempt to deny to the great officers of the palace their established right to sit in judgment in cases involving a peer. The movement was the natural assertion by the great nobles of their right to be judged by their equals.[3]

Attitude of the monarchy toward the peerage. The attitude of the monarchy toward the development of the institution is not easy to ascertain. But it would not appear to have been one of special favor. Far from establishing a court of peers for the trial of John, as has been claimed, the sovereign, at most,

---

[1] Text Brussel, "Usage", 1: 272. This trial has been criticised by Pardessus ("Bibliotheque de l'École des Chartes" IV: 285) and Luchaire, "Instit. Monarchiques" 1: 304.

[2] Tierri Galeran. Biographical notes, Luchaire Id. II: 305—7.

[3] This feeling finds expression in the promise of fidelity given by Theobald of Champagne to Philip in 1222, and its guarantee by some of his sub-vassals. They promise faithful service to the French monarch so long as the latter will do justice to the count of Champagne by those who can and ought to judge him: "quamdiu ipse mihi faciet rectum curiae suae per judicium eorum qui me possunt et debent judicare." Chantereau-Lefebvre, "Traité des Fiefs" proofs 115. Compare Id. 128, 132, 139.

summoned to the regularly constituted judicial assembly a number of those whom the duke of Normandy and of Aquitaine already recognized as his equals.[1] There is no intimation by the contemporary writers or in the declarations of Louis, thirteen years after, that this curia was any novel body; nor did John raise any question at the time of the summons regarding its competence,[2] as he would surely have done, had a tribunal been organized specially for him. In summoning these dignitaries the monarch created no special court. He simply guarded against possible denial of the competence of the curia regis by insuring the presence of some whose rank John could not despise. The parity of these persons, only one of whom could, in this instance, have been a layman,[3] was not a quality conferred by the king for a special occasion. It must have been a dignity accredited to them by general recognition. The peers, there is every reason to believe, were only a part, and probably a small part, of this judicial assembly, as was certainly the case in 1216 and 1224. In the latter instance, the decisive majority was in the hands of the lesser nobles and clergy, who were, for the most part, attached to the king and sensitive to his wishes. The vindication of the rights of the officers of the palace to sit in judgment on the peers must certainly be looked upon as favorable to the kingly authority. It is, like the declaration of the royal right to summon a peer without the intervention of a member of his order, a distinct denial of the pretentions of the great vassals, in the interest of the crown. The king desired the presence of the peers in the curia, if their presence would put the competence of that judicial body beyond question; but it is clear that, under Philip and his son, the monarchy was opposed to any exercise of separate judicial authority by the peers. It simply took advantage of a recognized distinction in honor among the subjects of the crown to strengthen the authority of the

[1] Pardessus, ("Bibliotheque" IV: 298—302), shows that but one lay peer the duke of Burgundy, could have been present at the trial of John and that the assertion of Beugnot ("Les Olim", I: xlvii) of a trial by a court exclusively composed of peers is without probability.

[2] John sought the judgment of the royal court, in 1201, in his controversy with Arthur over Anjou. (Scp. XVIII: 295). His objection in 1202 was not to the competence of the court, but to its right to compel him to go to Paris, alleging the recognized right of the duke of Normandy to refuse to go on the royal summons farther than the boundary between the duchy and the kingdom. Philip replied that he was summoned as duke of Aquitaine. Ralph Coggeshall, Stephenson, 136.

[3] See note above.

royal court over the high nobles; but this distinction was not created by the monarchy, and Philip and his son certainly were careful that the real control of the judicial assemblies should be in humbler and more docile hands than those of the peers.

The peerage advantageous for the monarchy

Thus limited, the peerage was an advantage to the crown. The condemnation of John to forfeiture by a court dignified by the presence of representatives of the high vassals, and the practical settlement of the succession to the most important fief remaining after John's possessions had been added, in large part, to the royal domain, put the competence of the curia regis beyond question in matters affecting the relations of the lay fiefs to the crown. The downfall of the count of Toulouse, and the absorption of John's territories, reduced the lay peerages to three, those of Flanders, Champagne and Burgundy; while the spiritual dignitaries all remained. But this change was not needed to render the control of the monarchy over the peerage much more effective than would have been the case, had the peers been exclusively lay nobles. The greater nearness of the ecclesiastical sees to the capital tended to make the attendance of these bishops on the councils of the king more constant than that of several of the lay peers could possibly have been, had they not purposely absented themselves from the court of France.[1] Their office was not subject to long minorities. It was therefore certain, in almost any contingency, that the majority of the peers present at a trial would be ecclesiastics, a class whose interests made them, as a rule, more devoted servants of the crown than the lay nobles. The clear recognition of the judicial equality of these prelates and the highest of the secular vassals, assured the easy assembly at all times of a court whose competency could not be gainsayed. And if the highest of the lay nobles must admit the authority of the royal court, much more those whose rank did not rise to the peerage.

Royal policy in trials involving lesser personages.

The same feeling of the necessity of trial by equals, which led to the recognition of the presence of peers as essential to the proper constitution of a judicial assembly before which one of their number was to be summoned, seems to have affected the composition of the court in cases involving prelates and nobles of lesser, but still exalted, rank. About 1210 Philip offered to judge the complaints of the bishop of Orléans before an assembly including the counts of Dreux

---

[1] The king of England naturally came rarely to the assemblies of the French monarch; the count of Toulouse never.

and Boulogne, the bishop of Lisieux, the abbot of Fleury, and many others whose names are not recorded.¹ The court before which the bishop of Paris appeared in 1221 contained the archbishop of Reims, prince Louis, the bishop of Senlis, the royal chamberlain, the constable, the counts of Brittany, Dreux, Blois, and Beaumont, beside many advisers of lesser prominence.² The succession to Beaumont was adjudged to Theobald d'Ully in 1223, by the king, assisted by the archbishop of Tours, the bishops of Angers and Senlis, the princes Louis and Philip, the chamberlain, the constable, Enguerran de Couci, Archambaud de Bourbon, and the count of St. Paul; beside many barons of lesser note, clerks, and royal counselors.³ The effort in all these cases was plainly to secure the presence in the judicial assembly of some, at least, whose rank was fully equal to that of the contestants. By this means, as in the case of the peers, any pretext for refusal to appear, based on the inequality of the judges and the person summoned, was avoided; while the real power remained in the hands of those closely attached to the interests of the king.

It is no impeachment of this policy that the two bishops, whose cases have just been cited, successfully refused to submit their complaints to the decision of the royal court. Their refusal was based not on any inequality in rank between themselves and the assembly before which the king invited them, but on the incompetence of any secular tribunal to adjudicate their claims,⁴ a pretention which the growth of the power of the curia regis made idle within a few years after Philip's death.⁵

But this action of the bishops of Orléans and Paris was exceptional. Before the reign of Philip closed, the competence of the royal court, backed as it was by the arms of the monarchy, was well-nigh unquestioned. Under his guidance, it had compelled the respect of a large proportion of the great vassals by actual adjudicature of their quarrels; others had avoided appearance before its bar only by taking arms. In 1186, the duke of Burgundy, defeated in arms, was glad to throw himself on the royal mercy and

Results of the curia regis under Philip.

---

¹ Text Boutaric, "Actes du Parlement de Paris" I: ccc.
² Delisle, Cat. 2034. Teulet, "Layettes, I: 514,"
³ Boutaric, "Actes du Parlement de Paris" I: ccci. Martène, "Amp. Coll." I: 1163.
⁴ "Episcopus vero dixit publice quod non debebat judicari, nisi per episcopos Francie, et ita recessit, domino rege offerante jus". Boutaric, "Actes du Parlament de Paris" I: ccc.
⁵ Id. ccxciii—iv.

offer to make reparation to the despoiled churches of his territory, as the curia regis should decide.¹ John, king of England, willingly sought the decision of the same court, in 1201, between his claims to Anjou and those of his nephew, Arthur. A sentence from the same tribunal, the year following, executed by the arms of Philip, cost the English sovereign the fairest part of his continental possessions. Arthur of Brittany, doing homage to the king of France in 1202, was willing to stipulate that any disputes with his uncle, the king of Castile, should be settled by the decision of Philip's court.² Three year later, the bishop of Clermont was glad to invoke the same authority against rebellions vassals who claimed the protection of the king of Aragon. William the Breton records that Philip offered to restore his lands to the traitorous Reginald, count of Boulogne, were he inclined to sustain a trial before the court, an ordeal which Reginald was unwilling to endure.³ A similar refusal on the part of Ferrandus, count of Flanders, to lend aid to the French monarch, or to justify his conduct to the court of the latter, was the immediate cause of the great invasion of Flanders in 1213.⁴ The preceeding year had seen the decision, by peaceful settlement, of the rival claims to the succession to Bourbon, which had been brought before the court.⁵ The great trial of 1216, in the contest ever Champagne, is a crowning tribute to the authority of the tribunal.

Arbitrations. One method of adjudicating disputes between the holders of the great fiefs, without recourse to the curia regis, was, indeed, open, and was employed with considerable frequency. The contestants might agree on arbitrators, to whose adjustment they would submit their quarrel. But it would appear that, under Philip, such a method of settlement usually required the approval, or at least the consent, of the king.⁶

The system of examination into rights and offences, by special commissioners,⁷ has been spoken of as the third factor in the growth

---

¹ Rigord, Delaborde, I: 52.
² Teulet, Layettes, I: 236.
³ Guil. Amor, Delaborde, I: 245.
⁴ Id. 249, 250.
⁵ Delisle, Cat. 1337.
⁶ Delisle, Cat. 1742, 1953, 1954, 2047, etc. In 1208 Reginald of Boulogne and Blanche of Champagne agreed to leave their quarrel to the king in case their arbitrators should disagree. Chantereau-Lefebvre. proofs 34.
⁷ Beugnot, "Les Olim", I: 947—959 has some valuable observations on the system of inquests.

of the power of the curia regis. These inquests occupy an intermediate place between the judicial assemblies, held in the presence of the king, and the local courts of the royal officers. They were investigations made at the scene of the controversy itself, or sufficiently near it to allow the ready summoning of witnesses. The persons by whom they were conducted were often the local officers of the monarchy, as we shall have occasion to see when considering the functions of the bailiffs. But they differ from the inquiries which every judicial officer of the crown doubtless had a right to institute, in being made at the direct command of the king,[1] conducted by persons designated by the monarch for the special case, and intended to serve as a basis for action by the king or his court.

The system of Inquest.

As might be anticipated from the want of separation between the distinctly judicial and the administrative branches of government, these inquests were oftener examinations into rights and titles, to serve as a basis for governmental action, than determinations of the merits of a controversy which had been brought before the court. The procedure was not wholly unknown before Philip;[2] but, as a means of extending the influence of the central administration to the remoter districts of the royal domain, this system gains increasing importance as his reign advances. A single register of Philip's acts records 132 such inquests between 1195 and 1220.[3] These investigations embrace such questions as the rights of the king and barons regarding the clergy of Normandy;[4] the value of the revenues due from Bonneville, Falaise, or Domfront;[5] the title to the regalia at Bourges;[6] the right to administer justice at Roie,[7] Mondidier, Liancourt, and in the châtelaincy of Vernon;[9] the quarrels between the bishop of Amiens and the burghers of that city;[10] the claims of the monks of Longport, and the canons of Valséri, to the use of the

Questions inquired into.

---

[1] The record of inquests in register E. (Delisle's enumeration) begins: "Hic incipiunt inquisitiones facte, de mandato domini regis, super diversis rebus qui inferius sunt conscripte." Beugnot "Les Olim" 1: 956.
[2] Id. 952, 953.
[3] Register E.
[4] Text, Martène, "Amp. Coll." 1: 1059. "Les Olim" 1: 978.
[5] "Les Olim" 1: 961, 962. text.
[6] Id. 959. text.
[7] Id. 963. text.
[8] Delisle, Cat., Appendix, p. 522.
[9] "Les Olim" 1: 969. text.
[10] Id. 989. text.

forest of Retz;[1] the pretentions of the canons of St. Aignan at Orléans as to various taxes levied on the men on their lands;[2] the quarrel between Simon d'Equancourt and the burghers of Péronne regarding pasture lands,[3] or between these burghers and the archbishop of Reims in reference to the admission of those whom they had banished from their commune;[4] the possession of the right of hunting in the forest of Othe, claimed by the archbishop of Sens;[5] or the quarrels between the monks of Écharlis and the men of Vaumort.[6]

Procedure.

It is possible that in one or two instances, as, for example, at the preparation of the declaration of the rights of the king and barons in Normandy, the assembly itself appointed scribes, who drew up a deposition to which its members swore.[7] But this was rarely the case, and was only practiced when the question was more administrative than judicial. The inquests were usually conducted by one[8] or more commissioners, generally two or three, who were sometimes representatives of both parties to the dispute;[9] but customarily agents of the king only. These inquirers proceeded, by royal order to the scene of the controversy, and summoned such witnesses as could be obtained. The latter were sworn by fitting oaths and interrogated.[10] The substance of their testimony was reduced to writing, and embodied in a report, stating also the names

[1] "Les Olim", 1035. text.
[2] Id. 1010. text.
[3] Delisle, Cat. 1557.
[4] Delisle, Cat. 1986.
[5] Id. 1755.
[6] Id. 1778.
[7] "Notum facemus preterea, quod jura domini regis et nostra que nobis memorie occurebant, sicut vidimus tempore Henrici et Ricardi regum ea observari, advocato consilio prudentum virorum, scilicet Ricardi de Willikier, Ricardi de Argentiis, Ricardi de Fonteneto, et Radulfi Labbe, et quorundam aliorum bona fide scripsimus." Teulet, Layettes, I: 296, 297. "Les Olim" I: 980.
[8] For the employment of only one commissioner see Delisle 1755. "Les Olim" I: 1010.
[9] "Interim autem vos duo ballivi, cum duobus canonicis Belvacensibus, inquiriatis similiter bona fide per juramenta legitimorum hominum patrie." Order for inquest into the right of justice at Liancourt. Delisle, Cat. Appendix p. 522.
[10] "Jurati et interrogati, dixerunt". Les Olim I: 959. "Dominus Albericus, miles et conversus de Sancto-Eligio-Fonte, abjuratus super ordinem suum, dixit". Id. 960. "Major et Jurati Calniaci dixerunt, super sacramentum quod fecerunt regi". Id. "In verbo sacerdotis dixerunt." Id. 1012.

and stations of the witnesses; in some instances the seals of the commissioners, or of those testifying, were added.[1] This document was then transmitted to the king,[2] who, if the inquest concerned a matter in dispute and was not simply an administrative inquiry, issued a charter in his own name,[3] sometimes apparently in that of his court also,[4] announcing and confirming the result.

This system of procedure was really an extension of the curia regis to the local scene of the investigation. The testimony was taken where it could best be had, but the inquest was no local court. It simply ascertained the fact, — the action to be based on that fact was decided by the king and his counselors, not by the commissioners who made the inquiry. This local extension of the central judical power greatly aided in rendering effective the royal authority. It facilitated the recourse to appeals from the decisions of the courts of the royal vassals to that of the king, of which we begin to find traces as an officially recognized legal procedure late in Philip's reign,[5] but which even his strong hand could not introduce as general custom. It helped to prepare the way for the wide recognition of the authority of the Parlement of Paris under the reign of St. Louis.

An extension of the curia regis.

The organs of the central administration, as existing under the reign of Philip Augustus, have now been passed in review and their

The reregency of 1190—91.

---

[1] "Les Olim" I: 969, 980. Teulet, Layettes, I: 297, 298.

[2] "Quod inde cum canonicis predictis inquisieritis, per vestras litteras patentes nobis renuntiatis." Order for Liancourt investigation." Delisle, Cat. appendix 522.

[3] Delisle, Cat. 436, 1572—3, 1778, 1986 etc. Teulet, Layettes, I: 417.

[4] Boutaric, "Actes du Parlement de Paris." I: ccxcviii.

[5] Of course, appeal to the curia regis for refusal of justice to a subvassal was always recognized. The appeal of the barons of Poitou, against John, in 1201—2, is a case in point. One of the earliest charters recognizing the right of appeal from a judgment rendered in due form by a vassal's court is the following, of uncertain date, but surely of the latter half of Philip's reign. It regulates the relations of the bishop and the commune of Noyon. "Philippus... noverint universi quod, si episcopus Noviomensis habuerit querelam contra communiam vel contra aliquem de communia de querela sua propria, decernimus et volumus ut judicium fiat per liberos homines episcopi, sub hac conditione quod, si judicium illud placuerit communie vel illi de quo conqueritur episcopus, stabile erit et gratum habebit; si vero displicuerit, ad nos poterit appellare, et tunc tale judicium tenebunt quale curia nostra eis dixerit." Delisle, Cat. appendix p. 523.

relation to the monarch examined. Before turning to the consideration of the local administration, however, we must glance at the means employed for the conduct of government in the absence of the king, — the regency of 1190—91. During the eighteen months spent by Philip on the crusade,[1] the monarch was represented in France by the queen-mother, Adela, and her brother William, the archbishop of Reims. The importance of the latter as a counselor of the king, as well as his commanding station as primate of France, made his selection for the post fitting and proper, while the motherless prince was doubtless safest in the hands of his grandmother. The appointment of regents during the absence of the king on a crusade was no new experiment; Louis VII. had entrusted the government to Suger and to Ralph, count of Vermandois, on his departure for the Holy Land in 1147. Then, as under Philip, the consent of the assembly was asked:[2] but, under Louis VII. and his son alike, the real decision as to the personality of the regents was made, previous to the meeting of the vassalage, by the king and his counselors, and the assembly simply ratified the royal act. In 1190 the king and his familiares drew up an elaborate rule for the administration of the kingdom during the regency, — the testament of Philip Augustus. This document shows that it was no unlimited power that the crusading monarch entrusted to the regents. After providing for the local administration by bailiffs, provosts, and their local advisers, he orders the regents to hold a court once in four months, at Paris, to hear complaints and to administer justice; and also to receive reports from each city and from the bailiffs regarding the course of local affairs.[3]

---

[1] Philip set out from Vezelai, probably on July 6., 1190; he spent Christmas, 1191, at Fontainbleau, on his return, and two days after was in Paris. Benedict of Peterborough II: 112, Ralph de Diceto, II: 104. Rigord, Delaborde I: 99, 118.

[2] For the assembly at Étampes Feb., 16–18, 1147, and the election of Suger and the count of Nevers, who was replaced by Ralph of Vermandois, see Luchaire, "Instit Monarchiques," I: 262. Sep. XII: 93. On the choice of 1190, compare Rigord, 99, 100.

[3] "Preterea volumus et precipimus ut carissima mater noster A. regina statuat cum carissimo avunculo nostro et fideli Guillelmo Remensi achiepiscopo, singulis quatuor mensibus, unum diem Parisius, in quo audiant clamores hominum regni nostri, et ibi eos finiant ad honorem Dei et utilitatem regni. Precipimus insuper ut eo die sint ante ipsos de singulis villis nostris et baillivi nostri qui assesias tenebunt, ut coram eis recitent negotia terre nostre." Testament, sections 3, 4. Rigord Id. 101. An instance of the exercise of this judicial power by the regents is to be found in Boutaric, "Actes du Parlement

The state of the kingdom, as evinced by these thrice-yearly inquiries, was to be announced by letter to the king, together with the proofs of such malfeasance of the local officers as was not embraced under the designations of murder, rape, homicide, or treason.[1] Only when guilty of the heinous crimes included under the four catagories just enumerated, could the regents summarily remove a bailiff, or the bailiff a provost.[2] All other offences were reserved for the personal cognizance of the king.[3] Yet even these investigations and audiences were not conducted by the regents alone. "Others", as to whose exact station the document does not inform us, were to be present to assist the regents in adjudging the delinquencies of the bailiffs.[4] These were, in all probability, members of the palace council, the familiares of the monarch when at home; and among them were probably the burghers of Paris, who are expressly mentioned as receivers and custodians of the royal revenue,[5] and who also attested the expedition of charters,[6] and were the guardians of the great seal during the regency.[7] Nor were the regents free to carry out their will in ecclesiastical affairs. Though unrestrained election of bishops and abbots was to be granted on petition of the canons or monks, minor vacancies, occuring while the regalia were in the hands of the regents, were to be filled in accordance with the advice of brother Bernard of Grammont.[8] These provisions for the assistance of the

Share of the counselors.

de Paris" I: ccxcvii, where the fief of Flavigni is adjudged to the bishop of Autun.

[1] "Si autem aliquis de baillivis nostris deliquerit, preter quam in murtro, raptu, vel homocidio, vel proditione, et hoc constabit archiepiscopo et regine, et aliis qui aderunt ut audiant forisfacta baillivorum nostrorum, precipimus eis ut nobis singulis annis, et hoc ter in anno, literis suis nobis duobus (diebus) predictis significent quis baillivus deliquerit, et quid fecerit, et quid acceperit, et a quo pecuniam, vel munus, vel servitium, propter quod homines nostri jus suum amitterent, vel nos nostrum."

"Similiter regina et archiepiscopus de statu regni nostri et negotiis ter in anno significent." Testament § 5, 8. Rigord, Delaborde, I: 101, 102.

[2] Id. § 7.

[3] Id.

[4] Compare note above. "Aliis qui aderunt ut audiant forisfacta baillivorum nostrorum".

[5] "Preterea precipimus quod omnes redditus nostri et servitia et obventiones afferantur Parisius per tria tempora .... et tradatur burgensibus nostris predictis, et P(etro) Marescallo". Id. § 14. Rigord, 103.

[6] Delisle, Cat. LXII.

[7] "In presentia nostrorum burgensium, qui sigillum nostrum custodiunt". Charter of Dec. 1190. Delisle, Cat. LXIII, 332.

[8] Testament § 9, 10, 18.

regents in their work show that the government, during the absence of Philip on the crusade, was essentially one of regents and counselors, not one of regents alone. The humble origin of many of these advisers exhibits the influence already exerted in the discussions of the palace, though not as yet in the assemblies of the kingdom, by members of what was later to be known as the "Tiers État". But, though the powers of the regents regarding the ordinary administration were in many ways limited, they, and not the council, were, nevertheless, the representatives of the king. This is especially noticeable in controversies involving the higher nobility. Such an instance is to be found in the action of the archbishop of Reims in regard to the disputes over the succession to Flanders, consequent upon the death of Philip of Flanders in June, 1191, at the siege of Acre. Rumors of that event having reached Baldwin of Hainault, through the energy of Gislebert, before the messengers of the French monarch could arrive in France,[1] the count of Hainault was able to take unhindered possession of a large part of Flanders. But the regent was not backward. At the instance of Philip he received the homage of the district of Péronne;[2] and although he soon had to relinquish the idea of gaining Flanders entirely for his royal nephew, he appointed a court at Arras, in October, 1191, to adjudge or compromise the contests between Baldwin and Margaret, widow of the late count Philip, thus asserting, as representative of the king, his right of jurisdiction over even the highest of the nobles.[3] At this court he secured a peaceful settlement between the contestants and advanced also very materially the interests of the French monarchy.

The regency was, in the nature of things, a temporary makeshift, and, as such, was likely to meet with more difficulties than the rule of the sovereign himself. But the regency of 1190 encountered no such opposition as Suger had experienced during Louis VII.'s sojourn in Palestine. Many of the more turbulent of the nobles of France had accompanied Philip on the crusade, but a large share of this comparative peace was due to the strength which the central government had acquired in the forty-three years which had elapsed since the previous experiment, an increase in strength which made it possible

---

[1] Gislebert, 228.

[2] See the letter sent by Philip in June, 1191, from Acre to the men of Péronne, announcing the death of Philip of Flanders, and ordering them to swear allegiance to him and to prince Louis before the bearers of the letter, William of Reims and others. Delisle, Cat. appendix p. 500.

[3] Gislebert, 223.

for the king to make the rule of the regency contemporaneous with the general introduction of a great change in the local government which it will soon be our task to consider.

III) The actual local administration of the monarch during the reign of Philip Augustus, as under his predecessors, extended only over the domain proper of the crown, that is, over those territories in which the king himself exercised the authority of a duke or count, and those places outside the domain itself in which the king shared the sovereignty with lay and, especially, with ecclesiastical suzerains. All local government outside this region was in the hands of the local feudatories; and if the king was able to interfere for the protection of churchly interests or the regulation of local customs, in occasional instances, within the territories of his great vassals, that interference was effected by influence or force from without, not by the action of royal officers within these fiefs.[1]

Philip's local administration.

Had such officers existed, the distinguishing feature of the French monarchy during the eleventh, twelfth and thirteenth centuries would have been wanting: — the predominently feudal character of the relations of the nobles to the crown. But if the king had few actual claims on the lay barons beside those of military service, aid, and counsel in legal and administrative exigencies,[2] the power of a strong monarch like Philip over them was, nevertheless, not small. The church throughout most of Northern and Central France, was the direct tenant of the crown in temporal matters. On the vacancy of a bishopric or of a royal abbey the king, as the rightful overlord, assumed full administration of such rights and possessions of the see as were not distinctively ecclesiastical. This ancient right of regalia was not

---

[1] The distinction between the domain and the kingdom is clearly made in a sentence of banishment pronounced by Philip, in 1202, against Riulph, Corvin and Hector le Meure, infractors of the peace at Laon: "Inde est quod nos eosdem de omni terra nostra et omni feodo nostro et regno bannavimus, ita quod nullus eorum amodo responsionem sive clamorem facere poterunt erga communitatem Laudunensem vel erga aliquem de pace Laudunsi. — Sciendum est etiam quod, si nos eosdem infra terram nostram dominicam vel regnum nostrum post bannitionem istam capere poterimus, nos ipsos in carcere nostro, quamdiu vixerint, tenebimus." Teulet, Layettes, I: 238.

[2] "Si . . . . . resilerent a pactionibus . . . . ego post quadraginta dies postquam submoniti, id emendare nollent, nullum servitium nec auxilium nec consilium eis praestarem." Guarantee sworn by Blanche of Champagne, in 1215, for the fulfillment of the contract of betrothal between Philip, Louis and Hervey of Nevers. Brussel, Usage, I: 161, 162.

— 98 —

The king an the Church. The regalia.
enjoyed by the king in Aquitaine[1] or Languedoc.[2] In the west of France it was possessed by the Angevins throughout their territories,[3] and by the dukes of Brittany in their fief.[4] In Normandy,[5] Angers, and Maine[6] it came to the monarchy only by the conquest of those domains in the opening years of the thirteenth century. But in the province of Sens,[7] in most of the episcopates subject to Reims,[8] and in certain

[1] In 1137, when ruler of Aquitaine, as husband of Eleanor, Louis VII. granted exemption from regalia to the whole province of Bordeaux, Brial Sep. XIV: lviii, lix. Poitou was conquered by Philip in 1203, but whether he reintroduced the right does not appear.

[2] Raimond VI., of Toulouse, obtained absolution, in 1209, on condition of renouncing the regalia which he had previously enjoyed. This included certain bishoprics in the province of Bourges, (Cahors, Albi, Rodes). Text Sep. XIV: lx note. Louis VII. had given many such charters of exemption in his efforts to gain the support of the bishoprics of Southern France. In his case they cost the crown nothing which it actually possessed. Some of these privileges were confirmed and augmented by Philip. Compare charters for Lodève. Bibl. de l'École des Chartes, XXXVII: 382.

[3] For the possession of the regalia of Normandy by its dukes, compare Brussel I: 281—286. The oath of the bishop of Angers to Louis VIII., in 1223., claims: "illis libertatibus quas habuimus temporis felicis memoriae Philippi .... et regum Angliae Henrici et Ricardi." Id. 296. For Mans, see Martène "Amp. Coll." I: 1172. Tours was in dispute till the reign of Philip. Sep. XIV: lvii.

[4] Brial. Sep. XIV: lvi, lvii.

[5] About 1208 Philip declared that during a vacancy at Rouen, the administration, spiritual and temporal, should be in the hands of the chapter. But in 1222 the chapter prayed him to deliver the regalia to their bishop-elect Theobold. Delisle, Cat. 1109, 2137. For Evreux, see Teulet, Layettes I: 505, The rights of the Norman dukes were investigated, in 1205, as a basis for the relations of the king and Norman churches, Brussel II: xxiv. Teulet, Id. 296.

[6] For the enjoyment of these regalia by the king after the conquest, see Delisle, Cat. 1500, and note 3 above.

[7] All churches in the province of Sens owed regalia. For Sens itself, see Delisle, Cat. 80; Chartres, Sep. XXIII: 681; Orléans, Delisle 1395; Paris, Martène, "Amp. Coll." I: 989; Troyes, Brussel, II: clxxx; Meaux seems to have been somewhat in dispute with the count of Champagne, for, in Dec. 1222., Philip forbade the bailiffs, provosts, or sergeants of that count to touch the goods which the bishop of Meaux had bequeathed by will; thus asserting the royal supremacy. Delisle 2182, compare Brussel, I: 311. Auxerre obtained the relinquishment of the regalia to the chapter in 1207, through large money payments Sep. XVIII: 732. Nevers received the same exemption in 1208 or 1209. Martène, "Amp. Coll." I: 1080; also by payment, Sep. XVIII: 240.

[8] Philip received regalia from Reims in 1202, Brussel, II: clxxviii. The king relinquished the regalia of Arras, in 1203 or 1204, for 1000 livres, Martène, "Ampl. Coll." I: 1042, Brussel I: 307, 543. At Châlons the king enjoyed the regalia. Brussel II: clii. Delisle, Cat. p. 503. Amiens, Beauvais, Laon,

belonging to Bourges¹ and to Lyon,² this right was an effective means of filling the royal treasury,³ and even more advantageous to the monarchy as affording political power.¹ The return every few years of the temporalia of these great sees to the royal control, enabled the king to resist the encroachments of the neighboring vassals on the ecclesiastical fiefs;⁵ and, for a time at least, to use the whole force of a bishopric, in addition to his own proper resources, against any lay subject whom he might wish to curb. The right of regalia carried with it the privilege of appointing to the benefices ordinarily in the gift of the bishop; thus allowing the king to fill these territories, often in the heart of the lay fiefs, with his partisans.⁶ The exigencies of the treasury, and possibly the necessity of

Soissons, Térouanne and Tournai were apparently also under the royal control. Cambrai, however, was declared by the king to be outside the kingdom. Martène, "Amp. Coll." I: 1079.

¹ At Bourges and Limoges. Brial, Sep. XIV; lvi.

² In 1189 Philip recognized that the regalia of Lyon belonged to the bishop of Autun, during a vacancy, and those of Autun to the archbishop of Lyon. Delisle, Cat. 235. He surrendered the regalia of Langres to the dean and chapter in 1203 or 1204, "Gallia Christiana" IV, inst. 197. In 1202 the bishop-elect of Mâcon recognized the king's right to the regalia; but Philip renounced it in 1209. Delisle Cat. 713, 714, 1115. Martène "Amp. Coll." I: 1087.

³ The sums received from the regalia were very considerable. In the treasury account of 1202, those of Châlons were paid in to the amount of 2047 livres Provins. Those of Reims — in 18 weeks only — amounted to 2668 l. Paris and 216 l. 11 s. Provins. Those of Troyes were 100 l. Brussel II: clii, clxxviii, clxxx.

⁴ For example, when danger was threatening from the growing power of Otto IV. in Germany, the men of Reims swore to admit the king and his army into their city and to aid him against the emperor and other enemies. Philip lent them 4000 l. Paris to finish the fortifications of the city. — Dec. 1209. In May 1210 the king offered 2000 livres to hasten the fortifications of Châlons. These are not, indeed, exercises of the right of "regalia;" but they show the close connection between the monarchy and the bishoprics, which that right must have done much to foster. "Gallia Christ." X: inst. 57. Delisle, Cat. 1212.

⁵ E. g. the resistance to the interference of the "vicedominus" of Châlons, about 1202. Delisle, Cat. p. 503; or to the interference of the count of Champagne at Meaux in 1222. Id. no. 2182.

⁶ "Preterea precipimus quod si prebenda vel beneficium aliquod ecclesiasticum vacaverit, quando regalia in manu nostra venient, secundum quod melius et honestius poterunt regina et archipiscopus viris honestis et litteratis, consilio fratris Bernardi, conferrant; Salvis, tamen donationibus nostris, quas per literas nostras patentes quibusdam fecimus." Will of Philip. 1190. Rigord Delaborde. I: 102, 103.

winning support in the border territories, in meeting the great peril which threatened the monarchy from Germany, induced the king to relinquish the regalia and grant free elections to the chapters of a few bishoprics, in instances especially where the neighboring lay vassals were comparatively dependent on the crown;[1] but the gain in strength and territory which the monarchy derived from the victorious outcome of its contests with England and Germany made good the loss. Motives of policy, too, moved Philip to continue the abolition, begun by his father, of the barbarous custom of spoil, by which the palace of the deceased prelate was stripped of its furnishings for the royal profit, and even the bequests of its former occupant confiscated,[2] though the king's action was by no means uniform in this regard.[3] In the main, Philip retained and improved the advantages which his rights over the clergy gave him.

Ecclesiastical elections.
Not less important in securing the royal influence over the churches was the custom which required the king's assent to the election of a bishop, a custom which prevailed throughout the region

---

[1] At Arras, in 1203 or 1204, for 1000 livres; At Auxerre in 1207, and Nevers in 1208 or 1209, for large payments; Langres was privileged in 1203 or 1204 and Mâcon in 1209. Arras was in the domain itself through the acquisition of Artois. The counts of Nevers and Auxerre were specially dependent on the king.

[2] For the extensive abolition of this abuse by Louis VII. see Luchaire, "Inst. Mon." II: 64, 65. In 1190 Philip renewed or increased his father's concession for Paris, Delisle, Cat. 290; and the same year granted like exemption to Reims. "Gallia Christ." X inst. 51.

[3] How far the king sometimes pushed not only the right of regalia, but that of spoil also, a letter of Innocent III. regarding the proceedings of the royal officers after the death of Hugh, bishop of Auxerre, in 1206, shows: "Rex, audito quod . . . Hugo . . . naturae debitum exsolvisset, statim fecit per servientes suos episcopales res quas vocat regalia occupari; qui more praedonum debacchantes in eis crudeliter, ecclesiae nemora passim fecere succidi, eadem venalia omnibus exponentes; stagna quoque fecerunt dirui et penitus expiscari, et, ejusdem Ecclesiae hominibus captis, ipsos tormentis ad redemptionem miserabilem compulerunt, et abducentes animalia universa, frumentum, vinum, foenum, ligna etiam et lapides expolitos, quos idem episcopus ad construendam capellam et alia aedificia praepararat, nequitur asportarunt; episcopalibus domibus supellectili qualibet spoliatis, ita ut in eis praeter tectum et parietes non fuit aliquid derelictum . . . . Bona quae praefatus episcopus ecclesiis et pauperibus diversorum locorum . . . . legaret, sicut apparet in testamento ipsius . . . . idem rex penitus confiscavit." Sep. XIX: 488, 489.

It was only after much contest, in 1207, that Manasses of Orléans secured the gems set in his predecessor's rings; the king keeping the gold setting, on a strict interpretation of his father's privilege of 1157. Sep. XVIII: 732.

where the right of regalia was enjoyed,[1] and which extended also to the choice of the heads of many abbeys.[2] It emphasized the dependence of the religious establishments on the crown at every new succession. It made it possible for the king to resist the choice of persons specially hostile to his plans. Even where the prelate was not personally attached to the king, the lay noble in the neighborhood was more an object of his fear than the distant monarch. Hence the readiness of many bishops, on the outskirts of the territories immediately subject to the crown, to do homage to the king and put themselves under his protection. This movement was especially marked in central France, where the bishops of Cahors, Clermont, and Limoges in particular profited by their attachment to the king.[3] Hence, too, the constant appeals of the clergy to the Capetian sovereigns, for aid against the encroachments of the baronage; and the alacrity with which such monarchs as Philip responded to their calls.[4] The royal

Appeals for royal protection.

[1] "Si forte contigerit sedem episcopalem vel aliquam abbatiam regalem vacare, volumus ut canonici ecclesie vel monachi monasterii vacantis veneant ad reginam et archiepiscopum, sicut ante nos venirent, et liberam electionis ab eis petant". Will of Philip, 1190. Rigord, 102. William, bishop of Auxerre, when dying in 1181: "clericos coepit cum lacrymis monere et exhortari, ne inter eos discordiae ... irreperet flagitium; sed statim eo sepulto regem adirent, obitum suum nunciaturi, et debitam eligendi licentiam ab eo petituri". Scp. XII: 404.

[2] The "Abbatiae regales"; enumerated in Philip's registers are to be found in Scp. XXIII: 682. The king enjoyed their regalia. In 1186 Philip actively interfered in the affairs of St. Denis, compelling the abbot to resign. Rigord, 65. As an example of the frequency with which permission to choose was asked of the king, the charters regarding election in the years 1221 and 1222, may be cited. Lira. Delisle 2084, 2085, Corbie, Id. 2091. Cormeilles. Id. 2100. Ste. Geneviève de Paris, Id, 2148—2150. Lessai, Id 2184—2185. Massai, 2186, 2187.

[3] The bishop of Cahors was received as liege vassal in 1211, after consultation between the king and his advisers. The king promised to favor his claims against the count of Toulouse. Text, Brussel I: 31.

In 1205 Philip adjudged the castle of Vertaizon to Robert, bishop of Clermont, its holders having received the bishops enemies and having failed to respond to the summons of the royal court. Boutaric "Actes du Parlement" I: ccxcix. In 1212 the king gave the bishop various fiefs in Auvergne, which the latter pledged himself never to deliver to the count Auvergne or any enemy of the king. Delisle 1876. Further gifts were made in 1220, Id. 2000. His fidelity was guaranteed by the countess of Champagne in 1218. Brussel. 1:21.

Philip received the homage of John, bishop of Limoges, in 1204, and promised that the bishopric should be permanently attached to the crown. Delisle, Cat. 875.

[4] To repress attacks on the churches was the object of a large part of the minor military expeditions of the king, who thus crippled the power

protection was ever ready to be extended to monastic bodies and to religious foundations, partly, doubtless, from motives of piety, but chiefly because every such protection gave the monarchy a point of vantage from which the lay nobles could be held in check.[1]

Philip availed himself of the censures of the church to secure his agreements with the baronage.[2] The body of the clergy supported him in a manner strongly contrasting with the rebellious spirit of many of the lay nobles. His treatment of them was firm; he insisted on the performance of their military duties;[3] he endeavored, with

of the baronage under cover of repressing wrongs to the clergy. Thus in 1180, at the very opening of his reign, the king took part in expeditions against Hebo of Charenton in Berri, and Imbert of Beaujeu, and William of Châlon; thus making the nobles, as far as the Rhone, feel the power of the monarchy. Rigord, 16, 17. Nor did he hesitate to attack more powerful vassals on the same pretext. In 1186, complaints having been laid before Philip that Hugh III., duke of Burgundy, had exacted 30,000 livres from the churches, he summoned his army and took Châtillon-sur-Seine. The duke, being unable to regain the lost fortress, submitted and offered to make amends to the churches in accordance with the judgment of the "curia regis." Rigord, 45, 53; other examples might be cited.

[1] Such protection removed the ecclesiastical establishments from the interference of the lay advocati, and other neighboring barons, thus carrying the royal authority into the heart of the great fiefs. They are very numerous. More than forty instances may be found enumerated in the Catalogue of M. Delisle — several of these embracing a large number of monasteries in a single privilege. A few of the more remote may be mentioned. In 1180 Philip took the monastery of Charlieu in Beaujolais under his protection, Delisle 13. The church of Sarlat, in Périgord, received a similar privilege in 1181, Id. 19. In 1189 Philip assumed protection of the district of Saint André, an ecclesiastical dependence, probably in Burgundy, Id. 229. Ord. XI: 252. The conquest of Normandy was preceeded by several such privileges — e. g. in 1189 for Notre Dame du Bec; 1194, Foucarmont, Id. 502; 1200, Bonport, Id. 637. The abbey of Saint Maixent in Poitou was declared permanently under the protection of the crown in 1204. Id. 833. In 1221 or 1222 Philip assumed protection of the religious establishments of the order of Cîteaux, Id. 2099. Ordon V: 142, of which most had been privileged in 1190; Cat. 314.

[2] The employment of this means was comparatively rare. Instances are — the promises of fidelity and aid made to the king by Baldwin count of Flanders and Reginald count of Boulogne in 1196, which were guaranteed under church censure by the archbishop of Reims and the bishops of Arras, Térouanne and Tournai. Delisle, Cat. 498, 500. That of Theobald III. of Champagne was similarly secured in 1198. Brussel I: 118--119.

[3] On the assembly of the army designed for the capture of Guarplic, in 1210, the two brothers William, bishop of Auxerre, and Manasses, bishop of Orléans, returned home from the rendez-vous at Mantes, with their followers, alleging that they were not bound to service when the king did not person-

varying success to make them submit controversies to the decision of his court;¹ he limited their legal jurisdiction as far as possible.² But he was a generous patron and a vigorous defender of their rights when attacked by others; and the return he received in support from the clergy was worth to the monarchy all that the favors cost it. Had it not been for his more direct control over the churches, Philip could not have withstood the desires and combinations of the baronage as he did.

An inestimable advantage in his dealings with the clergy and baronage alike was derived from the relation of the monarch to the non-noble class. The reign of Philip Augustus was characterized by the rapid spread of communes. These associations seldom, if ever, owed their inception to the efforts of the monarchy. During the 150 years previous to Philip's reign their growth had been rather in spite of, than owing to, the king.³ And, though certain general feelings of humanity undoubtedly existed in Philip,⁴ his favor toward this class of the population was based far more on considerations of their value in furthering his policy than on any sympathy with their oppressions. The two chief cities of the royal domain, Paris and Orléans, were not communes. The commune of Étampes was abolished by Philip himself.⁵ But Philip understood well the benefits to be derived

The king and the non-noble class.

Communes.

---

ally accompany the expedition. They refused satisfaction to the king, who confiscated their regalia. After much discussion, and many attempts on the part of pope Innocent III. to effect a settlement, the matter ended with the recognition of their obligation by the two bishops, in 1212. The king, indeed, granted the bishop of Auxerre a personal dispensation from army service, but this did not include his knights and was given distinctly as an act of grace. Guil. Amor I: 229. Sep. XIX: 537—556. Martène, "Amp. Coll." I: 1110.

¹ About 1210 Manasses of Orléans refused to recognize the competence of the royal court to judge his rights regarding certain procurations, and alleged that he could be judged only by the bishops. Delisle, 1241. His brother, then become bishop of Paris, held the same conduct in 1221, Id. 2034. Both were able to avoid judgment at the time. Compare this essay p. p. 88. 89.

² See Sep. XVIII: 248, Delisle, Cat. 1477, 1707. See especially the articles of agreement between the king and barons respecting the claims of the clergy to legal jurisdiction. Martène I: 1083. Brussel II: xxvii.

³ Compare Luchaire, "Instit. Monarch." II: chapter III, for a careful examination of the royal policy toward the communes, before Philip Augustus.

⁴ As illustrated, for example, in his prohibition of wrecking. Delisle, Cat. p. 498.

⁵ In 1199 or 1200. Ordon. XI: 277. Other examples are Châteauneuf, at Tours, in 1184, Sep. XVIII: 292; and Laon, in 1190—1, Delisle, Cat. 331, both effected by churchly influence.

from these organizations where a local authority, obnoxious to him, was to be overcome. He was not able, indeed, to control the communes within the territories of his greater vassals; there his interference extended only to an occassional confirmation of a charter, as in the case of the commune sanctioned at Dijon by the duke of Burgundy;[1] but, in general, his consent was not so much as sought by the principal suzerains, not even by the closely related rulers of Champagne. Throughout his own domain, and the bishoprics over which the king exercised the right of regalia, the communes multiplied rapidly, especially during the early years of his rule.[3] And there can be no doubt that the institution conduced greatly to the effectiveness of the royal control over the domain proper, and the adjacent territories. True, the king had to surrender something to the commune. The interference of the royal servants in purely local affairs was limited by the charter of communal privileges; and the inconveniences of this limitation were certain to be felt as the kingdom grew more consolidated. But in the stage of developement which the monarchy of Philip represented, the benefits of the communal system outweighed its disadvantages. The acquisition of local self-governement was gladly paid for by a notable increase in the

---

[1] Delisle 88, 196. Ordon. V: 237.

[2] Compare Brussel I: 183—187. Even so dependent a baron as the count of Ponthieu could grant communes in his territory without royal interference. Those granted by William, count of Ponthieu, were not confirmed till 1221—2. Delisle 2097, 2098. Ordonn. XII: 297. Several had been in undisputed operation for years previous. Compare Id. XI: 310.

[3] Philip established communes at Chaumont, in 1182; Cerni and dependences, 1184; Crespi-en-Laonnois, 1185—6; Tournai, 1187; Pontoise, 1188; l'oissi, 1188; Montreuil, 1188; Saint Riquier, 1189- 90; Sens, 1189—90 (a new charter, the commune was older, Ordon. XI: 244, 262); Hesdin, 1192; Montdidier, 1195; Villeneuve-en-Beauvaisis, 1200; Andeli, 1204; Pont Audemar, 1204; Nonancourt, 1204; Filliêvre, 1205; Péronne, 1207; Brai-sur-Somme, 1210; Athies, 1211; Chauni, 1213; Crespi-en-Valois, 1215; Poitiers, 1221 (a new charter).

The registers of Philip give the communes subject to him as: Arras, Péronne, Noyon, Amiens, Tournai, Montdidier, Roie, Bapaumes, Corbei, Compiègne, Soissons, Laon-St. John, Laon-Condé, Bruyères, Vailli, Cerni, Crespi, Chelles near Paris, Senlis, Beauvais, Montreuil, Chaumont, Pontoise, Meulan, Poissi, Mantes, Sens, Villeneuve-en-Beauvasis, Sens, Hesdin, Ferrieres (Fillièvre). Rouen, Verneuil, Caen, Falaise, Pont Audemer, St. Jean d'Angeli, Poitiers, Niort these with the customs of Rouen. Sep. XXIII: 684. Athies, (Ord. XI: 298); Andeli, (Delisle 804); Brai-sur-Somme, (Ord. XI: 295); Nonancourt, (id. 289); St. Quentin, (id. 270); and St. Riquier, (Ord. IV: 548 ; Beauquêne and Ham, (Boutaric, "Institutions militaires" 207) should be added to this list.

revenue returned to the king, the amount being sometimes doubled,[1] and, for the aims which Philip had in view, a large revenue was of the utmost importance. The king obtained considerable bodies of troops direct from the communes, whose services were not subject to the delay and vexations which attended requisitions through an unwilling noble.[2] The communes afforded him, in some instances, the advantages of a garrisoned border fortress, without its expense; and the service of their soldiery in the field was probably such as to contribute something to the success of the royal arms. Their presence, as organized bodies of troops, at the battle of Bouvines, is deemed worthy of record in the account of the contest which William the Breton gives us; but the day was still distant when a great battle was to be decided by these foot soldiers of the towns.[1] The chief advantage of the commune to the monarchy was that it diminished the power of the neighboring noble, bishop, or provost. The latter, through royal officers, often occupied a

---

[1] E. g. Cerni-en-Laonnais. Ord. XI: 234. Villeneuve-en-Beauvaisis agreed to pay 100 livres yearly, Sens 600 l. money and 1200 modii grain, etc. (Ord. XI: 279, 263 etc.). The king usually obtained a definite revenue, in large part in money, in place of the variable receipts of tonlieu, forfeits, police justice, mortmain, etc.

[2] All communes owed service; charter of Crespi-en-Valois, Ord. XI: 308. Confirmation of communes founded by thechurchof St. Jean de Laon, id. 277. The connection between the king and communes being direct, the former suzerain of the place was no longer responsible for the raising of troops in the region under the communal charter; see charter for the church of St. Jean de Laon just quoted. Compare Boutaric. "Institutions Militaires de la France" 156—160, 204, regarding the military services and obligations of the communes.

[3] E. g. Mantes, whose citizens were always active in securing the royal interests, against aggression. In 1188 they successfully withstood the march of Henry II. up the valley of the Seine. Philippide, III: 357 etc. ed. Delaborde, II: 79.

[4] While there can be no doubt that the troops of the communes of Amiens, Arras, Beauvais, Compiègne and Corbie were of service in the battle of Bouvines, it is difficult to attribute to them any such decisive weight in the conflict as many historians do. Though this value is attributed to them by Luchaire (Instit. II: 187) and Winkelmann ("Philipp von Schwaben" II: 374) among others, William the Breton represents them as promptly driven back by the attack of the Germans, who penetrated to the position occupied by the king himself. The king was saved by his knights, and the share of the communes in the battle after this repulse does not seem to have been important. Delaborde I: 282. M. A. Molinier (Revue Historique Jan.-Feb. 1888, pp. 192, 194, 195) supports this estimate of the work of the communal soldiers at Bouvines as comparatively insignificant.

semi-feudal station and practiced abuses which made it hardly less the interest of the monarchy than that of the cities to place a limit to their power.[1] The territory endowed with communal privileges was in an especial sense king's land; its charter and its protection alike came from the royal hand; and the influence of the commune in weakening the power of the smaller nobles on the outskirts of the domain, and of the great ecclesiastics beyond its border, can hardly be overestimated.

The privileged towns. In a less degree, these advantages accrued to the monarchy from that great class of towns whose privileges did not go so far as to provide the local self-government of the commune.[2] These privileges, of every variety of fullness, were given by Philip, as by his predecessors Louis VI. and VII., to a great number of cities, villages, and territorial districts. It is not our purpose here to enter into any minute examination of them.[3] Their primary effect was doubtless to limit the power of the king and his officers in the regions thus privileged. But by bringing a certain degree of fixity into the customs by which the particular regions were ruled and by freeing from odious burdens, these concessions stimulated trade and fostered population, and, hence, increased the influence of that non-noble class whose growth in power signified the weakening of the nobles. How far these concessions are to be attributed to the wisdom of the monarch may be an open question, but there can be no doubt that their ultimate effect was greatly to consolidate and strengthen the position of the crown in opposition to the feudal vassals.

The king and the nobles. Great as was the aid which Philip derived from his relations to the church and to the non-noble class, their support alone would never have enabled him to withstand the forces against him. Though the king was able, as has already been noticed, to secure the formal assent of the barons, who were present in his assemblies, to such features of his policy as he announced to them, the bond uniting the great

[1] The semi-feudal character of the provosts and the efforts of Philip's immediate predecessors to check their abuses of power are discussed by Luchaire, Inst. I: 228—233, II: 139.

[2] E. g. Orléans, Bourges, Lorris, Bois-commun, Wacqmoulin, Voisines etc. Paris has, curiously, no charter of liberties reaching back to this period. The non-communal form was preferred and often enforced by the king in the territories more immediately under his control.

[3] The admirable discussion of these privileged cities in the "Institutions Monarchiques," II chapter of M. Luchaire, is as true, in its essential features, of the reign of Philip, as of the times of his immediate predecessors, to whom it is consecrated.

vassals to the throne was, in general, very weak. Any diminution in the king's prospects of success was followed by the loss of a large part of his supporters, as Philip had bitter occasion to prove repeatedly in his early contests with the Angevins and the counts of Flanders. If they intrigued with the vassals of others, his rivals solicited his own followers no less. His real hold over the baronage of Artois and Vermandois, of Normandy, and even more of Anjou, Maine, Poitou and the Touraine, where his arms overcame the forces of the Plantagenets, was based far more on a well grounded fear of the consequences of the royal displeasure, than on any attachment to the throne as a center of national unity. It was the good fortune of Philip, or rather the result of his political wisdom and insight, that he early recognized the party whose territorial situation and whose affiliations with the monarchy made their interests in a large degree those of the crown. During the first few months of his reign he leaned, indeed, as his father had done, on the support of the count of Flanders. But that dependence was brief. The ascendency of Henry II. over the young monarch was accompanied by such material aid as enabled Philip to make head against the great combination which the count of Flanders and his maternal uncles brought against him. But, fortunately for the history of Philip's reign, he speedily broke with the Angevine rulers and entered into closer relations with the members of his mother's family and those politically connected with them. Thenceforth his main support, outside his own domain, lay in the territories subject to the family of Champagne and the dukes of Burgundy. They sustained the king in his life and death struggle with Richard, when all the nobles of the west were banded against him.[1] They were the foremost to uphold him in the conquest of John's territories; and in counseling him to resist papal interference in the completion of his work.[2]

Philip supported by his mother's family.

---

[1] In 1197 and 1198. Before the contest ended Richard had on his side Baldwin of Flanders, Reginald of Boulogne, Philip of Namur and his brother Henry, the count of Blois, beside the Normans, his nephew Otto of Poitou, later emperor, and the Bretons. He even secured some of the nobles of Champagne through bribing (Hoveden IV: 19); but on the death of count Henry of Champagne occuring at Acre in 1197, Philip made a new and specially close treaty of alliance and support with the new count, Theobald III., guaranteed by many nobles of Champagne, on receiving his homage in April, 1198. Text Brussel I: 116—119. In Nov. of that year a similar alliance was effected with Odo, duke of Burgundy. Rymer, Foedera I: 1: 71.

[2] See this essay p. 69, note. Blanche had renewed the close alliance with Philip. Homage, Marlène, "Amp. Coll", I: 1029, 1033, May 1201.

When the final struggle between the king and the Plantagenets became that of France against Germany and England, it was again chiefly the nobles of eastern France who rallied to the assistance of the king at Bouvines.

Dependent condition of Champagne. This close connection between Philip and the representatives of the family of his mother, already existing under counts Henry II. and Theobald III., was fostered by the dependent condition of the great county of Champagne when the death of Theobald in 1201 left an unborn heir and a disputed title.[2] Not only was the dependence of Champagne, under the administration of the widowed countess Blanche, sufficient to allow Philip to draw large sums of money from that fief,[3] and to secure for himself the control of certain of its military defences;[4] he was able to exercise a positive influence on the local administration of the country. The king was enabled

---

[1] Guil. Amor. Delaborde, I: 276.

[2] Henry II., count of Champagne, died in 1197, leaving two daughters, Alice und Philippa, who would naturally have been the heiresses of Champagne. Their legitimacy was extremely doubtful. Their mother Isabella, younger daughter of Amalaric, king of Jerusalem, and, after the death of her sister Sybilla at the siege of Acre, the heiress to the title, had been the wife of Umfred de Toron. From him she had obtained a divorce through the aid of Conrad of Monteferrat, whom she married in 1190—1. The validity of this divorce was never recognized by the pope. On the murder of Conrad in 1192 she married Henry of Champagne, then the leader of the crusaders in Syria. Of their two children, Alice married Hugh I of Cyprus; Philippa was unfortunate in her marriage as in her birth, becoming the wife of Érard of Brienne, in 1211, who was related to her within the prohibited degrees. The couple raised claims to the succession to Champagne, and found some following, especially among the relatives of Érard. Philip Augustus had already, in 1209, agreed not to bring the case to trial before the majority of Theobald V. Martène, Coll. I: 1094. This he repeated in 1213. Delisle, 1456; and in 1214, Id. 1502. But the case was forced to trial by the warlike attitude of Érard, compare Delisle, 1657. In July, 1216, it was decided at Melun by the court of the peers and barons in favor of Blanche and Theobald. Brussel, I: 651, 652. The case was thus practically ended, though the claims against Theobald continued till into the reign of Louis IX. For papal interference in favor of Blanche and Theobald see Sep. XIX: 582—586, 590, 597, 602. Migne, "Patrologia Latina" CCXVI: 971—992.

[3] e. g. Blanche paid Philip 15000 livres for the agreement of 1209. Martène, I: 1094. Delisle, Cat. 1216, 1250.

[4] At the time of her homage, Blanche delivered Brai-sur-Seine and Montereau, to be held by the king in security for her fidelity till the heir should come of age. Martène, "Anvp. Coll.", I: 1033. This was repeated in 1213, and it was further agreed that the cities of Meaux, Lagni, Provins and Coulommiers, could not be fortified till Theobald should come of age. Id I: 1125.

to make agreements respecting the Jews, which placed those of Champagne and of the royal domain under the same regulations, thus securing their permanent residence in the respective territories, and regulating their manner of business in the interests of good order and the mutual security of creditors and debtors.¹ Nor did he rest here. In August, 1215, the king issued an order regulating the weapons to be used by champions throughout Champagne, and enjoined upon the countess-regent to publish and cause it to be observed throughout her domains.² Doubtless, the unusual circumstances then existing alone rendered this exercise of the royal authority possible, but it was none the less a true intervention in the local administration of a great vassal and one which marks the highest authority attained by the monarchy under Philip Augustus over the internal affairs of a great fief, not bodily annexed, as was Normandy, to the domain.

But, in general, the power of the king to interfere in the affairs of a fief, not in the domain proper — i. e. one over which the king did not possess the direct authority of a duke or count, — was exceedingly limited. If favoring circumstances permitted Philip to prescribe certain regulations respecting the local administration of justice in Champagne, the instances were wholly exceptional. The count of Champagne, like other great vassals, had the acknowledged right to make war on the king, should the latter deny him justice in his court,³ though this right was of course limited in practice by the

Independence of the nobles.

---

¹ See text of these agreements, Brussel 1: 571 (1198 with Theobald III.), This was renewed by Blanche in May, 1201, and provided that Jews belonging to the one contracting party should not be allowed to reside or do business in the territory of the other. The case of Cresselin, in 1203—4, was in conformity with this agreement. Brussel I: 575. This was again renewed in 1210. Id. 579. In Sept., 1206, Philip entered into an elaborate convention with Blanche and Guy of Dampierre regulating the business of the Jews, the interest allowable, sealing of bonds, their custody, etc. Id. 578.

² This order is as follows: "Philippus Dei gratia Francorum rex; dilectae et fideli suae B. comitissae Trecensi, salutem et dilectionem: Noveritis quod nos, consilio bonorum virorum, et pro communi omnium utilitate statuimus quod campiones non pugnent de cetero cum baculis qui excedant longitudinem trium pedum. Proinde nobis mandamus, et per fidem quam nobis debetis vos requirimus quatinus per totam terram vestram id publice clamari faciatis et firmiter observari. Actum Parisius anno Domini Mᵘ CCᵒ XVᵒ mense Augusti." Brussel I: 320. A slightly altered text is to be found in Ordon. I: 35.

³ Charter of fidelity of Theobald V. of Champagne Feb. 1222, to Philip: "Quod ei (regi), sicut domino meo ligio bene et fideliter serviam contra omnes homines et feminas qui possunt vivere vel mori; et quod ei non deficiam de bono et fideli servitio, quando ipse michi faciet rectum curiae suae per ju-

physical possibility of opposing the king; he coined his own money,[1] and could forbid the circulation of that of others, even of the coinage of the king, in his fief;[2] he levied such taxes as he chose, and the complete administration of justice throughout his domains was in his hands. These powers of the count of Champagne were the possession of every great vassal of the crown. Under such circumstances it was the true policy of the king to add as many of these nearly independent territories to the actual domain as his force or political shrewdness could compass, and to limit the power of the other vassals in such a way as to make them increasingly dependent on the sovereign and, if not under his direct control in local affairs, at least unable to resist his will in matters of general policy.

The conquest of the Plantagenets necessary for the monarchy

As long as the king of France was overshadowed by the Anglo-Norman power in the west, and was compelled, as was Louis VII., to depend on the friendship of a vassal,[3] almost as independent and not less self-seeking, in order to resist the attacks of the Angevine rulers, the power of the king to influence the course of events in the other great fiefs of France was very slight. The whole policy of Philip was therefore bent, from the time he attained maturity enough to have a policy, toward the destruction of the Plantagenet supremacy. For this end he refused to hear the urgings of the pope that he should engage actively in the Albigensian crusade: a proposition, which, involving as it did the punishment of a vassal against whom he had good cause for anger, would, doubtless, under other circumstances have gained his ready assent.[1] For this end, he intrigued with the electors in Germany and supported rival candidates for the im-

---

dicium eorum qui me possunt et debent judicare". Text Brussel 1: 349 (date given wrongly as 1220). Chantereau-Lefebvre, "Traite des Fiefs". Proofs 115.

[1] Vuitry, "Études sur la régime financier de la France", 455 et seqq.

[2] Compare the charters of Odo III. of Burgundy, in 1195 and 1206 making agreement with the bishop of Langres that the sole standards of value at Châtillon-sur-Seine should be those of Langres and Dijon: "Quod nullae aliae monetae ibi currant, nisi Divionis et Lingonarum, aut ad scambium secundum valorem ipsarum". Brussel, I: 198.

[3] The count of Flanders, Philip d'Alsace.

[4] Letter of Philip to Innocent III. about 1208. "Et si materiam habetis conquerendi de eo (comite Tolosiae), nos similiter multam habemus materiam ad conquerendum de eo .... Et bene sciatis quod de omnibus guerris quas habuimus nullum auxilium de eo habuimus, nec per ipsum, nec per gentem suam, quamvis de nobis teneat unum de majoribus baroniis de regno nostro." Delisle, Cat. p, 512, 513.

perial throne.[1] The annexation of Normandy was, in a certain sense, a foreign conquest. The duke of Normandy was, in theory, the chief vassal of the king of France; but the real relation between the Angevins and the Capets had become that of equals and fellow-sovereigns, far more than of superior and inferior. Homage was, indeed, performed to the king of France, and the latter could, when public opinion supported him, employ the legal forms of the nominal relation to make a conquest seem the execution of a judicial sentence.[2] Yet the homage and the sentence alike were based on relations which had no longer more than a shadow of reality. The generally accredited murder of Arthur of Britanny was a most fortunate incident for the furtherance of Philip's policy; the horror which that deed awakened was speedily turned to the profit of the crown. In attacking the Plantagenet supremacy in Normandy, as in resisting the claims of the papacy to dispose of Languedoc,[3] Philip was ready to gain what aid he could from the generally accepted feudal principles of the time. But he was as ready to proceed contrary to feudal precedent when he could not otherwise attain his ends. There can be no doubt that a king who intrigued to prolong the imprisonment of Richard would have readily attacked John without the justification which the latter's relations with his vassals afforded, had he possessed the strength and had opportunity favored. It would be aside from our purpose to enter into a detailed examination of the steps which resulted in the conquest of a large part of the Angevine possessions. But it may not be inappropriate to notice that the policy which won Normandy for the crown was no ex-

---

[1] The relations of Philip to the contest in Germany have been minutely examined by Scheffer-Boichorst, "Forschungen zur deutschen Geschichte", VIII: 565—563.

[2] Compare this essay p. p. 78—80, where the attempt is made to show that the condemnation passed on John was not occasioned by the supposed murder of Arthur but was brought about by complaints on the part of his sub-vassals of Poitou in 1201 and 1202.

[3] Philip asserted the principle that in case of malfeasance on the part of the vassal the fief reverted to its overlord, which was the basis of the condemnation of John in 1202, in his letter to Innocent III. respecting the Abigensian crusade, which has been already quoted: "De eo autem quod vos predicti comitis (Tolosinae) terram exponitis occupantibus, sciatis quod a viris litteratis et illustratis didicimus quod id de jure facere non potestis, quousque idem de heretica pravitate fuerit condempnatus. Cum autem inde condempnatus fuerit, tantum demum id significare debitis et mandare ut terram illam exponamus tanquam ad feodum nostrum pertinentem." Delisle, Cat. p. 513.

ception to Philip's usual methods of procedure. The Plantagenet rule was never popular in Normandy itself; it can scarcely be said to have been more than tolerated outside of Anjou, Maine and Poitou. And the policy of Philip completely mined the ground from beneath the feet of the English sovereign. The French king was unscrupulous enough in the means he used, not only with Richard and John, but with their followers. It was a contest in which neither side hesitated to employ any weapon within its power; but if the substantial fruits came to Philip, it was through his superior insight and calculating patience, rather than through any methods which his opponents would not have stooped to use. He won the sub-vassals of the Norman duke for himself, as he had previously won the count of Boulogne and Baldwin of Guines from allegience to Flanders.[1] The chief men of Normandy were secured by gifts, promises and bribery;[2] not by

Philip's policy regarding Normandy.

---

[1] Compare Gislebert, 243.

[2] The nobles guaranteeing the peace made between John and Philip at Le Goulet, May, 1200, were Baldwin, count of Aumale, Earl William Marshall, Hugh de Gournai, William du Hommet, Robert de Harcourt, John de Préaux, William de Caieu, Roger de Toeni and Warren de Glapion. Rymer, Foedera I: 1: 79. All these were sureties on the side of John. There remained faithful to him in the contest for Normandy, Baldwin of Aumale, William Marshall and Roger de Toeni. The latter was excepted by name from the privileges of the capitulation of Rouen. Of the others, Hugh de Gournai surrendered Montfort treacherously to Philip in 1203; but the same year turned traitor to his new lord and Philip confiscated his goods. Scp. XVIII: 342. Delisle, Cat. 990. William du Hommet was a hearty supporter of Philip. Scp. XVIII: 192; Delisle, 761. Robert de Harcourt held a fief of Philip after the war, Scp. XXIII: 710. John de Préaux was on Philip's side, Brussel II: XXIV; William de Caieu also, Delisle, Cat. 1495. (in 1214). Warren de Glapion whom John had made seneschal of Normandy, was won by large gifts, Delisle, Cat. 817 B. 825 A. 933 A.

Philip gave holdings to the Mayor of Falaise immediately after the surrender of the city, Delisle, Cat. 816. The mayor of Verneuil was similarly rewarded in 1205, Id. 906, while extensive gifts were made to the nephews of the mayor of Rouen, immediately after the capture of the city, it would appear, Id. 836. The same policy was pursued in Anjou and Poitou. In 1204, Philip made agrement with Geoffrey Martel that the latter should win as many of the nobles of Anjou as possible, to the royal cause. "Noverint etc. quod nos habebamus pro imprisio nostro Galfridum Martelli, et ipse promisit nobis bona fide et sine malo ingenio quod ipse nobis serviet . . . . et nobis attrahet barones de terra quoscumque poterit." Delisle, Cat. p. 507. About 1205, Philip proposed to the count of Eu that he advance the royal cause in Poitou. To this end the king will yield to him all the royal domain in Poitou for five years and give him yearly 4000 livres, and 100 knights with 1000 foot soldiers for three months military service. Text Id. p. 510.

force, unless force was absolutely needed. The church and the monks were made his friends by protections and concessions;[1] and the growing power of the commercial classes was recognized by the establishment or confirmation of communes in many of the Norman cities.[2] The work was also aided by a policy fostering commercial intercourse with France proper.[3] Through such means Philip won the judgment of a majority of the Normans in his favor; a work which the Norman hatred of the Angevins and weariness of the long wars doubtless assisted.

Nor were Philip's measures to secure the great province so won less painstaking. The property of the comparatively small body of nobles, who refused to recognize his authority, he confiscated;[4] and he exchanged estates near Paris, lying therefore under his immediate supervision, for the holdings of some whose loyalty to the new regime, though not wholly refused, was yet questionable.[5] The lands which came into the king's hands, as successor to the Norman dukes or by confiscation from the baronage were, in large part, distributed among his followers, so that the country was well leavened

---

[1] Philip granted freedom of election to all the sees in Normandy. Philippide, VIII: 241. His protection was extended to great numbers of monasteries. Delisle, Cat. 637, 689, 827, 839, 899, 1062, 1125 etc.

[2] Such privileges were granted or confirmed, in 1204, at Andeli, Falaise, Caen, also at Niort, Poitiers and St. Jean d'Angeli, Delisle, Cat. 804, 815, 830, 847, 877, 878. In 1207 the commune of Rouen was confirmed. Id. 1024.

[3] About Oct., 1204, Philip issued an ordinance making the money of Tours, rather than that of Angers, the standard of exchange in Normandy. Text, Delisle 507. In Feb., 1205, he exempted the inhabitants of Nonancourt, Verneuil and Breteuil from many taxes for rights of passage in Normandy, Poitou, Anjou, Maine, Brittany and Gascony. Ordon. XI: 289, XII: 506. In Jan., 1210, regulations for commerce were made by the representatives of Paris and Rouen, in the presence of the king. Delisle. 1185, 1186.

[4] About 1204 Philip announced that he had added to his domain the barony of Gravenchon, which had belonged to the count of Évreux, the lands of the count of Varenne, of the earl of Arundel, of the earl of Leicester, of Geoffrey de Sai, of lord Clare, of the count of Meulan; the barony of Montfort, which had been held by Hugh de Montfort; the lands of Robert Bertran, of William de St. Jean, the barony of Moutiers-Hubert, and all the lands of knights then in England. Delisle, Cat. 887. The territories expressly named in this charter were but a part of the confiscations; compare Id. 799, 906, 907, 933 A, 935, 972, 982 etc.

[5] Instances will be cited in considering Philip's general policy of territorial exchanges.

with a distinctively loyal element;[1] yet, in Normandy at least, this change did not displace the ancient tenants of the fiefs to an extent sufficient to render Philip's rule generally unpopular among them. But the chief means by which Normandy was made an integral part of the kingdom was by its direct incorporation with the royal domain; a step which placed the province under the immediate administration of the king and made the monarchy master of forces greater than those of any single vassal of the crown.

and other territories gained by him. Substantially the same policy was pursued in respect to Vermandois and Artois; though the latter, as the heritage of the crown prince Louis, was placed under his more immediate oversight. The less settled state of Maine, Anjou and Poitou compelled Philip to adopt a modified system of administration for those provinces, as we shall have occasion to see, yet even there the general policy of the king was not essentially different. In Brittany, Philip instituted a new line of dukes by the marriage of its heiress with Peter Mauclerc, a son of a line nearly related to the royal house,[2] but whose unforeseen disloyalty was yet to tax the powers of Philip's successors. But, though Brittany thus remained outside the royal domain, the king was careful to reserve to himself the fidelity of the Breton sub-vassals.[3]

Favoring circumstances. The methods employed against the Angevins were those used by Philip against his other neighbors. He embraced any opportunity to enter into negociations with their sub-vassals and create a party for himself. And in this policy his statesmanship was greatly aided by

---

[1] The catalogue of M. Delisle enumerates over fifty such gifts made during the four years from Oct., 1203, to Oct., 1207. They were little less numerous for many years thereafter. These fiefs were not only presented to distinguished nobles, such as Robert de Courtenai, Robert, count of Dreux, or Bartholomew de Roie; they were given also to commanders such as Henry Clement the Marshall, and Cadoc the leader of the mercenaries. Squires, sergeants, archers, falconers and even servants of the royal kitchen were recipients of the same bounty.

[2] Peter Mauclerc was the son of Robert II. of Dreux and great grandson of Louis VI. He married Alice, daughter of Constantia, duchess of Brittany, by her third husband, Guy de Thouars, about January, 1213, and received with Alice the duchy from Philip, who had held control of it since the defection of Guy in 1206.

[3] Peter, in doing homage to Philip for Brittany, Jan. 27, 1213, agreed not to receive the homage of his Breton subjects without reserving the fidelity which they owed to the king of France. "Ego Petrus..... juravi.... quod ego hominagia et fidelitates Britonum nequaquam accipiam, nisi salva fidelitate domini nostris regis Francie Philippi". Teulet, Layettes, 1; 387.

the accidents of his situation. Not to speak of the quarrels between king John and the baronage in England, and the contests for the imperial crown in Germany, the situation of many of the fiefs of France was such as to further his plans. The early death, or crusading zeal, of several of his most powerful vassals, notably Baldwin of Flanders and Theobald III. of Champagne, left minorities which permitted active royal interference in their fiefs. Baldwin's absence from France, and his death soon after attaining the imperial crown at Constantinople, removed from Philip's path the one who would have been his chief opponent in the conquest of Normandy. The lapse of a large number of fiefs into the female line, and among them some of the most important, Flanders, Brittany, Boulogne, Nevers, afforded opportunities for the exercise of the royal prerogative of regulating the marriages of such heiresses, which the king was not slow to use to secure those suzerainties for those whom he believed would be his partisans. A great movement of religious fanaticism reduced the whole south of France to political helplessness, without an effort on Philip's part in the slightest degree commensurate with the benefit which the monarchy derived from the destruction of the well-nigh complete independence of Languedoc.

These events, partly the result of fortunate circumstances, but made fruitful by a political skill which could turn them to profit, rendered Philip the strongest power in France. The failure of any combination of the barons to break his purposes, the steady growth of the royal domain and consequently of the royal resources, rendering the king increasingly superior to his great vassals in the forces at his disposal and increasingly independent of their aid, made Philip a sovereign who, instead of shrinking before the Angevins and depending for support on the count of Flanders, as his father had done, was a foe worthy of the forces of England and Germany. No serious opposition from the baronage disturbed the years after the battle of Bouvines. The result.

Much of this success in bending the vassalage to his plans was doubtless due to the system of guarantees which Philip began to employ early in his reign, and which he used, with increasing frequency, to its close. By this device the nobles of a district were bound under pledges, sometimes of definite sums of money to be forfeited in case of non-compliance with the royal wishes, sometimes of personal aid to the king in compelling their fellow vassals to perform The system of sureties.

agreements with the monarch or to remain faithful to him.[1] During Philip's later years scarcely any important contract was entered into between the king and his baronage, the fulfillment of which was not thus secured to him. The faithfulness of the individual was thus made the concern of all the nobles of the district, and not only of the nobles, the communes also lent their guarantee to enforce the wishes of the king. The result of this system was to make the

[1] A few examples, from the years 1211 and 1212, when the danger of attack from England and Germany was imminent, and Philip was planning counter-moves to frustrate the schemes of Reginald of Boulogne, whose treachery had just been discovered, may be cited to show the application of the system.

In Sept., 1211, Enguerran, vicedominus of Picquigni (near Amiens) promised fidelity to Philip and that he would not aid Reginald of Boulogne, Otto, or John. This was guaranteed by Thomas de St. Valeri and Reginald d'Amiens. The latter, in the following month, made a similar pledge to Philip, guaranteed in turn by Enguerran of Picquigni. Delisle, Cat. 1302, 1304. On Jan. 22. 1212, Ferrand of Portugal, the new count of Flanders, made a promise of fidelity which he was distined soon to break, but which was guaranteed by the châtelains of Ghent and Lens, by John de Nesle and the dowager countess Matilda. Sep. XVIII: 589. Delisle 1323—27. Teulet, Layettes, I: 374.

Philip felt sensitive to the danger of attack from the possessions still held by John beyond the Loire, and fearful of the effect of John's promises and money on the fickle nobles of Anjou and the Touraine. A marriage having been agreed upon between Drogo de Mello the younger, to whom he had intrusted the important fortresses of Loches and Châtillon-sur-Indre in 1205 (Martène "Amp. Coll." I: 1053), and a daughter of Sulpicius d'Amboise, Philip had the young man's fidelity guaranteed by his father, Drogo de Mello, then constable of France, his two brothers, G. de Trainel and Guy de Dampierre, and by Itier de Touci, William de Garlande, and Manasses de Mello. Teulet, Layettes, I: 377. Probably he felt more apprehension regarding Amauri de Craon than the son of his constable. At all events, he required the sureties of the latter to pledge a money forfeit should Amauri fail to put his castle of Chautocé, near Angers, at the king's disposal. The pledges were Robert, count of Alençon, 1000 livres; Juhel de Mayenne, 1000; William des Roches, [1000?], Bernard de la Ferté, 300; Ralph, viscount of Beaumont, 500; Robert de Pernai 300; Rotrod de Montfort, 500; Gervais de Pruillé, 300; Hamelin de "Rootra", 200 and Guy Turpin, 200. Teulet, Id. 375, 376. Marlène "Amp. Coll." I: 1099. (Both instances are of Feb. 1212). Meanwhile the over-hasty crown prince had compelled Ferrand of Flanders to yield him Aire and Saint-Omer. Philip, probably partly to restrain his son and partly to secure the fidelity of the territory just acquired, had the fidelity of Louis guaranteed by the nobles and cities of Artois. (Feb. and Mch., 1212). The sureties were Michael de Harnes; John, châtelain of Lens; William of Béthune; Alard and Reginald of Croisilles; Baldwin de Commines, châtelain of Aire; William, châtelain of St. Omer and the mayors, officers, and communes of Aire, Bapaumes, Hesdin and St. Omer. Teulet, Layettes, I: 374, 375.

smaller vassals almost wholly dependent on the crown in matters affecting the general policy of the king. It was impossible for them to go counter to the royal wishes so long as the powerful vassals in their neighborhood were their sponsors to the king and were favorable to the monarch. On the other hand, the great nobles were strongly restrained by the necessity of encountering the opposition of their sub-vassals and numerous small neighbors.[1] The system of guarantees enabled Philip greatly to extend the employment of a strict mode of tenure for such of the border fortresses as were held in fief — a tenancy at the pleasure of the king — the return of the castle at the king's demand being assured by the pledges of the nobles and subjects of the vicinage, the representatives of the non-noble class being the mayors and communes of the cities.[2]

According to the statement of Rigord, the cognomen Augustus was given by that writer to Philip by reason of the increase in the royal domain effected by the king.[3] The title was a happy one, for it describes at once the most striking fact of Philips reign and the

Extent and increase of the domain.

[1] The fidelity of the great vassals was often pledged by their vassals, who entered into agreement to turn against them in case of disloyalty to Philip. The agreements of Blanche, regent of Champagne, in May, 1201, (Brussel II: xxii); of Alice, the widowed duchess of Burgundy, in 1218, (Delisle, Cat. 1844—1848); and of Theobald IV. of Champagne, in 1222, are examples of the use of this security.

The charter of Odo III. duke of Burgundy, in 1201, guaranteeing to Philip that William de Chanlite would not fail to answer Hervey, count of Nevers, before the royal court, and abide by the conditions that the king might fix (Teulet, Layettes I: 225); and the pledge of future good conduct, given by Peter, châtelain of Béthisi, in 1220, for Stephen le Gruier, whom the king had pardoned of murder (Id. 501), may be cited as illustrations of the use of pledges of nobles for their dependents. Sometimes the nobles appealed to were unwilling to take the responsibility. Thus, in 1202, Hugh count of Rethel, being unable to obtain Blanche of Champagne as surety, assigned one of his fiefs in pledge to Philip. Id. 231.

[2] Examples of such pledges to give up fortresses at the royal demand are fairly numerous. E. g. for Ivri and Avrilli, in 1200, (Delisle, Cat. 632); Beausart, 1203, Id. 767—769; Montrésor, 1205, Id. 947—950; Argenton, 1209, Id. 1149—1154, 1165; Cours, Id. St. Paul, 1210, Id. 1188; Guarplic, Id. 1238; Palluau, 1211, Id. 1254; Marcheville, Id. 1293; Lavardin, 1212, Id. 1338; Chantocé Martène, Coll. I: 1099; Sulli, 1218. Id. I: 1133; Chantecoq. 1218, Delisle, 1829; St. Remi-des-Plains, Id. 1810; Amboise, Montrichard, Fresnai, Beaumont, St. Suzanne, 1221, Id. 2049; Aigremont, 1222, Martène, Coll. I: 1164, Dreux, 1223, Delisle 2223; Ham, Id. 2226 etc. On the system of tenure returnable at the royal pleasure, compare Boutaric, "Institutions Militaires de la France". 130—132.

[3] Delaborde I: 6.

means by which he was able to raise the monarchy to a degree of power far beyond that of any of the kings of the third race who had preceeded him. The exact extent of the territory of which the king was the immediate proprietor, at the beginning of the reign of Philip Augustus, is difficult to ascertain. The former view, that the domain was a compact and circumscribed entity, like the duchy of Normandy for example, has been abandoned in the face of evidence that, beside the two hereditary territories of the Capetians, the Ile-de-France and the Orléanais, and the estates in the neighborhood of Bourges to which Philip I. added that city and Dun-le-Roi by purchase in 1101, the monarchy possessed various scattered holdings in territories outside of what has usually been considered the royal domain.[1] The first exact information regarding its extent is the treasury account of 1202,[2] — a period at which Philip Augustus had already made significant additions. But, though we do not know its composition under Louis VII. in the minutest detail, the portions beyond the limits of the Ile-de-France, the Orléanais and Berri were comparatively insignificant; the scantiness of our information regarding them is a proof of their unimportance. Such a domain did not equal the possessions of the house of Anjou, it was not as large as the territories ruled by the family of Champagne and Blois.

Conquest and inheretance It was Philip's good fortune to increase the domain to more than double its size, as held by his father, and to make the French monarch the immediate lord of by far the largest single holding in the kingdom of France. The conquest of the Angevine possessions of Normandy, Anjou, Maine, Touraine and Poitou, with the Norman dependency of Brittany, was followed, as has been noticed, by the addition of all save Brittany to the domain. Through the death of Elizabeth, countess of Flanders, in 1182, Philip became heir to Vermandois, and entered into full possession after the demise of Philip of Flanders

---

[1] The work of Brussel is a source from which writers have not hesitated to declare the exact extent of the domain under Louis VII., and under even earlier kings, by elimination from the record of provostries in the account of 1202. Even M. Vuitry, "Etudes sur le régime financier de la France", 169, 190, has fallen into this error. But M. Luchaire, Inst. Mon. I: 86, points out that the royal domain cannot be so strictly defined.

[2] Brussel. Usage des Fiefs, II: cxxxix et seqq. Philip had added Amiens and dependencies, Arras, Lens, Pierrefons, Péronne, Bapaumes, Vernon, Evreux, Paci-sur-Eure, Anet, Meullent, Gien and Montargis, at least, to the list of 1202. See Vuitry's correction of Brussel's list, "Etudes" etc. 168.

and Eleanor, countess of Beaumont, the sister of Elizabeth.[1] Eleanor's death added Valois also to the royal possessions. Artois came to him as the dowry of his first queen and the heritage of prince Louis.

But force of arms, or hereditary succession, were not the only means by which the direct possessions of the crown were increased under Philip's wise policy; though from these two sources, naturally, the greatest additions were derived. The king strove to gain and keep positions of strength on the borders of the territories owning fealty to the great vassals. Acting on this principle in 1196, Philip assigned crown property near Senlis, worth 800 livres yearly, to Richard de Vernon and Richard, son of the latter, whose allegiance had been transferred to him by the terms of the peace made with Richard of England, on Jan. 15, of that year. The king received in exchange Vernon and Longueville.[2] He thus secured immediate control of a strong position on the Seine, just as it crosses the Norman border and commanding the usual route of travel between Paris and Rouen; while the barons who had lately owned the suzerainty of his rival were removed to a region distinctly faithful to the crown. When Normandy had been won, the same policy of exchange served to strengthen the royal grasp on the new acquisition. Thus in the latter part of 1204, Philip assigned St. Leger-en-Iveline and its dependencies to Amicia de Montfort, who, in turn, transferred to him Breteuil, and all that her brother, the earl of Leicester, had possessed

Exchanges.

---

[1] Elizabeth, wife of Philip of Flanders, was heir of her brother Ralph II. the Leper, and received of him Vermandois, Amiénois and Valois. She was great-granddaughter of Henry I. of France. In default of other heirs, Philip could claim succession "jure hereditario" (Rigord 40), or as relapsing to the crown. One such heir existed in her sister, Eleanor, countess of Beaumont-sur-Oise, wife of Matthew the royal chamberlain. Philip of Flanders being too powerful a claimant for Eleanor to resist, the latter was glad to relinquish her claims to the Amiénois and Vermandois to the king, in exchange for the enjoyment of Valois, After much contest the count of Flanders had to consent to the retention of the Amiénois and Vermandois by his royal nephew and Eleanor of Beaumont, with the exception of a small portion. (1185) Gislebert 164, 165. Philip at the same time gained Noyon, Corbie, Montreuil-sur-mer and St. Riquier as well. (Id.) A treaty in 1191, with Eleanor, allowed the latter the continued enjoyment of the Valois, with St. Quentin and some other places in Vermandois in addition. Delisle, Cat. 354. These territories were left by Eleanor to Philip, on her demise without children, about 1213; compare Id. 1587. The homage of certain portions being due to the churches of Amiens and Noyon, Philip secured these rights in 1185 and 1203, respectively, by concessions to the churches, Martène "Amp. Coll." I: 965, 1112.

[2] Martène "Amp. Coll." I: 1008. Teulet, Layettes I: 186. The peace, Id. 182.

on the Norman side of the channel.¹ About the same time, a similar exchange transferred the dowry which the widowed queen of Richard of England, Berengaria, enjoyed at Falaise, Domfront and Bonneville-sur-Touque, to the French monarch, who gave in return the newly captured city of Le Mans.² The fief of Domfront, thus acquired, was speedily made over by Philip, with other holdings, to Reginald of Boulogne, in exchange for the fortress of Mortimer; gaining for the monarchy a strong advance post on the boundary of Normandy and Ponthieu.³ The same policy induced Philip, as early as 1193, to strengthen his line toward Flanders by the acquisition of Pierrefont, by the gift of lands near Paris to Gaucher de Châtillon.⁴ He had already obtained the suzerainty of Pierrefont, by surrender of the right of entertainment enjoyed by the king at the expense of the bishop of Soissons.⁵ An additional position of strength, on the same exposed side of the domain, came wholly into the king's hands by the purchase, in 1210, of Brai-sur-Somme from Walter, châtelain of Péronne, for 4100 livres, money of Paris.⁶ The frontier of the Loire attracted no less of the royal notice. In 1206 Philip strengthened his position in the Touraine by assigning a Norman fief and certain revenues to Andrew de Vitré and his brother Robert, the "cantor" of the church at Paris, in return for Langeais, which Robert had held from the unfortunate Arthur of Brittany.⁷ The new administrative regime in those regions was ushered in by the assignment of most of Anjou to its seneschal, William des Roches; but the king expressly reserved for his immediate control the border land of the Touraine and the fortresses of Chinon, Bourgueil, Loudon and Saumur.⁸ These reservations were, for the most part, repeated when Amauri de Craon succeeded William de Roches in 1222.⁹ Similiar motives induced Philip to add the fortress of Issondun to his estates in Berri, in 1221, by exchange and purchase from the heirs of Culan.¹⁰ The royal policy was evidently to gain control of the strong posts on the frontiers.

[1] Martène "Amp. Coll." I: 1048. Teulet, I: 271.
[2] Martène, Id. 1046.
[3] Compare Id. I: 1047 and Teulet, I: 269, 270.
[4] Martène, "Amp. Coll." I: 1004.
[5] In 1185 or 1186. Teulet, Id. I: 144.
[6] Martène, "Amp. Coll." I: 1097. Teulet, Id. I: 350.
[7] Martène, "Amp. Coll." I: 1067.
[8] Sep. XVII: 215.
[9] Martène, Id. I: 1166.
[10] Id. I: 1158. Teulet, Layettes, I: 521.

The opportunities afforded by changes in the succession to fiefs were made sources of increase to the domain. The history of Nevers affords several illustrations. Its count, William V., having died in 1181, Philip took the wardship of the county and, in 1184, married its heiress, Agnes, to Peter of Courtenay, his cousin.[1] The latter resigned Montargis to the king, as the price of his favor.[2] A quarrel having arisen in 1199 between Peter, now count of Nevers, and his neighbor, Hervey of Donzi, Philip aided the latter with mercenaries, and the defeated Peter of Courtenay was compelled to give up his daughter and heiress, Matilda, whom he had affianced to Philip of Namur, to the victorious Hervey and, together with her, all the county of Nevers save a life tenure of Auxerre and Tonerre. But the new count of Nevers had to pay for the royal aid by the relinquishment of Gien to the king.[3] The homage due from this fief to the bishop of Auxerre was purchased by the monarch, in 1204, (in conformity with the principle always asserted by Philip that it was beneath the dignity of the crown to do homage to any authority, lay or ecclesiastical), by the surrender of the procurations due at Auxerre and Varzi,[4] and the union of Gien with the domain was complete. By an agreement of betrothal, made between Hervey and Philip Augustus, in 1215, the royal domain would eventually have been further increased, through the union of Hervey's daughter and heiress, Agnes, and Philip, eldest son of Prince Louis.[5] The untimely by death of the young prince frustrated the plan; but the marriage of Agnes to Guy, count of St. Paul, in 1221, brought a third gain to the crown from its relation to Nevers, — the young husband surrendering to the king the rights possessed in common with his brother at Pont-Sainte-Maxence, near Senlis, as the price of the royal approval.[6] The years 1218 and 1219 brought another acquisition of the same nature. Theobald VI., of Blois and Clermont, having

Opportunities through successions.

---

[1] Scp. XVIII: 251.

[2] Martène, "Amp. Coll." I: 1047.

[3] Scp. XVII: 658. The quarel was over the abbey of St. Lawrence, not far from Donzi. Id.

[4] Scp. XVIII: 726. The principle involved is expressed in Philip's charter relinquishing the procurations due from the church of Amiens in return for release from homage due that church for the newly acquired Amiénois, (1185): "voluit haec ecclesia, et benigne concessit, ut foedum suum absque faciendo hominio teneremus, cum utique nemini facere debebamus hominium, vel possimus". Martène, Id. I: 965.

[5] Scp. XVIII: 783.

[6] Teulet, Layettes, I: 516, 517.

died in the former year, his fiefs were divided between his two daughters, Margaret and Elizabeth; the former gaining Blois and the latter Chartres. For the redemption of her inheritance Elizabeth induced her sister and her brother-in-law, Walter of Avênes, to surrender Nogent to the king, — she giving an equivalent from her county of Chartres to reimburse her sister of Blois.[1]

Directly north of Paris, at a distance of only a few miles and separating the Ile-de-France from Vermandois, lay the county of Clermont-en-Beauvaisis, almost an island in the domain. The death of Theobald VI. of Blois and Clermont in 1218 left several candidates for the succession; but the king secured their rights by purchase, granting an annuity of 100 livres to Matilda, countess of Dammartin,[2] and gaining the titles of two others, Robert de la Tournelle and Guy of Senlis, the butler, by gifts of land.[3] The county of Clermont thus passed into the royal domain. The county of Alençon was gained by a similar arrangement with its heirs, in 1221, after the death of count Robert.[4] Nor was Philip less successful in securing the county of Beaumont, which lay even nearer to Paris than that of Clermont and, like that fief, was almost entirely surrounded by the royal domain. A judgment of the royal court having decided the succession in favor of Theobald d'Ulli, cousin of the late count, in 1223,[5] the new possessor abandoned to Philip a large portion of the county outright and the suzerainty of all its fiefs save four. In exchange, the king allowed him to retain certain places in the county for his profit, and paid him 7000 livres in money.[6]

Sharings. A smaller, but effective, source of increase to the royal domain was derived from the sharings effected between the king and the lesser vassals. These partitions were a source of great protection to the weaker territorial lords against their powerful neighbors, for they secured the guarantee of the sovereign to the integrity of the fief. Naturally they were usually resorted to by ecclesiastical establishments, but sharings between the king and lay vassals were not unknown. Though the small holder obtained protection, and often an increase

---

[1] Delisle, Cat. 1865, 1870, 1891. Teulet, Layettes.: 474—477.
[2] Payable by the provostry of Crespi. Delisle, Cat. 1826.
[3] Id. 1820, 1821, 1834, 1841.
[4] Id. 2020, 2028, 2142, Martène, "Coll. Amp." I: 1165, Teulet, Layettes, I: 506, 509.
[5] Martène, Id. I: 1163. Boutaric, "Actes du Parlement de Paris", I: ccci.
[6] Martène, Id. I: 1173, Delisle, Cat. 2205, 2210. Teulet, Layettes, I: 559, 561.

of privileges,[1] by dividing the benefits of his fief with the king, the gain to the monarchy was even more. The partition was usually made on the basis of an equal division of the income, save that distinctively churchly impositions like tithes, and certain portions of the church lands or buildings, were reserved as the exclusive property of religious establishments. The administration was in the hands of officers chosen jointly by the monarch and the sharer,[2] or, if not so chosen, bound by oath to each of the contracting parties. It is easy to see how such an arrangement would inure to the profit of a strong monarch, allowing him, as it did, to have control of the local administration of the fief and to use its fortifications in the interests of the crown. Philip thus gained points of vantage in the duchy of Burgundy,[3] the counties of Bourbon,[4] Sancerre[5] and Dreux,[6] the bishoprics of Auxerre,[7] of Beauvais,[8] of Laon[9] and elsewhere. How dangerous these sharings, with their usually accompanying privileges, were felt to be by the neighboring great vassals is shown by the care of Blanche, countess of Champagne, to secure a promise from Philip, in 1207, that he would effect no more such sharings on a small section of her border in the region of Sens.[10]

A similar desire to enjoy the protection of the growing monarchy led the inhabitants of certain places outside the royal domain to secure the king's pledge not to suffer them to go out of his hands. The control thus obtained by the crown was not immediate, as in the case of a sharing, the cities were not added to the actual domain,

Retention in the king's hands.

---

[1] E. g. In Jan., 1208, Philip, having been admitted to a half share in the fair of St. Taurin at Evreux, decided that the fair should continue seven days instead of one as heretofore. Delisle, Cat. 1070. Teulet, Layettes. 312, 313.

[2] "Prepositus qui in villa fuerit, per dominum regem et nos communiter ponctur, et fidelitatem nobis monachis faciet". Charter of the monks of the Charité-sur-Loire, sharing Dixmont with Philip. Teulet, Layettes, I: 148. "Prepositus autem qui ibi erit faciet fidelitatem regi et nobis." Convent of St. Lawrence. Id. 169, 170.

[3] In 1201, at Parai, Beaumont (Saône et Loire), Rigni and other places. Delisle, 865.

[4] In 1181 at Valigni, Id. 30 and in 1184 at Cusset, Id. 106. Ordon. IV: 205.

[5] Concressant, 1182, Delisle, 65, 204.

[6] Mills at Anet, 1195, Id. 458. Teulet, Id. 180.

[7] Nine mills and other property of the convent of St. Lawrence (-des-Aubats). 1192—3. Id. 374. Teulet, Id. 169.

[8] At Arnelle and Neuvi, belonging to abbey of St. Quentin de Beauvais, 1190. Delisle. 298.

[9] At Rozei in 1180, Id. 14. At Dizi, 1196. Ordon. XI: 275.

[10] Delisle, Cat. 1055.

and it was not always possible for the king to fulfil his promises; but the advantage of such agreements is obvious, — they afforded easy stepping-stones for further advances of the immediate royal administration, and they gave the monarch special claims over territories whose future was so closely linked with that of the crown. Thus, in 1204, Philip received the homage of Elias V., count of Périgord, and agreed that his territories should not go out of the royal hands.[1] At the same time the monarch made a similar promise to the commune of the city of Périgueux, which swore fidelity to him.[2] This pledge was renewed to the count of Périgord when the second successor of Elias V., Archambaud II. did homage to the king, in 1212.[3] Philip entered, at the same time, into like relations with Bertran de Born, and pledged the retention of the fortress of Hautefort under the royal protection.[4] The king's reception of the homage of John, bishop of Limoges, in 1204, was the occasion of a promise to keep him and his successors attached to the crown domain.[5] In 1210 Philip declared that the town of Charlieu was similarly placed under the care of the monarch, thus securing a place of importance in Beaujolois, situated close on the southern border of Burgundy.[6]

Protections, Where the royal promise did not go as far as to pledge the inseparable union of the territory with the crown, the royal protection, nevertheless, gave a real extension of the king's control. The frequency with which such protections were granted to religious bodies and their importance in enlarging the influence of the monarchy, has already been noticed. By far the greater number of such charters relate to ecclesiastical foundations, and such as were given for the benefit of villages and towns were usually for places belonging to convents or churches, since ecclesiastical establishments naturally felt their weakness more than lay fiefs. Thus Philip assumed protection of the village of Méves, near Bourges;[7] of that of Chevreville, near Nanteuil;[8] of Boissi-Mauvoisin, near Mantes;[9] the district of Saint-

---

[1] Delisle Cat. 821, 822. Teulet, Layettes, I: 249.
[2] Id. 823, 824. Teulet Id. 249.
[3] Delisle. 1409.
[4] Id. 1409.
[5] Id. 875.
[6] Ordon. XI: 294.
[7] In 1182—3. Delisle, Cat. 57.
[8] Belonging to Notre-Dame de Nanteuil. In 1186. Id. 169.
[9] Depending on the abbey of Fécamp. Id. 226, 897. Teulet, Layettes, I: 149—281.

André, probably in Burgundy;[1] and the village of Escurolles in Auvergne.[2] These protections not only extended the royal influence, they gave definite rights to the monarchy. At Saint André the king received half of all the revenues, at Escurolles he obtained a provost, a share in the exercise of justice, and certain taxes.

The royal protection was even extended by special charter to individuals of the non-noble class.[3] A real, if less definite, assertion of the same authority is to be seen in the privileges offered to merchants visiting the fairs of France, as for example when Philip announced, in 1185, to the traders of Flanders, Ponthieu and Vermandois that all merchants visiting the lenten fair at Compiègne should be under his guardianship.[4] Similar concessions were made to the merchants of Ypres in 1193, and, in 1209, like privileges were extended to those of Italy and other countries who should come to the fairs of the countess of Champagne.[5]

The brief chronicle recorded on the Easter tables of St. Denis declares that Philip Augustus gained, during his reign, the counties of Vermandois, Poitou, Anjou, Tours, Maine, Alençon, Clermont, Beaumont and Ponthieu.[6] It might well have added Artois, Amiénois, Valois and the great duchy of Normandy. But, had it done so, it would still have told only half the truth. The domain grew in multitudinous instances, less noticeable to the public eye, but none the less sources of strength. And when the body of the ruler had been laid to rest in the vaults of St. Denis, and the calculating and skillful brain had ceased to plan, the new monarch received a kingdom whose growth was certain, even under his bungling hand, and which was powerful because Philip had made the royal fief the largest and strongest of all the holdings of France.

Results of the reign.

This rapid increase in the territory owing immediate allegiance to the king made the question of local administration one of growing

Local Administration.

---

[1] Depending on the monastery of Montier St. Jean. In 1189, Ordon. XI: 252.

[2] Depending on the abbey of Cluni. In 1189. Ordon, XI: 261.

[3] In Oct., 1211, Philip took under his protection, for a period of ten years, Raimond Archambaud, burgher of Cahors. Delisle, Cat. 1305.

[4] Id. 123. Philip was admitted to a share in the profits of their fair Id. 147.

[5] Id 392, 1181.

[6] Sep. XVII: 423.

importance under Philip's reign. And it was a problem whose solution he attempted with his usual vigor.

<small>The Provosts.</small> At the time of his accession to the throne the immediate local representatives of the monarchy were the provosts and their sub-officers, the vicars and city beadles;[1] together with the mayors and sergeants of the villages.[2] All these officers were known by the collective title of servientes or ministerii.[3] The institution of provosts had existed, certainly, since 1046.[4] Their number was very considerable, though any enumeration before 1202 is fragmentary and uncertain.[5] It would appear, however, that one or more of these officers exercised his functions in each district of importance of which the king was the immediate territorial proprietor, or where the crown could claim a permanent revenue.[6] During the early years of Philip, as under his predecessors, these functionaries were the collectors of

---

[1] Luchaire, Instit. Mon. I: 209—215. "Tenendum esse precipimus ut prepositus noster per aliquem de servientibus suis de domo et mensa sua, qui bedelli vel abscultatores appelantur, contra burgensem aliquem nihil omnino disrationare possit". Confirmation of the privileges of Orléans, about 1187. Delisle, Cat. appendix p. 499.

[2] The mayors of communal cities were chosen by the communes: "burgensibus nostris de Bapalma concedimus ut de singulis quatuordecim mensibus in singulos quatuordecim menses, faciant novem majorem". Charter for Bapaumes, 1196, Ordon. XI: 275. But the smaller places, not enjoying communal privileges, had mayors, in some instances, who were royal officers. E. g. at Bagneux, Brussel, account of 1202, civ, ccii. At Dampierre, Delisle, Cat. 2147. A similar officer at Dun le Roi was the sergeant. In 1209 Philip ordered Hugh de la Chapelle to take this office from a certain Arnoul and give it to Hélinaud who promised to pay 10 marks yearly. Delisle, 1169. Compare Luchaire I: 215, 224

[3] "Servienti nostro, tanquam nobis ex omnibus agendis respondebitur". Charter of Roie, Ordon. XI: 231. "Neque prepositus nec aliquis serviens noster" Orléans. Delisle, appendix 498. "Quod nec ab illo episcopo nec a successoribus suis poterimus exigere procurationem, aut successores nostri, aut servientes aut nuncii nostri Terouenam venientes". Exemption for the bishops of Térouanne, 1193, Martène, "Amp. Coll" I: 1001. "Quittavinus omnes textores .... de omni demanda et introitu ministerii". Privilege for the weavers of Étampes, 1204, Ordonn XI: 286.

[4] Luchaire I: 209.

[5] Brussel, on the basis of the account of 1202—3, enumerates 45 provostries held by Philip at that time, and 4 assigned in dower to the queen mother. Usage, I: 434—440. But, unless a reduction in number had taken place since the reign of Louis VII., this list cannot by exhaustive. Compare Luchaire, II: 297 appendix.

[6] Luchaire I: 86, 211.

the royal income and the administrators of the royal estates.[1] Save in places exempted by special privilege, their judicial cognizance extended to all but the most flagrant crimes. They superintended the execution of judicial sentences, exercised police authority and possessed certain military powers.[2] They represented the interests of the king in the places which enjoyed the degree of local self-government granted by a communal charter. They were, therefore, the direct agents of the crown in all matters of local administration. Their aggressiveness and persistence in attacking the powers of the clergy and small nobles, as well as their exactions from the non-noble class, doubtless aided the process of consolidation of the royal power in the crown domain which had gone on under Louis VI. and VII., and which had broken down serious opposition to the king, on the part of the vassals in the neighborhood of Paris, before the accession of Philip. Nevertheless the system was, at best, very imperfect. A large part of the efforts of the crown were required to repress the tyranny and exactions of these agents. A certain degree of control was exercised over the provosts and their assistants by the seneschal, — how or to what extent the absence of definite record makes it impossible to define.[3] But this superintendence by a single person, whose office was a fief of honor and not a mere tenancy at the king's good pleasure, and who was moreover a noble with vast estates of his own to draw his interests away from the royal service, was not likely to be very effective, even if the nominal powers of the seneschal over the provosts were considerable. Two causes tended to render the provosts comparatively independent of the royal authority though acting in the name of the king, and hence greatly reduced their value to the crown. The first was the semi-feudal character of their tenure of office, going so far, in some instances, as to render the post hereditary,[4] and tending to makes its holder a petty vassal rather than a direct exponent of the central authority of the sovereign.

---

[1] In 1185 the Patriarch of Jerusalem and prior of the Hospital came to France to ask aid for the Holy Land: "quo audito Philippus..... honorifice recepit diligentissime prepositis terre sue sive dispensatoribus precipiens, quod, ubicunque per terram suam irent, de reditibus regis sufficientes expensas illis ministrarent". Rigord, Delaborde I: 47.

[2] Compare on the powers of the provosts, Luchaire I: 219—223.

[3] Compare this essay, page 41.

[4] See Luchaire I: 231, 232 and the Charter of Joscelin de Thouri relinquishing his provostry of Flagi, which he held "jure hereditario," to Louis VII, 1177. Id. appendix II: 307.

The second and even more disastrous cause is that, by the time of Philip, much of the revenue of the provostries was made a matter of sale, being farmed out for a definite yearly sum to their holders.[1] It became, naturally, the concern of the provosts to make as much as possible out of their charges; a desire which was not likely to advance the interests of the crown. Hence the curious spectacle, which meets us all through the twelfth and early part of the thirteenth centuries, of the granting, by the monarchy, of exemptions from the jurisdiction of the royal officers, to most of the cities and many of the country districts of the domain.

Independence of the sub-officers.
Nor was the independence of the minor officers, who still survived from the old Carolingian constitution, less considerable. Certain of the vicars had become wholly feudal and hereditary. Their rights were bought and sold, they passed into the hands of new possessors by marriage.[2] In many of the cities the vicars were still removable, but at Paris, at least under Philip, the office was given for life.[3]

The great nobles had local administrative officers similar in name and function to those of the crown.

Necessity of a reform.
It is plain that the necessity of reform must have impressed itself on a young and vigorous ruler whose plans for conquest abroad demanded a vigorous judicial and financial administration of his own domain. Possibly one of the great nobles may have shown the monarch the path to be persued by an earlier change in his own

---

[1] In the account of 1202—3 the provostries are accounted to the treasury in three equal payments, at the three reckoning terms of the year. Thus, for example, the provostry of Sens paid 200 l. at each term, Orléans 406 l. 13 s. 4 d. Compiègne etc. 876 l. 13 s. 4 d. Lorris, 193. 6. 8. Paris, 1233. 6. 8. etc. A few are reported in one or two payments, e. g. Poissi, Meulan, Villeneuve-en-Beauvaisis. These were not the sole returns of the provosts, as we shall have occasion to see; but they prove clearly that, in 1202, the greater part of the revenues of each provostry were in farm. A custom as universal as this could not have been a sudden change of policy, and it is therefore well-nigh unquestionable that the provostries must have been held in farm before the reform of 1190.

[2] In 1202, Theobald de Maudâtour gave the church of St. Denis his rights over the vicarage of Boissi-Laillerie. Delisle, Cat. 721. In 1207, Payen de Reuil sold his vicarage, "voirie," to the prior of St. Denis for 600 l. to satisfy his debts to the king's Jews. Id. 1065. A sale of the post at Chatillon is recorded in 1205, Id. 919. Instances of claims by marriage. Id. 1389.

[3] In Mch., 1222, Philip gave Hescelin, his sergeant, a life tenure of the vicarage of Paris. He was the son of Aleaume Hescelin or de la Porte, who had been freed from tallia in 1192. Delisle 366, 2140.

officers.¹ But, however that may be, Philip embraced the occassion offered by the installation of the regency and the readjustment of his government at home, on the eve of his departure for the crusade of 1190, to introduce the change in the local administration. It was no hasty step. It had been discussed in the circle of the king's immediate council,² and was proclaimed in the charter defining the powers of the regency. The essence of the reform consisted in the appointment of an officer, to be known as the bailiff, baillivus, in each important district of the royal domain.³ This officer should administer justice in the weightier cases, collect the more valuable and more uncertain revenues and have a general superintendence of the work of the provosts. To aid in the latter task, and probably to render the introduction of the new system more effective by restraining any opposition that the provosts might be disposed to make to it, the bailiffs were, during the absence of the monarch on the crusade, to appoint four men of good reputation in each provostry, without the consent of at least two of whom no business was to be transacted.⁴ In cases of flagrant crime, the bailiff was empowered summarily to remove the provost; for minor offences he should report

<small>The Bailiff's.</small>

---

¹ M. A. Lefèbvre, "Bibliotheque de l'École des Chartes" 1860, pp. 179—188, attempts to prove that bailiffs existed in Brie under the rule of the counts of Champagne as early as 1161. He does not, however, demonstrate that they held the position in the administrative hierarchy given them by Philip in 1190, nor is the term bailiff in the charter of 1161 and 1178, which he cites, necessarily employed in other than the general sense commonly given to it in the XII Cent.; that of agent.

² Compare this essay p. 61.

³ "Et in terris nostris que propriis nominibus distincte sunt baillivos nostros posuimus". Will of Philip Rigord, Delaborde 100. We have no information as to which lands these were in 1190. Probably they were substantially the same as appear in the account of 1202—3. i. e. Paris, Senlis, Arras, Gisors, Étampes, Sens, Orléans and apparently Vermandois. In the "Scripta de Foedis", Sep. XXIII, we find Berri; (compare an order of Philip to Gilbert de Chanceaux and Matthew Dreu, Jan. 1213. "balliviam vestram". Martène Thesaurus Anec. I: 825.) Philip extended the system to his conquests. The "Scripta de Foedis" gives us the bailiwicks of Rouen, Caen, Côtentin, Bayeux, Bonneville, Caux and Verneuil in Normandy. The later bailiwick of Amiens seems to have been administred by the provost under Philip. Brussel I: 487. That of Paris was accounted for by the two provosts in 1217 and 1219. Id. 482, 483. Brussel gives a bailiff at Tours in 1217. Id. 489. compare also Sep. XVII: 305 where a bailiff of Tours is recorded in 1220.

⁴ Will of Philip, section I. The king himself appointed the advisers at Paris, who were there six in number. Their special functions have already been considered.

the delinquent to the king.¹ The bailiff himself was required to hold a monthly court for the prompt administration of justice, or, if the crime was one demanding royal cognizance, for preliminary examination and record.² The results of these assizes were to be reported three times a year to the regents at Paris, on the day specially appointed for considering the state of the kingdom.³ Such are the main features of the system, at its introduction, as presented by Philip's testament.

<small>Not a new title; but a new office.</small> The term bailiff was not a new one. It was in general use previous to 1190, but not as indicating an officer superior to the provost. Its employment was rather indefinite, indicating customarily an agent; though it was occasionally used to designate an officer subordinate to a provost, as the term balliva sometimes denoted a subdivision of a provostry.⁴ This loose use of the title persisted, in some instances, even after the system introduced in 1190 had long been in operation.⁵ But if the designation was not novel, the office, as instituted by Philip, was new; and the bailiff was thenceforth the most important representative of the monarchy in the field of local administration. Being distinctly a royal rather than a feudal officer, holding his position by crown appointment and never by purchase or heredity, the bailiff was far more likely to serve the interests of the crown than the provost, whose prime concern was naturally to recoup himself for the outlay required to secure his post. His official superiority to the provost was strengthened by his social preëminence, for the bailiffs were usually, though not invariably, selected from

---

¹ Will of Philip sections 6, 7. "Baillivos autem nostros non poterunt amovere regina et archiepiscopus a bailliviis suis nisi pro murtro, vel raptu, vel homicidio, vel proditione; nec baillivi prepositos, nisi pro aliquo istorum". Rigord, 102.

² Id. section 2.

³ Id. sections 3, 4.

⁴ Compare Luchaire, Instit. Mon. 214. See Delisle, Cat. 224, where Philip invites the mayor of Étampes and the provosts and bailliffs of Janville, Dourdan and Poissi to meet a St. Jean-en-Vallée. 1188. In 1183 Philip granted privileges to those dwelling in Orléans, the bailiwick of St. Martin, of St. Jean etc. Ordon. XI: 226. In one section of the "Scripta de Foedis" balliva seems to be used in the sense of the provostry itself. Scp. XXIII: 689—693.

⁵ In 1217 Philip ordered the bailiffs of Meulan, Mante, Vernon, Andeli and Rouen charged with the collection of water customs, to grant free passage to the boats of the monks of Notre-dame de Voeu. Delisle, Cat. 383. In 1203 Philip gave Beaumont-le-Roger to Guy de la Roche, and the next year, probably, the king addressed an order. "Amico et fideli suo Guidone de Rupe, vel ballivis ejus", requiring the prompt payment of certain alms to the monks of Lyra. Martène, "Amp. Coll." 1: 1042.

the noble class;[1] while the provostries fell more and more into the hands of wealthy burghers. In general, the bailiffs seem to have come from the same rank of lower nobility which furnished so many of the royal counselors.

The prime function of bailiffs and provosts alike was the administration of the revenue. It was from their position as officers of finance and agents in the management of the domain that their other attributes followed; but, as we have seen in the case of the royal counselors, they united the most varied powers. Yet the establishment of the bailiffs, dividing as it did the authority hitherto exercised by the provosts, was a decided step toward that subdivision of governmental employment essential to administrative effectiveness.

Duties of Bailiffs and Provosts.

The Account of 1202—3 shows us the nature of the partition in the collection of the revenues between the bailiffs and provosts. That record is in two main divisions, entitled respectively, praepositurae and balliviae. Under the former head the receipts from the fixed rents paid in by the provosts are entered. The sources of this income are not given, only the sum paid for the farm is recorded in the treasury roll. But the revenues sold to the provosts were those derived from ovens, mills, presses, taxes on markets, halls and stalls, imposts on certain trade organizations, the products of meadows, streams, etc.[2] In addition to the definite sum returned to the treasury for the farm of these items, the receipts of the praepositura included the payments formerly made to the seneschal, but received by the king since that office was in abeyance.[3] Charged against this indebtedness of the provosts to the treasury, were certain expenses for city guards,[4] for repairs of fortifications, granaries, bridges and other

The administration of the revenues.

---

[1] Compare the partially complete list of bailiffs given by Brussel, "Usage" I: 486. A striking example of a bailiff taken from the non-noble class is Cadoc, the chief of the mercenaries in Philip's service. He held court, as bailiff of the king, at Bernay in 1210. Delisle, "Mémoires de l'Acad. des Inscriptions," XXIV: pt. 2. p. 357.

[2] Brussel I: 432 enumerates these items, which are doubtless those usually farmed to the provosts. Probably the custom was not always uniform. In the account of 1202 the pressoragio of Samois is entered under the receipts of the balliviae, though paid to the provost. Brussel II: cl. The bailiff of Étampes receives "pro piscibus stamparum xl l." Id. cciv.

[3] Account of 1202—3. Brussel II. cxxxix—cxlvi. At Paris the receipt of the "tallia" on bread and wine was paid to the praepositura, Id. clxxxiv, clxxxix. That of Orléans under the title balliviae Id. cl.

[4] "XX servientes pedites Braii, lxx libras provinensis" provostry of Sens. Account. Id. cxxxix. "Viginti servientes Mosterolii" Moret Id. cxlii. These were the cities which Philip had received in pledge from Blanche of Cham-

structures in their charge;[1] for the payment of many chaplains and the discharge of various pensions;[2] for the maintainance of hunters, fishers, falconers, wolf and fox killers,[3] who were probably under the supervision of the provosts. The incidental expenses of some excercises of justice were also paid by them.[4]

In the account entitled balliviae, on the other hand, were entered the returns of the main items of the unfarmed revenue, whether collected by the bailiffs themselves, the provosts,[5] the châtelains,[6] or by special agents of the government without any official designation.[7] The income of the balliviae embraced the seigneurial expleta;[8] the payments in kind, such as wine, grain or fowls;[9] the forests;[10] the head-money, talliae, and mortmain exacted from the

pagne in May, 1201. "Simon et custodes turris xvii l & iiiis, de tertio anno." Pars. Id. clxvi.

[1] New gates, Orleans, Id. cxl. Granary, Chapelle, Id. Mills and ovens, Paci. Id. cxlvii, Bridges, Bréval, Id. cxlv. Tourotte, clxx etc.

[2] Chaplains at Sens, Chateauneuf, Étampes, Lorris, Pontoise, Paris etc. Id. Many pensions to private individuals, lepers, churches etc. may be found in the account of 1202. They are too abundant to cite examples. Compare also Delisle, Cat. 27, 1826, Sep. XVIII; 740.

[3] E. g. "pro venatoribus .. liiii, l & xi, s." Béthisi. Account of 1202, Id. cxliv. "Venatores, xx, l" id. clxxi. "Piscatoribus, xxxvs. Roie etc. Id. clxx. "Eustachius falconarius" Moret, Id. cxlii. "Giradus falconarius", Paris. id. cxlvi. "Lupari", Lorris, cxl. "Luparius", Moret cxlii etc. The number of these payments testify to the great prevalence of wolves and the efforts for their extirpation at this time. "Vulpeculator, de ultimo tertio, xix.l, vi,d. minus", Moret Id. cxc. "Gopillator", cxlii. etc.

[4] "Curia Dei x. lib." Orleans, Id. cxl. "Curia Dei c. s." Vitri Id. "Pro v judiciis et pro apparatu. xl.s Moret, Id. cxlii.

[5] E. g. "De praeposito Loriaci. De vavasoribus, lxxii.l . . . . et pro vasselamento Romandi, xxxv.l." Id. clxxv. "R praepositi Pontisariae. De bolengariis, xxxi.l & xs." R praepositi Gressi et Capellae. De taliis. iicl. Id. clxxvi. Such items, though paid in by provosts, are entered under the head of bailliviae.

[6] E. g. "R castellani Bitur. (Bourges) . . . . De Renando de Montefaucon, iic x. l. Canonici S. Stephani Bituricen. lxiii lib. Pro domino de Venre xxii.l. etc." Id. clxxix.

[7] Such appear to have been Aleaume Hescelin, Id. cxcvii, cciii (whose exemption from "talia" by Philip in 1192 has already been noticed, Delisle, Cat. 366); William Pulli, clericus, Id. cciii, and others, who accounted under the head of bailliviae.

[8] "R Willelmi de Capella (bailiff of Orleans) Petri de Tulleio, De expletis Aurelianesii, xixxl & x.s. & lx. marc." Id. clxxix.

[9] Id. cl. (Bailiwick of Sens) clii etc. cxcix etc.

[10] Id. clxxvii etc.

dependent classes;[1] the redemptions and reliefs due from the holders of fiefs and religious establishments;[2] the returns from certain mayors' offices;[3] the regalia of bishoprics and convents;[4] the profits of money exchanges;[5] the receipts from the Jews and fees for sealing their bonds;[6] and fines and forfeits for the higher exercises of justice.[7] Of all these revenues, classed as belonging to the bailiwicks, the treasury exacted an itemized record; and their amount and manner of collection was, therefore, far more under immediate government oversight than the incomes farmed to the provosts. Their collectors, whether bailiffs, provosts or special commissioners, were thus made strictly accountable for this branch of their employment; for in cases where, as at Paris in 1217 and 1219, the provostry and bailiwick were in the hands of the same persons only the provostry was farmed.

Payments to the treasury.

The accounts of all of these officers were presented at fixed periods, thrice yearly, to the royal treasurers at the Temple,[8] the net revenue paid in and a formal quittance entered on the record.[9] Thus far we are able to follow their transactions by the aid of their accounts; but the exact method employed in the collection of the revenue, the means by which the bailiffs and provosts secured the payment of their dues, and the precise degree of supervision and authority exercised by the former over the latter, is not made plain.

---

[1] Examples are too numerous to cite.
[2] "Pro racheto de Lancesse" (Longuesse) Id. cli. "Pro abbate Ferreriarum" id. cliv." Hoc debet recipere Willelmus de Capella: comes Sacri-Cesaris (Sancerre), C marchas et C. l, pro exercitu." Id. cliv. etc.
[3] Mantes, Id. cxlix. Bagneux (by the bailiff of Paris), clv, ccii.
[4] E. g. of Reims, Id. clxxviii. Troyes, Id. clxxx.
[5] Account of the bailiff of Paris: "Pro cambio M. marcharum Judaeorum c. l.; at pro cambio V c. marcharum xxv. l." Id. clv.
[6] „De sigillo judaeorum Bestisiaci, xxviii s. et iii d." Id. cxcvii. "De sigillo judaeorum Pissiaci de dimidio anno usque ad S. Johannem, xxv. l." Id. cxcix. "De Judaeis Par"(is) Id. ccii etc.
[7] Account of 1219 by the provosts of Paris, who were the bailiffs also, "De prisonibus evasis, M libras," Brussel I: 483; i. e. forfeits paid to the bailiffs by the sureties of prisoners.
[8] According to the Will of Philip in 1190 these periods were to be, I. the feast of St. Remi (Oct. 1.) II. the Purification of the Virgin (Feb. 2.) III. Ascension. Section 14. Rigord, 103. But, by 1202, the date first specified had been replaced by All Saints (Nov. 1.) The two others remained the same. The financial year began with All Saints. The usual receiving officer in the account of 1202 is brother Haimard of the Temple. He was occasionally supplemented by brother Warren, the later bishop of Senlis.
[9] "Et debet c. & iiii. l. & xii. s. Paris'. Frater Haymardus. c. & iiii lib. & xii. s. Et quitus." (Account of provost of Sens.) is the usual form of discharge.

But it is evident that the reform of 1190 placed in the catagory of receipts from the **bailliviae** all the more important revenues of the crown;[1] and though the bailiffs themselves did not always personally collect the items, the fact of their computation under the title of bailiwick accounts would seem to imply that the bailiffs were charged with a superintendance over their manner of collection.

Bailiffs as judicial officers.

The activity of the bailiffs as judicial and executive officers was scarcely less important than their services to the crown as agents of finance. The provision in Philip's testament of 1190, that these officers should hold a monthly assize, has already been noticed. At this court not only the trial of criminal cases occuring in territories immediately subject to the king was conducted, but the investigation of the civil rights of the crown and its dependents was a prominent feature. It held jurisdiction over usurers, Jews, and contracts,[2] even where the ordinary criminal administration was in the hands of the local holders of the land, as in the territories possessed by the abbey of Fécamp. Appeals from the decision of the assize seem to have been possible, though they certainly were not usual under Philip's rule.[3]

Investigations.

But, whether in the assize itself, or as special commissioners, the bailiffs were the ordinary agents of the king in legal investigations affecting local rights. On the basis of their inquiries the royal decision of matters in dispute was often given. Thus a quarrel be-

---

[1] E. g. In 1221. Philip ordered Gilles de Versailles, Reginald de Béthisi (bailiffs) and Sibert de Laon to make inquiry at the first assize at Amiens regarding the wine excise of that city. Thierry, Monuments, I: 196.

[2] "Remanent autem domino regi usurii, recognitiones et Judaei," Charter acknowledging the concession of the "placita spadae" or criminal jurisdiction, to the monks of Fécamp throughout the lands held by them, 1211, Teulet, Layettes, I: 373. "Item Judaei Normanniae coram ballivo suo, in assisis quae habent recordationem, vel coram ballivo, presentibus decem militibus habebunt recordationem debitoris de summa debiti, et de assignamento; ut ibi inrotulentur tam debita quam assignamenta." Regulations of 1219 respecting the Jews. Ordon. I: 36. In 1218 Philip ordered all his bailifis to adjudge at the request of the archbishop of Rouen and his suffragans the usurers under excommunication. Delisle, Cat. 1792.

[3] An instance of such an appeal occured at the Easter term of the Exchequer of Normandy in 1211; "Eremboure contra Aalesiam cepit breve de feodo (et) gagio. Juratum fuit quod terra illa antecessor' ... Eremborgio, et ipsa et sponsus saisiti fuerant de ea quando iverunt per guerram in Francia; sed de feodo et gagio nihil sciunt. Robertus Brunet (apparently the bailiff) et alii in assisia judicaverunt quod Erembeure haberet saisinam. In scacario judicatum fuit quod illud judicium erat falsum, et habuit Aelesia saisinam suam." Brussel II: 1029.

tween the abbey of St. Denis, the church of St. Aignan, and Gaucher de Joigni was settled through an inquiry by William de la Chapelle, bailiff of Orléans, in 1201—2.[1] A similar royal confirmation was given, in 1213, to the result of an investigation by Gilbert de Chanceaux and Matthew Drogo, bailiffs of Berri, regarding the rights of widows in their bailiwick.[2] The following year a royal commission of four examined into and declared void the claim of the count of Rouci to a tax on wine at Cerni, near Laon.[3] The same bailiffs terminated, in 1215, a dispute concerning pasture rights between Simon d'Equancourt and the burgers of Péronne, which had been submitted to their investigation by the king.[4] Adam Heron, bailiff of Étampes, decided in 1217 that the right of hunting in the forest of Othe belonged to the archbishop of Sens.[5] A similar examination by three bailiffs was the basis of the royal settlement of the quarrel between the monks of Écharlis and the men of Vaumort, near Sens.[6] A joint commission composed of Warren, bishop of Senlis, and Reginald de Béthisi, bailiff of the same city, ascertained, in 1220, the respective rights of the archbishop of Reims and the communal officers of Péronne.[7] About the same time the two bailiffs, Giles de Versailles and Reginald de Béthisi were ordered by Philip to examine into the right of high justice at Liancourt, then in dispute between the king and the chapter of Beauvais.[8]

---

[1] About an elm situated between the lands of the parties. Delisle, Cat. 682. Regarding these investigations see this essay, pp. 91, 92.

[2] "Mandamus vobis et praecipimus ut inquisitionem quam fecistis de viduis mulieribus Bituricis faciatis observari" Order of Philip. Martène, Thesaurus. I: 825.

[2] The investigation was conducted by Giles de Versailles, Reginald de Béthisi and William Paste, royal bailiffs. Therri de Beaurieux, though appointed one of the four commissioners failed to take part. Teulet, Layettes, I: 409.

[4] I. e. the three bailiffs who appear in the previous note. Delisle, Cat. 1557.

[5] Id. 1755.

[6] The bailiffs were William de la Chapelle, Bartholomew Drogo and Garnier du Pré. Id. 1778.

[7] Id. 1986.

[8] "Interim autem vos duo baillivi, cum duobus canonicis Belvacensibus, inquiratis similiter bona fide per juramenta legitimorum hominum patrie, tam clericorum quam laicorum et militum vicinorum, cujus debeat esse magna justicia predicti ville et loci ubi factum est malefactum, et quod inde cum canonicis predictis inquiseritis, per vestras literas patentes nobis renuntietis." Delisle, Cat. appendix p. 522.

The bailiffs also served as representatives of the crown in the adjudication of questions affecting the rights of the king and his great, semi-independent vassals; as, for example, when the royal bailiff, William de la Chapelle, and Oudard, marshal of Champagne, decided against the attempt of Guy de Chappes to institute a market at Champlost;[1] or when the royal bailiff and the bailiff of the countess of Champagne adjudicated together between the provost of St. Martin of Tours and the inhabitants of Chablis.[2] In Normandy at least, it was the bailiff who represented the king in controversies affecting church patronage.[3]

<small>General agents of the king.</small> The financial and judicial services of the bailiffs were only a part of their functions as agents of the crown. They shared with the provosts the protection of religious establishments, and carried out the royal orders granting freedom of conventual elections.[4] The bailiffs exacted and received guarantees of fidelity to the king;[5] they assigned the lands, in some instances, which were given as equivalents in royal exchanges;[6] they could, if ordered by the king, compel a commune to take oath of allegiance to its bishop, or forbid its burghers to resort to an ecclesiastical court.[7] They regulated the course of money in conformity with the sovereign's command.[8] They reported on the condition of the royal fortresses and the movements of the king's enemies. At the monarch's order, they could summon all

---

[1] Delisle, Cat. 1676.
[2] Id. 1908.
[3] In cases of disputed right of patronage the question was to be submitted to a commission of four priests, chosen by the archbishop or bishop of the diocese, and four knights, chosen by the bailiff of the district. Agreement of 1207. Ordon. I: 26, XI: 292.
[4] Instances of orders to bailiffs and provosts to protect religious establishments are too numerous to cite. In Aug. 1221 Philip announced to the bailiffs of Normandy his authorization that the monks of Liru should choose an abbot. Delisle, 2085.
[5] Delisle, Appendix pp. 519, 520. Teulet, Layettes, I: 240, 442, 563.
[6] Delisle, 2020, 2021, 2104.
[7] In Jan. 1214, Philip ordered William du Châtellier and Reginald de Béthisi to forbid the burghers of St. Quentin to plead regarding real property in the church court. Id. 1477. March 1217. Philip ordered Giles de Versailles and Reginald de Béthisi to compel the commune of Beauvais to swear allegiance to the bishop of that city. Id. 1705.
[8] "Mandamus .... sicut multociens vobis mandavimus, monetam nostram Bituricensem per totam balliviam vestram currere faciatis et aliam pravam monetam penitus aboleri". Order to the bailiffs of Berri, 1213. Martène, Thesaurus I: 825.

the military forces of their bailiwicks.¹ They were the regular local administrative organs of the monarchy, as well as its financial and judicial agents.

The less settled state of Anjou, Maine and Poitou compelled Philip to modify the policy of local government adopted in the other regions of his domain. Instead of a number of bailiffs, each responsible for a comparatively restricted district, he appointed, or confirmed, two local seneschals; one for Anjou, and the other for Poitou and such part of Guienne as he might hope to win. It would appear that Philip at one time intended to continue a similar officer in Normandy, for he confirmed the seneschalship to Warren de Glapion, who had held a similar position under the English king John.² But the completeness of the subjugation of Normandy enabled him to dispense with so powerful and dangerous a representative of the local nobility as early as 1204. There is every reason to believe that the local seneschal was, in the district under his charge, the equivalent of the general seneschal, whose office Philip had suspended when the death of Theobald of Blois left it vacant in 1191, shortly after the establishment of the system of bailiffs. The local seneschal was a noble of the region, appointed as representative of the king, and holding his office as a fief of permanent and hereditary tenure.³ His financial duties embraced the collection of the same items of revenue which appear

<small>The local Seneschals.</small>

<small>Their duties and rights.</small>

¹ Compare report of Milo de Levis and Reginald de Villa Terrici, bailiffs of Côtentin and Bayeux about 1220. "Excellentisimo domino suo Philippo ... Milo de Leviis et Renaldus de Villa Terrici, salutem. Nobis per literas vestras precipiendo mandastis quatenus submoneremus omnes milites et servientes feodatos balliarum nostarum qui vobis debent servicium, ut essent, omni occasione remota, apud pontem Ursonis, die jovis proxima ante festum sanctindree, apostoli. Sciatis nos mandatum vestrum adimplevisse, et milites et servientes qui vobis debent servicium ad mandatum ipsum bene venerunt, et . . ·. . venimus apud Gaiclinum (Guarplic) cum domino Willelmo de Melloto .... et dictus Willelmus munivit dictum castellum coram nobis, et infra castellum posuit quinque milites. XX servientes .... Posuit etiam intus castellum XXIII dolia vini et frumentum cujus quantitatem non potuimus numerare certissime, quia afferebatur cum equis et quadrigis et difficilis erat via ...." They then report the character of some fortifications erected by Peter de Guarplic and that they had forbidden Gervais de Mayenne to receive Peter onto his lands or allow the work of fortification to continue. Delisle, ap. pp. 521, 522.

² Compare Delisle, Cat. pp. cxxii, 507. A seneschal of Touraine, Thierri de Gallardon, appears in 1219 or 1220, Id. 1928.

³ Charter of Philip for Aimeri viscount of Thouars. 1203—4. Notum ... quod nos amico et fideli nostro A. vicecomiti Toarcensi dedimus in homagium ligium senescalliam Pictavie et ducatus Aquitanie ultra Legerim, quando Deus eam nobis dederit vel per nos vel per amicos nostros acquirere, in perpetuum

under the head of bailliviae in the accounts of those portions of the kingdom which were administered by bailiffs and provosts. He raised all special taxes or talliae and accounted for them to the treasury. He gathered and had a share of one third in the forfeits, exploits and services. Of the seigneurial income, as customarily raised by the provosts, he had no part, save a fee of one mark of silver for every fifty livres collected by the provosts under his charge.[1] He exercised the judicial duties which accompanied such functions in the case of the bailiffs.[2] He was the general administrative agent of the monarchy in his district.[3] But the chief advantage which the crown derived from the office was that it concentrated a large military power in a single hand. The restless nobles of Anjou would have refused the summons or despised the force of a bailiff; they could not afford to treat so lightly the orders of one whose holdings made him the most powerful noble among them. But the same concentration and localization of power which made the local seneschalship a valuable governmental agency in turbulent districts, made it a dangerous weapon also when turned against the monarchy. The history of the two seneschalships which remained after the speedy suppression of that of Normandy shows well the merits and defects of the system. That of Anjou and Maine was given to William des Roches by the unfortunate Arthur of Brittany in 1199 and confirmed

William des Roches, seneschal of Anjou.

tenendam ab eodem vicecomitem et herede suo de uxore sua desponsata. Martène, "Amp. Coll." I: 1043. Teulet, Layettes, I: 247.

[1] The charter given by Philip in Aug., 1204, defining the rights of the seneschal of Anjou contains the following provisions: "Ipse nihil capiet de dominicis redditibus nostris Andegaviae, Turonum et Cenomanniae. Sed id senescallus debet habere de praepositis et praepositurus; de singulis quinquaginta libris unam marcham argenti ad pondus Turonense, quas praepositi persolvent pro praepositurus..... Et si nos fecerimus demandam vel talliam in Christianis vel Judacis de senescallia Andav. Tur. Cenomanniae, illa demanda levabitur per manum dicti senescalli, ad opus nostrum, per legitimum compotum et scriptum; sed idem senescallus nihil habebit de demanda illa vel tallia. De omnibus aliis tam forisfactis, explectis et servitiis, quae praedicto senescallo fiant, habebimus duas partes, et senescallus tertiam partem." Brussel I: 644. The same provisions were made in a charter for the seneschal of Poitou at the same time. Martène, "Amp. Coll." I: 1049. These charters are also in Teulet, Layettes, I: 267.

[2] Delisle, Cat. 892, 1316, Martène, Thesaurus, I: 804. Teulet, Layettes. I: 331.

[3] E. g. In 1214, Philip ordered William des Roches and G. d'Athies to deliver the regalia of Mans to the new bishop, reckoning it from the day when the confirmation of his election became known to the king. They are ordered first to ascertain whether the bishop of Mans ought to swear fidelity or not. Delisle, Cat. 1500. See also, Id. p. 507.

by Philip in May of that year.¹ The death of Arthur and the conquest of Anjou and Maine having intervened, Philip, now become the immediate lord of those territories, continued the office in the hands of William des Roches. His rights and duties were prescribed by a charter of Aug., 1204. Further privileges gave him, in addition to the seneschalship, the actual enjoyment of Angers, Baugé and a large part of Anjou, to be held at the pleasure of the king.² The seneschalship and these fiefs he retained till his death in 1222;³ when he was succeeded by his son-in-law, Amauri de Craon.⁴ His appointment was amply justified by his defence of Anjou against invasion from Poitou in 1208 and his faithfulness to the crown in the great crisis of 1214, when almost every other noble of the Southwest was won by John.⁵ Had it not been for William des Roches it is doubtful whether the advance of the English monarch could have been checked in time to allow the main forces at the command of Philip to meet the allied army at Bouvines.

The other seneschal, Aimeri, viscount of Thouars, was given his place in the royal service about the same time as William des Roches; and his rights as seneschal of Poitou were identical with those enjoyed by the latter in Anjou.⁶ It was not long, however, before he was in full rebellion against Philip, and it required the most vigorous efforts on the part of William des Roches and the marshal, Henry Clement, to check his attacks on the royal territories, continued from 1206 to 1208. Thenceforward he continued an active enemy of the French monarch, till the general truce between Philip and Henry III. of England, in 1220, brought about similar terms of amnesty between the former and the viscount of Thouars.⁷ His seneschalship, though given him in hereditary tenure, was brief and unprofitable to the French crown.

Aimeri de Thouars, seneschal of Poitou.

The system of local seneschals was probably the best governmental device possible for the monarchy of Philip August in the

---

¹ Charter, Brussel, I: 643: "in feodum et hereditatem."
² Compare the charter of May, 1206, summarized in Delisle, Cat. 997, and that of Jan., 1207, given in full in Sep. XVII: 215.
³ Sep. XVIII: 302.
⁴ Martène, "Amp. Coll." I: 1166. Compare Delisle, Cat. 1884.
⁵ Sep. XVII: 61, 102.
⁶ Philip received his homage, reserving the rights of Arthur, should he be delivered, about Nov. 1202. Martène, "Amp. Coll." I: 1041. He received the seneschalship, by a charter already quoted, during the winter of 1203—4. Id. 1043. His rights were defined by charter in Aug. 1204. Id. 1049.
⁷ Teulet, Layettes, I: 498.

stormy regions where it was employed. But it was a prolongation of the feudal administration of the early Capetians, such as had existed previous to the reforms of 1190. It placed the administration in the hands of a single noble, a resident and a large holder in the district so governed, and possessed of his office by a tenure which made him not easily amenable to the king.

The effect of Philip's administration on the revenue.
Under the combined influence of the enlargement of the royal domain and the improved efficiency of its administration, the increase in the revenue of the king was rapid. It is not our purpose to enter into an examination of the sources from which the treasury derived its income, most have been pointed out in a general way already, and they differ little from those enjoyed under the Capetian sovereigns immediately previous to Philip.[1] But, if we may trust the report of a chance attendant on his obsequies, the annual revenue rose from about 228,000 livres, at his accession, to 438,000, at his death.[2] The sums can, at best, be only a rough estimate; but they probably exhibit truthfully the relation of the revenues at the two periods. The great bequests contained in Philip's will and made possible because the revenues of the kingdom were regarded as the private property of the sovereign, testify also to the financial success of the reign.[3]

Results of increased income. Military strength.
This increase in the income enjoyed by the monarchy, strengthened the royal power in every direction. It enabled Philip to interfere actively in the politics of Germany, it contributed largely to extend the royal authority in Normandy, Anjou and Poitou. But one of the chief benefits conferred by a full treasury was the mili-

---

[1] These sources of the royal revenues have been fully treated by Vuitry, "Études sur le régime financier de la France," and Luchaire, "Instit. Mon." 1: 84—127.

[2] Conon, provost of Lausanne, was in Paris at the time of Philip's death, and records: "Sepultus autem fuit com insigniis regalibus, et vix erat annis 59, et regnavit annis 45, et ditavit regnum et auxit ultra quam credi possit; quia com Lodovicus rex, pater suus, non dimiserit ei in redditibus, sicut officiales regni referebant, mense, 19 milia librarum, ipse dimisit Ludovico, filio suo, qualibet die, 1200 libras Parisiensium in redditibus." Mon. Ger. XXIV: 782. See also Luchaire, I: 126.

[3] The will provides for the distribution of over 410,000 livres, and apparently a large sum further was left to Louis VIII. The latter clause is now illegible. Teulet, Layettes, I: 549. According to a report of Conon of Lausanne, based, he declares, on what he has heard "a familiaribus regis et a publica fama," the amount bequeathed to Louis was 700,000 marks. This is probably considerably exaggerated. Mon. Ger. XXIV: 783.

tary strength which it made possible, through the hiring of bands of mercenary troups, and the raising of a paid soldiery at home, by means of the employment, for extended periods, of those whose feudal obligations bound them merely to a limited term of service. The feudal armies were always uncertain in numbers and, at best, an unsatisfactory basis of reliance, even where the more powerful nobles did not reduce their contingents to the beggarly minimum, which custom recognized as consistent with obedience to the royal summons.[1] Their forces served only for limited periods, and speedily disbanded, to return to their homes. Any strenuous warfare, in total dependence on such armies, was well-nigh impossible. Rigord relates a saying of Philip, which shows that he was keenly alive to the dangers and embarrassments which had been brought upon his predecessors, through their inability to obtain sufficient aid in time of need; and that, in spite of the unpopularity of the attempt, he early resolved to maintain a full treasury, for the defence of the kingdom.[2]

Feudal armies unreliable

The rulers of the Capetian line immediately previous to Philip, like most of the sovereigns and nobles of their age, had made use of mercenaries in their contests.[3] It was, therefore, natural that when the young monarch was brought into conflict with the nobles of his mother's family and of Flanders, struggles in which his supporters were the Plantagenets whose use of such troops was constant, he turned to the employment of mercenaries as a means of supplying his own deficiency in following. These bands of adventurers, composed of the off-scouring of society and whose sole aim was pay and

Mercenary bands.

---

[1] Boutaric, "Institutions militaires de la France" 191—197, gives a striking list showing the exceedingly small proportion of the forces at the command of the great vassals which were furnished by them to the king. In the reign of Philip I. it would appear that the count of Flanders could discharge his obligations by sending as few as ten knights to the royal army. Luchaire, "Inst. Mon." II: 48.

[2] Rigord records under 1194: "Thesauros etiam multos in diversis locis congessit, expensa modica contentus, dicens (rex) quod predecessores sui Francorum reges pauperes existentes, tempore necessitatis stipendiis militibus nihil ministrantes, ingruentibus bellis regni diminutionem possi fuerant non modicam. Principalis tamen intentio ipsius regis erat in thesaurorum congregatione, sancte terre Hierosolymitane a paganis libratio et Christianorum restitutio et regni Francorum ab inimicis strenua defensio, licet quidam minus discreti regis ignorantes propositum et voluntatem ambitionem et nimiam ei avaritiam objicerent." Delaborde I: 129.

[3] Compare Boutaric, "Institutions militaires de la France", 240—242. See also on the employment of these troops in the XII Century, the articles of Géraud, "Bibliotheque de l'Ecole des Chartes" III.

plunder, were popularly known as Braibanceni, Brebentiones,[1] Teutonici,[2] ribaldi or cotarelli; and were universally detested for their rapacity and cruelty. They were, nevertheless, a decided advantage to the monarchy, as compared with feudal levies. They possessed the merit, not inconsiderable in the eyes of the king, of owning no master save their employer; and if they were ready to enlist under a rival standard,[3] where better prospects of remuneration were offered, as long as the king could command a full treasury their services were his. We find such bands, in the employ of Philip, engaged in overrunning the lands of the count of Sancerre as early as 1181—2, or those of the count of Flanders, in 1184.[4] Forces of the same character resisted, in 1188, Richard's invasion of the territories of the count of Toulouse;[5] and, in the following year, won Tours from Henry II.[6] The use of such aids was, therefore, a well-established feature of Philip's policy, before his contest with John for the continental possessions of the Plantagenet house. In that struggle he was aided by many mercenaries, under the lead of Cadoc,[7] who was rewarded for his services with the gift of the château of Gaillon, and became eventually a royal bailiff. The services of his band contributed much to the conquest of Normandy and Anjou.[8]

A paid soldiery. But though these soldiers of fortune constituted a considerable part of the forces with which Philip overran the territories of John, they were by no means all the troops that the French monarch had in his pay. As Boutaric has pointed out, he supported a great number of knights, foot-soldiers, archers and engineers.[9] These were

[1] From their supposed Brabant origin, though it would appear that the bands were made up of men of all nationalities.
[2] Hoveden, II: 345.
[3] E. g. the readiness with which John's mercenaries, to whom the defense of Falaise had been entrusted, took service under Philip, in 1204. Sep. XVII: 80.
[4] Robert of Auxerre, Sep. XVIII: 250. Benedict, Petrob. I: 321.
[5] Hoveden, II: 345.
[6] Rigord, Delaborde, I: 95.
[7] Many biographical notes regarding this leader of the mercenaries, may be found in the article by Géraud, entitled "Mercadier" in vol. III of the "Bibliothèque de l'École des Chartes". That writer is in error, however, in his supposition that Cadoc perished during the invasion of Flanders in 1213. Compare Delisle, Cat. 1790.
[8] This band were the first to enter the Château-Gaillard at Andeli and they captured the city of Angers, Boutaric, "Institutions militaires de la France". 242.
[9] Id. 245. His remarks are based on the "Account of 1202", Brussel, II.

not irresponsible bands; they were a true national soldiery, whose services, either in excess of the time required by feudal custom, or outside the territorial limits within which they were bound to render aid, were paid from the royal treasury or by certain cities and ecclesiastical establishments from which the king had the right to require such service. A list,[1] prepared apparently between 1190 and 1202, gives the number of servientes due from these communes, cities, abbeys and ecclesiastical domains as 5,435; while other districts of the same class, which enjoyed the privilege of commuting their services for a money tax, owed 13,069 livres.[2] In the account for All Saints, 1202, the year in which the war with John began, there is to be found recorded the payment of sums amounting to 26,127 livres, expended for the maintainance of 8069 foot soldiers, servientes pedites.[3] These payments are drawn from the four bailiwicks of William de la Chapelle,[4] Hugh de Gravelle,[5] Reginald de Béthisi[6] and Robert de Meullent;[7] and are at the rate of about thirteen livres annually for each soldier, not far from the stipend attached to the chaplaincies founded by Philip.[8] As the writer just quoted has pointed ont,[9] the treasury account of 1202—3 shows that, in practice, money payments, instead of troops, were accepted by the king from many cities which were still reckoned as owing definite quotas of soldiers. In proportion to the increase in the employment of these sons of French soil as the paid servants of the crown, the use of the roving bands of mercenaries diminished. But, respecting both classes of troops, the policy of the monarchy was evidently to take the control of the army as far as possible into the hands of the royal officers, a policy which was made possible, on a large scale, only through the great increase in the royal revenues.

---

[1] Published by Boutaric. "Institutions militaires", 203, 204.

[2] Id. 205.

[3] Brussel, "Usage", I: 415—417, from the "Account" Id. II.

[4] His bailiwick included Orléans, St. Menim, St. Sanson, Checi, Châteauneuf etc." Brussel Id.

[5] Dourdan, Étampes, Morigni, Montl'heri. Id.

[6] Compiègne, Noyon, Senlis, Mondidier, Soissons, Corbei, Amiens, Péronne etc. Id.

[7] Paris, Villeneuve, St. Denis, St. Germain, St. Magloire, St. Martin des Champs etc. Id.

[8] E. g. Those established in memory of Philip's first queen, Elizabeth, at Notre-Dame de Paris, in 1190, at 12½ livres yearly. Ordon. XI: 269. Or at St. Jacques d'Etampes in 1192, at the same rate, Martène "Amp. Coll." 1: 995.

[9] Boutaric, "Institutions militaires" 205 and note.

The personal element. The principle features of the administration of Philip Augustus have now been considered. Other points of view might have been taken; but our study has sufficed to show that Philip reared the structure of government on foundations already laid. A developer, rather than an innovator, his reign brought into bloom the germs which had come into being under Louis VI., and even earlier sovereigns, and which the chill and feeble rule of Louis VII. could not destroy. If this essay has dwelt chiefly on the nature of his administration and the fortunate circumstances of his situation, we can never lose sight of the forceful personality which moulded and directed all to the attainment of a powerful and united monarchy; nor can we forget the skilful brain, without whose wise planning the accidents of situation would have remained unutilized and barren. To the clear insight into the nature of the difficulties by which he was surrounded; to the ready, if sometimes unscrupulous, skill with which he triumphed over most of them; to the patience with which he awaited his opportunity, and the promptness and vigor with which he struck when once the moment had come; to the facility with which he turned the customs and traditions of the feudal state about him into agencies for the increase of the power of the crown, — to these, personal qualities of the sovereign himself, are due the mighty and lasting results of the reign of Philip Augustus.

Biographical Sketch.

The writer, Williston Walker, was born at Portland, Maine, U. S. A., July 1, 1860, son of George Leon and Maria (Williston) Walker. His father is a clergyman of the Congregational denomination. The writer fitted for college at Brattleboro, Vermont, where he attended the public High School. In the autumn of 1879 he became a student at Amherst College, Amherst, Massachusetts, and received the degree of A. B. from that institution June 27, 1883. In the autumn of the same year he entered Hartford Theological Seminary, Hartford, Connecticut, and continued his studies there till May, 1886, paying special attention to Ecclesiastical History. He was matriculated a student in the University of Leipzig, November 5, 1886. At that University he has enjoyed the lectures of Professors Arndt, Biedermann, Heinze, Hildebrand, Maurenbrecher, Ratzel and Roscher. He has also taken part in the exercises of the Historical Seminars conducted by Professors Arndt and Maurenbrecher.

He was married, June 1, 1886, to Miss Alice Mather, of Amherst, Massachusetts.

His legal residence is Hartford, Connecticut, U. S. A.

www.ingramcontent.com/pod-product-compliance
Lightning Source LLC
Chambersburg PA
CBHW030310170426
43202CB00009B/944